OLD TESTAMENT STUDIES

Edited by

David J. Reimer

OLD TESTAMENT STUDIES

The mid-twentieth century was a period of great confidence in the study of the Hebrew Bible: many historical and literary questions appeared to be settled, and a constructive theological programme was well underway. Now, at the turn of the century, the picture is very different. Conflicting positions are taken on historical issues; scholars disagree not only on how to pose questions, but also on what to admit as evidence. Sharply divergent methods are used in the ever more popular literary studies of the Bible. Theological ferment persists, but is the Bible's theological vision coherent, or otherwise?

The Old Testament Studies series provides an outlet for thoughtful debate in the fundamental areas of biblical history, theology, and literature. The book of Joshua occupies a pivotal place in the Hebrew Bible. Found at the join between the books of Moses and the story of the Israelite kingdoms, it narrates events at a critical juncture of Israel's history. Graeme Auld's wide-ranging studies make a seminal contribution to the interpretation of this important yet sometimes troubling biblical book.

JOSHUA RETOLD

JOSHUA RETOLD

Synoptic Perspectives

A. Graeme Auld

T&T CLARK
EDINBURGH

T&T CLARK LTD
59 GEORGE STREET
EDINBURGH EH2 2LQ
SCOTLAND

First published 1998

ISBN 0 567 08603 8

British Library Cataloguing-in-Publication Data
A catalogue record for this book is available from the British Library

Typeset by Fakenham Photosetting Limited
Printed and bound in Great Britain by Bookcraft Ltd, Avon

CONTENTS

ABBREVIATIONS

AASF	Annales Academiae Scientiarum Fennicae
ATD	Das Alte Testament Deutsch
ATANT	Abhandlungen zur Theologie des Alten und Neuen Testaments
ATSAT	Arbeiten zu Text und Sprache im Alten Testament
BBB	Bonner Biblische Beiträge
Bib	*Biblica*
BK AT	Biblischer Kommentar – Altes Testament
BN	*Biblische Notizen*
BWANT	Beiträge zur Wissenschaft des Alten und Neuen Testaments
BZAW	Beihefte zur *ZAW*
CB	Coniectanea Biblica
CBC	Cambridge Bible Commentary
CBQ	*Catholic Bible Quarterly*
EI	Eretz Israel
EncBrit	*Encyclopedia Britannica*
ET	English Translation
FRLANT	Forschungen zur Religion und Literatur des Alten und Neuen Testaments
HAT	Handbuch zum Alten Testament
HSM	Harvard Semitic Monographs
ITC	International Theological Commentary
JBL	*Journal of Biblical Literature*
JerBS	Jerusalem Biblical Studies
JNWSL	*Journal for North-West Semitic Languages*
JSOT	*Journal for the Study of the Old Testament*
JSOTS	JSOT Supplements
KHC	Kurzer Hand-Commentar
LXX	Septuagint
MT	Masoretic Text
NCBC	New Century Bible Commentary
NICOT	New International Commentary on the Old Testament
OBO	Orbis Biblicus et Orientalis
OTL	Old Testament Library
RiB	*Rivista Biblica Italiana*
SBL	Society of Biblical Literature
SC	Sources Chrétiennes

SCM	Student Christian Movement
SCS	Septuagint and Cognate Studies
SDB	*Supplément au Dictionnaire de la Bible*
SH	Studia Hierosolymitica
SJOT	*Scandinavian Journal of the Old Testament*
SOTS	Society of Old Testament Study
SPCK	Society for the Propagation of Christian Knowledge
SVT	Supplements to *VT*
ThLZ	*Theologische Literatur-Zeitung*
ThZ	*Theologische Zeitschrift*
TOTC	Tyndale Old Testament Commentary
TRu	*Theologische Rundschau*
TSK	*Theologische Studien und Kritiken*
TWAT	*Theologische Wörterbuch zum Alten Testament*
VF	*Verkündigung und Forschung*
VT	*Vetus Testamentum*
WBC	Word Biblical Commentary
ZAW	*Zeitschrift fur die Alttestamentliche Wissenschaft*
ZDPV	*Zeitschrift des Deutschen Palestina-Vereins*

ORIENTATION

The biblical book Joshua is available to us whole in two substantially different versions – Hebrew and Greek; and, in addition, in Hebrew fragments from near the Dead Sea. The Greek book of Joshua, the Septuagint version, is not a translation of the familiar Hebrew, but of a (mostly) somewhat shorter form of the text. All first twelve studies in this volume bring into focus my fascination with different aspects of these facts. Presenting them in three groups is admittedly somewhat arbitrary.

The first four studies together with the ninth (in this volume, although the earliest published) launched me on the main argument of my previous book on Joshua: *Joshua, Moses, and the Land* (1980). The first two essays are essentially a pair: they are arguing the same case, but using different samples of the available evidence. They review portions of the book where the Hebrew and Greek texts are strikingly different – 1:1–4; 5:2–12; 8:9–17; 13:7–8, 14, 33; and also sets of recurring divergences – how the deity is named, how the individual tribes are styled, which tribes are explicitly said to have been assigned their territories by lot. Several of these issues overlap with long-standing problems in the literary history of Joshua. These papers suggest how fresh solutions become available when the evidence of the Septuagint is adduced.

The next pair of essays deals with the Levitical (Joshua 21) and refuge (Joshua 20) cities, in that logical order. The study of the cities of the priests and Levites tackles an almost isolated chapter within the book of Joshua by combining methods used in previous studies: close attention is paid to small but significant differences between the Hebrew and Greek texts of Joshua 21; and Joshua 21 is compared with the closely related material in 1 Chronicles 6, as in essay 9. These concurrent comparisons produce convergent results, suggesting that 1 Chronicles 6 preserved an earlier form of the material than Joshua 21 in either Greek or Hebrew, and that in Joshua 21 again the Greek largely represents an earlier textual form than the Hebrew as preserved.

The textual argument allowed me to propose that the list of nine priestly cities in Judah (and Simeon) was the kernel of the material. These were an unproblematic group in the context of the less regular structure of the older version in Chronicles; and they had resisted adjustment into the otherwise regular 4 × 12 structure developed

1

secondarily in Joshua 21. That historical result has, rather oddly, been adopted by Na'aman and Kartveit and some other specialists in historical topography who remain resistant to the text-critical ground-work on which it was based.

The fourth essay goes on to argue that Joshua 20 and 21 offer a harmonization of two approaches. The one is found in Deut 4:41–43 and 19:1–3 – Deuteronomy proposes three cities each, east and west of the Jordan, to which someone who had killed might flee the blood-feud till the case were settled. The other is the puzzling 1 Chronicles 6 which appears to imply that all cities of the Aaronites and Levites were cities of מקלט (conventionally rendered 'refuge'). Several criticisms of the main case over a decade or so are reviewed and answered in the fifth essay.

Questions raised in the second essay about the semantic development of גורל from 'lot' to 'allotment' and in the fourth about the original meaning of מקלט already showed that these textual studies had impor-tant implications for the meaning and religious associations of certain words. The early short note about a place-name in ancient Judah (essay 6) warns against basing scholarly castles in the air on an uncritical acceptance of the traditional Masoretic Text. The discussion of 'Crea-tion and Land' (essay 7) is based on a study of a relatively rare word (kabash) used in the opening chapter of Genesis and once in Joshua: interesting in itself, it also helps plot the relationship between Joshua and other biblical books. The eighth essay uses part of the argument in the opening one to document the semantic development within the Hebrew Bible of the terms שבט and מטה, uniformly rendered 'tribe' in translations of Joshua and Judges, and demonstrate that this developed meaning is much later than commonly supposed.

Links between Joshua 20–21 and Deuteronomy on the one side and 1 Chronicles on the other and between Joshua 18 and Genesis 1 have already been mentioned; and other such links are more explicitly the matter of the next group of essays. My first published article (essay 9 in this collection) has been particularly widely utilized by other scholars. It demonstrated that the opening chapter of the book of Judges depended on several notes scattered through the book of Joshua and was not itself their source: this chapter constituted a fresh and recent introduction to that biblical book and not, as long maintained, one of the earliest documents of which Judges was composed.

The last previously printed essay (essay 10) took me back to some Joshua issues in the light of questions I had raised and methods I had proposed in my *Kings Without Privilege* (1994). These helped me to join in two lively current discussions: the interconnectedness of the books of the 'Former Prophets' (Joshua, Judges, Samuel and Kings); and the significance of the not very many Qumran fragments relating to Joshua.

The eleventh essay sets in a wider context the earlier discussions of the cities of the Levites. This critique of Japhet's (indeed the consensus) position on the relationship between Joshua and Chronicles explores first some similarities and differences between the ways Joshua 13–22 and 1 Chronicles 2–7 portray the tribal structure of early Israel; and then offers a novel account of the relationship between Deuteronomy 31 and Joshua 1 on the transfer of authority from Moses to Joshua and 1 Chronicles 22–29 on the royal succession from David to Solomon.

Then essay 12 brings the discussion back close to where it began for me in terms of links between the neighbouring books of Joshua and Judges (essay 9). This twelfth essay explores some implications of taking seriously the LXX at the end of Joshua. That version is usually described as offering a longer ending to the book of Joshua; yet it talks of Israel in Eglon's hands immediately after it reports the death of Joshua. There is an obvious though marginal relevance for Joshua studies in that this link is found at the end of the LXX of Joshua. Yet much more important is the question of wider literary history it helps to pose. If what is widely recognized as the most 'Deuteronomistic' chapter of Judges (2:6–3:6) – the chapter which most clearly connects Judges as a whole to the surrounding books – is in fact a very late composition that (like Judges 1) draws material from the neighbouring books to frame a new introduction to a separate book of Judges, what does all this mean for the thesis of Deuteronomistic authorship of all of the Former Prophets? A review of Mieke Bal's work on Judges aids and abets the deconstruction of Deuteronomistic Judges.

A rapid and wide-ranging review (essay 13) of interpretations of the book of Joshua from Ben Sirach in the second century BCE down to 1995 brings to an end this baker's dozen of studies. And that phrase may usefully remind us how determinedly the biblical authors – not least among them those who told and retold the stories of Joshua – had to strive to maintain at precisely twelve the total of the entities they knew as Judah, Simeon, Levi, Benjamin, Joseph, Ephraim, Manasseh, Reuben, Gad, Zebulun, Issachar, Asher, Naphtali and Dan.

TEXTS

JOSHUA: THE HEBREW AND GREEK TEXTS*

In the book of 1914 whose title this article has borrowed, the Oxford scholar S. Holmes and the Press of Cambridge University were responsible for a study that was modest yet of far-reaching implications. It was a response to a German debate begun by J. Hollenberg's 1876 study of the character of the Alexandrian translation of the book of Joshua which 'was in many passages favourable to the LXX' while on the whole upholding 'the general superiority of the MT'. With the exception of C. Steuernagel (1899) subsequent scholars, signally A. Dillmann (1886), had adopted a much less favourable attitude to the Greek. Apart from his rebuttal of specific arguments of Dillmann and others, Holmes claimed to advance 'distinctly fresh reasons ... in favour of the superiority of the LXX' (1914: 1–2): (1) It can hardly be accidental that the LXX often lacks two or more instances of a given word or expression in the MT. (2) The circumstance that in several cases where the two texts vary from one another each text is consistent with itself suggests the hypothesis of a deliberate and systematic revision. Then (3) even some confused passages in the LXX, when turned back into Hebrew, give an intelligible text manifestly earlier than the MT.

He did have some immediate following. G. A. Cooke, in his revised edition of the Cambridge Bible volume on Joshua (1917), paid tribute to Holmes and adopted many of his conclusions. Then many of his results were endorsed by C. D. Benjamin in a thesis published in 1921. But there has followed a long period of neglect.

The first edition of Martin Noth's commentary on Joshua was published in 1938. The freshness of its attack might have weakened even more dangerously the malevolent grip of Hexateuchal criticism on that book had that not received a new lease of life in the same year from G. von Rad's essay on 'The Form-critical Problem of the Hexateuch'. An important year for modern study of the book of Joshua, 1938 saw too the publication of the last part of M. A. Margolis' uncompleted *The Book of Joshua in Greek* (Paris, 1931–8). This has been well described as the outstanding example of an attempt to recover the proto-LXX version of the text of an Old Testament book (Cross 1958: 130). Its handling of the Greek and other versions is superb. But it is much less

* This is a version of a paper read to the Summer Meeting of the SOTS in Cambridge, 1977; published in J. A. Emerton (ed.), *Studies in the Historical Books of the Old Testament*, Vetus Testamentum Supplements 30 (1979), 1–14.

clear that Margolis' all-too-brief comments are sound on the relationship between his reconstructed first Greek version and the Hebrew
tradition. In almost every case of divergence he opts for the priority of
the Hebrew. Noth had been responsible for the text of Joshua in the third
edition of Kittel's *Biblia Hebraica*, and in the commentary (1938: 7),
while he mentions Holmes, his statement that the Greek has shortened
and simplified its original at several points is an endorsement of
Margolis' view. Margolis apparently never cited Holmes; and this –
given the brilliance of the main part of his study – may have contributed
to that neglect of Holmes which it also shares.

Despite H. M. Orlinsky's paper at the Rome Congress on 'The
Hebrew *Vorlage* of the Septuagint of the Book of Joshua' (1969), and its
plea for a return to Holmes's starting-point, all recent studies have
continued to take the *Hebraica veritas* as their point of departure. E.
Otto's work on the festival of unleavened bread at Gilgal (1975) and M.
Wüst's on the geographical texts relating to the settlement of the
Transjordanian tribes (1975) are both eclectic in their use of the LXX.
J. A. Soggin's commentary (1972) is fairly scrupulous about noting
variants, but seldom discusses their significance. F. Langlamet's *Gilgal*
(1969) shows careful attention to detail, devoting a dozen pages to
variants within Joshua 3–4. Yet these, with Margolis and Noth, are
mostly found to be simplifications, harmonizations, or arrangements of
a *texte de base* of whose complexity the translator was only too
conscious. Holmes's name is beginning to reappear in the bibliographies
of studies on Joshua. Yet that normally tells us more about the
completeness of the bibliography than about the attention paid to
Holmes's work.

Holmes occasionally noted the relevance of his observations to the
literary analysis of Joshua (1914: 15–16, 37–8, 49); and it was concern
with this problem that led me to a scrutiny of the LXX in Joshua before
I knew of Holmes's work. There is no room in one article to discuss his
detailed conclusions, although most of them appear to be accurate or at
least responsibly argued. Some of the arguments presented here will
corroborate his case. Yet it will be with regard mainly to outstanding
problems of literary analysis that this paper will offer some character-
ization of the shorter Greek and fuller Hebrew of Joshua.

These vary from the very beginning. In the following translation from
the first chapter those elements in the MT not reflected in the LXX are
italicized:

> 1 After the death of Moses *the servant of Yahweh*, Yahweh said to Joshua the
> son of Nun, Moses' minister, 2 'Moses my servant is dead; now therefore
> rise, go over *this* (LXX: the) Jordan, you and all this people, into the land
> which I am giving to them, *to the people of Israel*. 3 Every place that the sole
> of your foot will tread upon I have given to you, as I proclaimed to Moses:

4 the desert and *this* Lebanon as far as the great river, the river Euphrates, *all the land of the Hittites*, and as far as the great sea towards the setting sun; it will be your territory.'

In this opening of the book there is no 'plus' in the LXX reflecting a longer text than the corresponding phrase in the MT. (It offers *Anti*lebanon in v. 4; but that will be an interpretation of the same text.)

Of such brief pluses, there are about twice as many in the MT as in the LXX in Joshua 1–4, 6, 8–9, 13–16, 18, 20–21, and 24; while in chapters 5, 7, 10–12, 17, 19, and 22–23 they are four or five times as numerous. But are we dealing with additions in one tradition or omissions in the other or a mixture of both? It is fair to observe throughout the book, as in the verses rendered above, that the shorter Septuagint is seldom an intrinsically unsatisfactory text; while the fuller Hebrew appears to possess an accumulation of detail and pedantry. Small *is* beautiful – but is shorter also earlier?

The LXX's accounts of the capture of Jericho in Joshua 6 and of Ai in Joshua 7–8 are considerably shorter than those in the MT. There are several divergences in the material common to them; but the most noticeable difference is that of length. A useful sample is 8:9–17 which takes up the story after the instructions given by Joshua for an ambush of Ai by 'thirty thousand mighty men of valour'. In the following translation the common tradition (which is also the shorter LXX) is given in the left-hand column, while the MT's pluses are to be found on the right.

9 So Joshua sent them forth; and they went to the place of ambush, and lay between Bethel and Ai, to the west of Ai

but Joshua spent that night among the people.

10 And Joshua rose early in the morning and mustered the people, and went up, with the elders

of Israel

before the people to Ai
11 And all the fighting men who were with him went up, and drew near before the city,

and encamped

on the east side (MT: north side)

of Ai, with a ravine between them and Ai.

12

And he took about five thousand men, and set them in ambush between Bethel and Ai, to the west of the city.

13

So they stationed the forces, the main encampment north of the city

with the ambush (MT: rear guard) west of the city.	But Joshua spent that night in the valley.
14 And when the king of Ai saw this, he and all his people made haste and went out early to meet Israel in battle; but he did not know that there was an ambush against him behind the city.	the men of the city, to the descent toward the Arabah
15 And Joshua and all Israel saw this and fled before him 16	in the direction of the desert. So all the people who were in the city were called together to pursue them;
and they pursued Joshua, and were themselves drawn away from the city.	
17 There was not a man left in Ai who did not go out after Israel; they left the city open, and pursued Israel	or Bethel

Small may be beautiful. But is the shorter Greek here a better (i.e. earlier) text or an improved (i.e. later) text? One of the all too few and all too brief fragments of Joshua from Qumran (cave 4) is of 8:3–18 (Callaway 1968: 319, n. 35). This Hebrew text is much shorter than the MT and shares a number of minuses with the familiar LXX. Now if the Hebrew tradition which our Greek has rendered *did* omit from the story of Ai the material in our right-hand column, it would cast suspicion on some at any rate of the other passages where the Greek differs from the Hebrew (MT) text. The LXX is free from the discrepancy of the numbers of the men in ambush; and one cannot help thinking that this has been the main reason why scholars have assented to the alleged inferiority of the Greek text. Yet if such difficulty had been felt, the simple expedient was open of making the numbers correspond. An editor or translator prepared to omit several words to avoid a difficulty was equally capable of altering a single number for the same end (compare Holmes 1914: 13). It is certain that at some stage in the growth of our familiar Hebrew tradition a complicated account of the capture of Ai was produced, perhaps in an attempt to do justice to conflicting information. Why not at a late stage in the MT tradition, rather than assume that a complicated account was first produced and then simplified in the LXX tradition? At this stage in the discussion only one further point will be noted: that 8:9, 13 share characteristics with MT pluses elsewhere. They attest the same pedantic concern for the location of the camp and the precise whereabouts of Joshua himself at any given moment as we find in 10:15, 43 (both absent from the LXX); 'Then Joshua returned, and all Israel with him, to the camp at Gilgal.' A further example of such specification in the MT will be mentioned below in connection with 5:10.

The LXX's pluses with respect to the common tradition are by no means homogeneous, but as a group they are of a different order from those of the MT. Three of them are clearly MT omissions: after 15:59 the Greek preserves the list of towns in Judah around Bethlehem; and after 21:35 the list of Levitical towns from the tribe of Reuben. The topographical gap in the MT's ch. 15 and the numerical asymmetry in ch. 21 leave no other option. Thirdly it may be argued that the longer conclusion of the LXX to the Danite town list (19:47–48) is not only prior to the shorter MT but also the source of the information in Judg 1:34–35 (Holmes 1914: 15–16). At no point within the LXX tradition of Joshua has there occurred an obvious substantial omission like these from the Hebrew. It is attractive to view this as a token of the greater reliability of this shorter tradition in its witness to a mostly shorter 'original'. If the text common to both Hebrew and Greek is also largely the original from which both have diverged, then the Greek is a version of a Hebrew tradition which has occasionally 'extended' this text, mostly with additional historical detail; while the MT represents a Hebrew tradition that has thoroughly 'expanded' it.

Commentators have often observed that the familiar Hebrew text of Joshua contains unnecessary detail. Noth for example describes many words and phrases as 'literary' or 'secondary additions'. Yet there is little recognition in his textual notes that many of these are MT pluses. A similar observation can be made about Langlamet's *Gilgal*, where he detects nine layers in Joshua 3–4. In none of the cases where he prefers the longer text of the MT and Holmes the shorter LXX does Langlamet ascribe the MT plus to any of his six narrative or catechetical sources. All are deemed to belong to one or other of the three redactional phases. Now, even if Holmes is correct, Langlamet is still close to the truth; for where a plus in the MT is also an *addition* to the *common* tradition, it does represent a redactional phase. The choice then is between asserting that the LXX reflects an improved edition in which unnecessary verbiage of earlier editors has been pruned, and asserting that the verbiage now in the MT accumulated at a stage after the separation of the *Vorlage* of the LXX. Of course, if Otto's subsequent *Mazzotfest in Gilgal* is to be believed, Joshua 3–4 should be divided almost without remainder into two parallel sources. And yet his account of Josh 8:1–29 is a further illustration of our case (1975: 26–50, 89). Within the story of the capture of Ai he assigns vv. 3a, 12, 13, 20b to his later source B and the remainder to A. All these are absent from the Greek apart from v. 3a, and that part-verse only disturbs the reader whose suspicions have been triggered by the Hebrew's vv. 12, 13.

In short, it appears we should disqualify our familiar Hebrew text from serving as a sure base for a close examination of the literary structure and relationships of the book of Joshua. It is from the more-or-less 'original' common text that better answers may come to our literary questions about the completed book of Joshua. This finds particularly clear confirmation in Joshua 5 with its discussion of the circumcision and first passover in Canaan.

The divergence over passover in vv. 10–12 is more straightforward and may be studied first. The central column below offers a retro-version of the LXX into a Hebrew as close to the MT as appears compatible with the Greek rendering:

10	10	10 ויחנו בני־ישראל
Καὶ ἐποίησαν οἱ υἱοὶ Ισραηλ	ויעשו בני־ישראל	בגלגל ויעשו
τὸ πασχα τῇ τεσσαρεσκαι-	את־הפסח בארבעה	את־הפסח בארבעה
δεκάτῃ ἡμέρᾳ τοῦ μηνὸς	עשר יום לחדש	עשר יום לחדש
ἀπὸ ἑσπέρας	בערב	בערב
ἐπὶ δυσμῶν Ιεριχω	בערבות יריחו	בערבות יריחו
ἐν τῷ πέραν τοῦ Ιορδάνου	בעבר הירדן [1]	
ἐν τῷ πεδίῳ		
11 καὶ ἐφάγοσαν ἀπὸ τοῦ	11ויאכלו מעבור	11ויאכלו מעבור
σίτου τῆς γῆς	הארץ	הארץ ממחרת הפסח
ἄζυμα καὶ νέα	מצות וקלוי	מצות וקלוי
ἐν ταύτῃ τῇ ἡμέρᾳ	בעצם היום הזה	בעצם היום הזה
12 ἐξέλιπεν τὸ μαννα	12 (וי)שבת המן	12וישבת המן ממחרת
μετὰ τὸ βεβρωκέναι αὐτοὺς	באכלם	באכלם
ἐκ τοῦ σίτου τῆς γῆς	מעבור הארץ	מעבור הארץ
καὶ οὐκέτι ὑπῆρχεν	ולא היה עוד	ולא היה עוד
τοῖς υἱοῖς Ισραηλ μαννα	לבני ישראל מן	לבני ישראל מן
ἐκαρπίσαντο δὲ	ויאכלו מתבואת	ויאכלו מתבואת
τὴν χώραν τῶν Φοινίκων	ארץ כנען	ארץ כנען
ἐν τῷ ἐνιαυτῷ ἐκείνῳ	בשנה ההיא	בשנה ההיא

The LXX plus in v. 10 offers a commonplace specification of the location of Jericho. As for the MT's plus in that verse, its concern to specify the location of the camp at any given time has already been discussed in connection with its pluses in 8:9, 13 and 10:15, 43.

However, quite the most significant difference is over chronology, and concerns the similar MT pluses in vv. 11, 12 – 'from the morrow (after the passover)'. For the tradition behind the LXX, the eating of unleavened bread from Canaanite grain was part of keeping the passover on the fourteenth day of the month. Hardly surprising that a book with so many Deuteronomic features should describe the first passover in Canaan according to the calendar in Deut 16:1–8. This text was economically altered through two neat additions to correspond to the 'Priestly' calendar of passover in Lev 23:5–6, where passover belongs to the fourteenth and the beginning of the feast of unleavened bread to the fifteenth day of the month. In both versions, *bʿṣm hywm hzh* has a strengthening function: in the Hebrew, to underline that it was on

---

[1] Haplography in MT?

the *following* day that unleavened bread was eaten; in the Greek, where the sentence division is earlier, to anticipate *b'klm* . . . – to highlight the coincidence of the feast and the end of manna (on the fourteenth). The deliberate nature of these 'corrections' to the tradition, and the consistency of the MT's interest in Joshua and the camp, put us on the ready to detect further examples of corrective reformulation of the text.

As for vv. 2–9, the most important difference between our versions is over the candidates for Joshua's circumcision as described in vv. 4–6a:

Greek	Hebrew	Hebrew
4 ὃν δὲ τρόπον περιεκάθαρεν	4 וזה הדבר אשר־מל	4 וזה הדבר אשר מל
Ἰησους τοὺς υἱοὺς Ισραηλ	יהושע את־בני־ישראל	יהושע
		כל־העם היצא ממצרים
		הזכרים
		כל אנשי המלחמה
		מתו במדבר בדרך
		בצאתם ממצרים
	5	5 כי־מלים היו
		כל־העם היצאים
ὅσοι ποτὲ ἐγένοντο	כל הילדים	וכל־העם הילורים
ἐν τῇ ὁδῷ	בדרך	במדבר בדרך
καὶ ὅσοι ποτὲ ἀπερίτμητοι	וכל הערלים	
ἦσαν τῶν ἐξεληλυθότων	בצאתם	בצאתם
ἐξ Αἰγύπτου 5 πάντας	ממצרים	ממצרים
τούτους περιέτεμεν Ἰησοῦς	² אלה מל יהושע	לא־מלו
6 τεσσεράκοντα γὰρ καὶ δύο	6 כי ארבעים ושנים	6 כי ארבעים
ἔτη ἀνέστραπται Ισραηλ	ישראל שנה הלך	שנה הלכו בני־ישראל
ἐν τῇ ἐρήμῳ τῇ Μαδβαρίτιδι	במדבר	במדבר
διὸ οἱ ἀπερίτμητοι ἦσαν	לכן ערלים היו	עד־תם
οἱ πλεῖστοι αὐτῶν	רבים מהם	כל־הגוי
τῶν μαχίμων τῶν ἐξεληλυ-	אנשי המלחמה	אנשי המלחמה
θότων ἐκ γῆς Αἰγύπτου	היצאים מארץ	היצאים
	מצרים	ממצרים
οἱ ἀπειθήσαντες	אשר לא שמעו	אשר לא־שמעו
τῶν ἐντολῶν τοῦ θεοῦ	³ בקול האלהים	בקול יהוה

The MT and LXX agree that circumcision had not been practised while the people wandered in the desert. But while the Greek is quite matter-of-fact in talking of others than the children of the desert requiring circumcision, the Hebrew is at pains to deny that any at the time of the exodus had not been circumcised. Did it hold that the rite was not universally practised among the Israelites in Egypt? Or did it hold that circumcision was practised later in life, perhaps at puberty, so that its

---

² The underlining points to similarities in consonantal texts with quite contradictory meanings.

³ The underlining points to a type of variation to be discussed at the end of the essay.

second category of candidates were still children at the exodus? In any
case, there is no motive for Greek translators or prior Hebrew editors to
have gone out of their way to alter a text to imply that the Israelites did
not universally practise circumcision while in Egypt. The MT is not
only longer, but more strident and more orthodox; and it is fair to
assume that this text has been reformulated for dogmatic reasons, and
probably in the light of God's command to Abraham (Genesis 17) that
the rite should be carried out universally and after but one week of life.
This helps us to understand the alteration to v. 2:

2 ...	... 2	... 2
Ποίησον σεαυτῷ μαχαίρας	עשה לך חרבות	עשה לך חרבות
πετρίνας ἐκ πέτρας ἀκρο-	צרים	צרים
τόμου καὶ καθίσας περίτεμε	ושב ומל	ושוב מל
τοὺς υἱοὺς Ισραηλ	את־בני־ישראל	את־בני־ישראל שנית

A combination of the Hebrew pluses in vv. 4, 5, that all were
circumcised in Egypt and that (only) the adults of the exodus generation
died in the desert, leads to the conclusion that those who left as children
were now being recircumcised. Hence the addition in v. 2 of *šnyt* to
guarantee the now proper understanding of *wš(w)b*. Its original sense of
sitting can be illustrated from ancient and recent Egyptian practice, and
may be taken to imply circumcision of adolescents (Pritchard 1954:
629; Durrell 1958: 157).

   Confirmation from this earlier part of the chapter that orthodoxy has
been at work on the text of Joshua 5 at some stage after the completion
of the common text of the book, and inspired by the 'Priestly' Genesis
17, invites a final comment on the MT's report of the passover.
Amongst the older literary critics, and their followers today, it is
precisely the phrase *mmhrt hpsh* that leads to these verses being claimed
for the 'Hexateuchal' P-source. Our account of the textual history of the
chapter has shown that this judgement is in a sense both right and
wrong: right in that both chronology and phraseology have been drawn
from 'P' contexts in the Pentateuch; wrong in that the phrase was no
part of the once complete original book – nor part of any P-document's
Joshua-story.

The detailed examples so far used in this essay have been of individual
passages in which it could be shown that the Greek tradition was shorter
and/or preferable – in the sense of a better witness to the 'original' book
of Joshua. To conclude the discussion it may be useful to mention a
number of recurrent variations. Some of these concern the designations
of an individual tribe.

   Tribes are called not only *šbt* and *mth*; they are referred to also by
their proper name, or that name can have *bny* or *mth bny* prefixed. In

Joshua 13–19 there are 69 references to individual tribes in the tradition common to Hebrew and Greek, with 12 more peculiar to the MT. Of the 69 common instances, 52 appear in the same *form* in both traditions while there is divergence in the case of 17. When the evidence is tabulated, some conclusions become clear:

	Common (52)	LXX (17)	MT (17)	MT + (12)
'simple' name	20	$8(3^A+5^B)$	2^C	3
bny	25	$3(2^C+1^D)$	$7(5^B+2^E)$	6
mṭh	0	3^F	1^G	1
mṭh bny	7	$3(2^E+1^G)$	$7(3^A+1^D+3^F)$	2

(1) Tribal names alone or construed with *bny* are much more common than forms including *mṭh*.

(2) The MT not only boasts 12 'additional' instances, but also uses a longer form in 12 of the common instances – the LXX has a longer form in only 5.[4]

(3) There is no instance in the common tradition of the tribal name construed with *mṭh* within the actual descriptions of allocations – only in the outer framework in 14:1–5 and 19:51.

(4) There is no case in which *bny* is used in one tradition and *mṭh* in the other.

(5) Apart from the 'framework' passages already noted under (3), *mṭh* and *mṭh bny* forms are used only in the opening and concluding formulae of individual allocations. It is to the same and similar contexts that all the Hebrew pluses and variants including *mṭh* belong. A decision on their reliability is indispensable before analysis can begin of the growth of this geographical material to its originally completed form, and before serviceable historical sources can be reconstructed. One likely conclusion of such analysis would be that *mṭh* is most securely embedded in the formula that concludes the regularly patterned reports in Joshua 19 of the allocations to the last six tribes (cf. Holmes 1914: 68); other reports will have been partially adjusted to this pattern.

Two recurring divergences can be detected in references to the deity. The first concerns the possessives construed with 'God'. The situation here too can be readily tabulated:

---

[4] The figures italicized in the above table are the totals within each tradition of each of the four forms of designation. The figures within brackets, with a letter from A to G attached, point to the specific types of divergence that have occurred. The key to the letters is as follows:

A   18:11, 19:24, 40
B   13:24, 18:11, 19:9, 10, 32
C   17:7, 19:1
D   18:21
E   19:9, 16
F   13:15, 15:1, 16:8
G   17:1

	Common	MT variants	LXX variants	MT +'s	LXX +'s
my	1	0	1	0	0
our	4	0	10	2	1
your(s)	3	1	0	0	0
your(pl)	15[5]	10	0	5	0
their	1	0	0	0	0

The Hebrew tradition most often offers the second person plural suffix, both in its own pluses and where it differs from the Greek. In 9 of the 11 cases of difference the Greek attests the *first* person plural. Of course inner-Greek corruption was a ready possibility as soon as the *ipsilon* of *īmōn* (your) became indistinguishable in pronunciation from the *īta* of *īmōn* (our). Yet if pronunciation affected the scribes one would expect more divergence within the Green textual tradition, which in this matter is remarkably unified (the text of LXX[B] has been followed here and throughout this essay). Then, whether the Greek or Hebrew tradition is in the end to be preferred, the variation has occurred in only one direction. Further, *hymōn* (your) overlaps perfectly with the Hebrew second plural suffix in all 90 or so instances throughout Joshua – and that is with all nouns. However, of the 54 instances of *hēmōn* (our), no less than 13 are in passages where the Hebrew reads the second not first person suffix – in the 9 cases already mentioned with 'God' and 4 more. The reason can hardly be accident. The very regularity of the Hebrew second person usage with the deity, given its already noted propensity to systematize, is suspicious in face of the Greek testimony. And our final topic too shows the Hebrew tradition ready to alter terminology for the deity.

The use of the proper name *yhwh* for the deity is almost completely regular in the book of Joshua. In the MT, *(h)ᵊlhym* refers independently to the God of Israel just 3 times. However, 10 further such instances are attested in the LXX. Of these, 7 are in chapters whose concentration of MT pluses and differences is much heavier than the norm for the book; while in the case of the other 3 the difference in divine name is not the only one in the verses in question. (One of the 10 cases closes our earlier quotation from v. 6a.) Happily in two passages there is more than just general indirect evidence for the priority of 'God' over 'Yahweh' (against Holmes 1914: 50).

According to Josh 9:27 (MT), Joshua concludes the affair of the Gibeonites by making them hewers of wood 'for the altar of Yahweh, to continue to this day, in the place which he should choose'. The Greek differs in two respects: in reading 'the altar of *God*', and in adding the subject 'Yahweh' to the final clause – 'for the altar of God, to continue to this day, in the place which Yahweh should choose'. It is easy to

---

[5] This total masks one verse (1:11) where the MT has 'your God' and the LXX 'God of your fathers'.

understand the Hebrew's omission of the final Yahweh as unnecessary once 'God' had been altered to read 'Yahweh' earlier. The alternative assumption, that the verse first suffered 'elohistic' corruption and then received a gratuitous 'Yahweh', is much harder to entertain.

Then there are two instances in connection with the famous poetic fragment in Joshua 10:

12   Then Joshua spoke to Yahweh in the day when *Yahweh* (LXX: God) gave the Amorites over to the men of Israel; and he said in the sight of Israel,
> 'Sun, be still at Gibeon,
> and Moon, in the Valley of Ayalon.'

13   And the sun was still, and the moon stopped, until *the nation* (LXX: God) took vengeance on its enemies. *Is this not written in the Book of Jashar?* (not in LXX) The sun stopped in the midst of heaven, and did not hasten to go down for about a whole day.

14   There has been no day like it before or since, when *Yahweh* (LXX: God) listened to the voice of a man; for Yahweh fought for Israel.

The tradition is united that Yahweh figures in the first and last comments. As for the LXX's three instances of 'God', its witness is to be preferred in v. 12 and v. 14. However in v. 13 its *theos*/God is a simple inner-Greek corruption of *ethnos*/nation – but a corruption facilitated by the presence of *theos* in the text immediately before and after. Holmes (1914: 50) conjectures that the original *gwy* was corrupted into *yhwh*, which was rendered *theos*.

Here is another textual conclusion with literary implications: it becomes likely that 'God' belongs to the 'source' of our poetic fragment – the 'Yahweh' notes at beginning and end will be the contribution of the Joshua editor, and Masoretic tradition will have later removed the resulting inconsistency. The Hebrew tradition which twice altered the divine name, and which – as we saw earlier – added the following v. 15, also cited in v. 13 the name of our 'source': but perhaps on no stronger authority than its editor's observation that David's elegy over Saul and Jonathan is similarly introduced in 2 Sam 1:18. Claims that we are dealing here in Joshua 10 with a fragment of an early *Yahweh*-epic and that we know that epic's name must be received with double caution (cf. Miller 1973 and Cross 1973: 70).

The evidence is far from exhausted.[6] Many more textual *cruces* could be studied, some of them with significance for the literary criticism of the book: normally only negative significance, in that they foreclose options.

Of course any shorter or variant text ought to be assessed on its merits. However, criteria – or at least local criteria – are often lacking

---

[6] For discussion of other details, see also chapters 2, 3, 6, and 9.

for a firm decision. Awareness of the whole context is vital. And in the case of the book of Joshua that means giving the Greek, not the Hebrew, the benefit of the doubt. . . . But not fanatically! I am not yet persuaded that its 'Shiloh' should be preferred to Masoretic 'Shechem' at the beginning of ch. 24 – that would entail the rewriting of too many books.

2

TEXTUAL AND LITERARY STUDIES IN THE BOOK OF JOSHUA*

1938 was an important year for the study of Joshua. It saw the publication of the fourth part of M. A. Margolis' unfinished study of *The Book of Joshua in Greek*; and of the first edition of M. Noth's commentary. The attention M. A. Margolis devoted to his reconstruction of the original Greek translation of Joshua was not matched by careful scrutiny of the relationship between this text and the familiar Hebrew – in all but a few instances the Greek or its *Vorlage* were simply inferior to the Masoretic text. M. Noth's literary conclusions have dominated study over the last forty years. And his view that most of the LXX's variants represent simplifications of a Hebrew text rendered complex by its literary prehistory is an apparent endorsement of M. A. Margolis' views on the Greek book. Little wonder that few studies since 1938 have given Greek variants more than a passing ritual mention. Even those recent scholars – such as F. Langlamet on Joshua 3–4 (1969), M. Wüst on the east-Jordanian settlement traditions (1975), or E. Otto on the Gilgal Mazzot-festival (1975) – who have paid closer attention to textual matters as part of their fundamental reconsideration of detailed portions of Joshua have confirmed, or been influenced by, our masters of 1938.

Yet study of some of the divergences between Hebrew and Greek texts which recur throughout the book of Joshua has convinced me that the generally shorter Greek is a better witness than the Hebrew to that common original from which both have diverged (see also chapters 1, 3, 6 and 9): that the LXX is not an improved text, but a basically better text. For some of the evidence I am indebted to S. Holmes's much-neglected work (1914). This essay will seek to illustrate from ch. 13–17 the necessary relationship between textual and literary criticism in the book of Joshua. If its conclusions can be sustained, then the familiar Hebrew is disqualified from serving as the basis for a *close* examination of details of the literary structure and relationships of that book.

It is well known that the evaluation of our book's conception of land division is complicated not just because the second start at ch. 18 for the seven remaining tribes is nowhere anticipated in the earlier chapters, but also because the allocation in the earlier chapters is prepared for twice and quite differently at the beginning of ch. 13 and 14. Which, if either,

* Published in *Zeitschrift für die Alttestamentliche Wissenschaft* **90** (1978), 412–17.

is the original preface to the geographical material in ch. 15–17? And how are the various sections of Joshua 13 related to each other?

That the opening command to Joshua, begun in 13:1 and now resumed in 13:7, to distribute the territory west of the Jordan to 9½ tribes should have suffered immediate interpolation in the form of a tradition about still unconquered land is obvious and typical (for a convenient discussion see Smend 1971). However, literary decisions about the flow and the growth of the remaining material in Joshua 13 and the opening of 14 are complicated by textual uncertainty at a number of key points.

The first of these concerns the transition between the command to Joshua ending in v. 7 and the Transjordanian review of v. 8ff.

LXX	MT
ועתה חלק את־הארץ הזאת בנחלה	ועתה חלק את־הארץ הזאת בנחלה
לתשעת השבטים וחצי שבט המנשה	לתשעת השבטים וחצי <u>השבט</u> המנשה
מהירדן עד הים הגדול	
מבוא השמש תתן אתה	
הים הגדול וגבול	
לשני השבטים וחצי שבט המנשה	<u>עמו</u>
(הראובני והגדי)	
	הראובני והגדי
	לקחו נחלתם אשר
נתן משה בעבר הירדן מזרחה	נתן להם משה בעבר הירדן מזרחה
נתן לו/להם משה עבד יהוה	כאשר נתן להם משה עבד יהוה
מערוער ...	מערוער ...

The problems of the inherited Hebrew text are three-fold: (1) חצי השבט המנשה is hard if not ungrammatical; (2) the double duty required of עמו, to refer in turn to both halves of Manasseh, is very forced; and (3) the repetition within v. 8 of a relative clause containing the words נתן ... משה is clumsy, while geographical descriptions beginning ... מערוער are not elsewhere left hanging syntactically as in v. 9 (cf. Deut 2:36; 3:12; 4:48; Josh 12:2; 13:16; 2 Kings 10:33). None of these difficulties attaches to the Hebrew text available to the Greek translators which gives every impression of being an original piece of simple drafting that comprises (a) a command to Joshua to settle 9½ tribes, (b) a note that Moses had already settled 2½ tribes, and (c) a brief description of the territory of these 2½ tribes. The retroversion quoted is that of S. Holmes, who feels that הראובני והגדי was not yet in the text available to the translators.[1] This Greek tradition is not just attractive in its own right; it also permits an explanation of how the difficult Masoretic tradition was produced: first a substantial omission prompted by the double occurrence of the half tribe of Manasseh, and then an attempt to save the situation by supplying information that the context showed was now lacking. Use was made of the phrase לקחו נחלתם which

---

[1] Yet it may be that the LXX's dative articles before the two names testify to the more regular לראובני ולדי – MT's הראובני והגדי are unique forms.

occurs in Num 34:14, 15 and within Joshua in 18:7, both concerning the allotment to the 2½ Transjordanian tribes. Talk of tribes *taking* their inheritances is foreign to most of the book of Joshua, which talks rather of their being given or assigned their areas; but is it not surprising at the beginning of ch. 18 which blames 7 tribes for their tardiness in taking up their inheritance.

The literary relevance of this textual discussion appears to be as follows. The LXX offers a good transition between v. 7 and v. 8, and between v. 8 and v. 9. If this text of the passage is original, there seems no reason to doubt that 13:1, 7–12 represent one stratum of the formation of the book. (Verses 13, 14 are also additions to the original stratum: v. 13 is the first of a series which continues in 15:63; 16:10; 17:11–13; 19:47; while רק in v. 14 is often the 'trade-mark' of the interpolator.) This can hardly be the case if we hold to the MT. The clumsy drafting noted there makes one suspect the hand of an inter- polator. And לקחו נחלתם, found elsewhere in Joshua only in ch. 18 with whose ethos it better corresponds, would be an odd part of the original command to Joshua which is to *assign* territory to 9½ tribes. The situation we encounter in Joshua 18 takes us quite by surprise: it will become even clearer later that it is unmotivated by anything in the preceding chapters.

The next two textual differences with possible literary ramifications occur just before and after the detailing in vv. 15–32 of the allotments to the 2½ tribes. The Masoretic tradition alone repeats at v. 33 the note found at v. 14 in the common tradition about the exclusion of Levi from the land distribution. Or so it seems. In fact the Hebrew v. 33 is far from a verbatim repetition of v. 14, and there is doubt about the text of v. 14 in the first place.

33 (MT only)	14 (LXX)	14 (MT)
ולשבט הלוי	רק לשבט הלוי	רק לשבט הלוי
לא־נתן משה נחלה	לא נתן נחלה	לא נתן נחלה
יהוה אלהי ישראל	יהוה אלהי ישראל	אשי יהוה אלהי ישראל
הוא נחלתם	הוא נחלתם	הוא נחלתו
כאשר דבר להם	כאשר דבר להם יהוה	כאשר דבר־לו

The LXX v. 14 offers a text midway between those of v. 14 and v. 33 in the familiar Hebrew: it supports רק as the opening word of the verse, and leaves the subject of נתן unspecified; yet like v. 33 it has יהוה only as the subject of the second half of the verse and offers plural suffixes at נחלתם and להם. This note is apparently indebted to either or both of Deut 10:9 and 18:1–2 for its content, and both of these Deuteronomy passages use singular suffixes. Why the textual differences? And why the repetition, or non-repetition, of the note?

On the textual question it is again most economical to assume that the

Greek is an accurate translation of the *original* note. The differences in v. 33 are trivial: the opening simple connective is adequate for a repetition of the note; and the specification of Moses as the grantor is unremarkable. The familiar Hebrew of v. 14 will represent a correction of the first drafting. The original had been but a loose reminiscence of the Deuteronomy passages; the MT, with its change to singular suffixes, brought it into closer conformity – and its mention of the fire-offerings, which produces an ungrammatical text, is clearly derived from Deut 18: 1. (It is just possible that אשי is a misplaced corruption of משה, which a few MSS and some Targumic evidence read in this verse too.)

From the point of view of literary development it is not just a tautology to observe that v. 14 is prior to v. 33 – its opening word רק suggests that attention is being called to a new piece of information. Furthermore it is unlikely that both verses belong to the same stratum of composition. If our textual conclusions were at all accurate, the original note will have been repeated – at least in the Masoretic tradition – with minor alterations at a time before the two greater changes were made to give the present Hebrew verse. If credence is given to the LXX's negative evidence, then the Hebrew v. 33 will have been but a spontaneous afterthought following the parting of the ways of the Hebrew and Greek traditions. Two considerations would support such an analysis: the Hebrew version of our book is expansionist at many points; and interest in the status of the Levites is manifest from different strata of the book's development – see 14:4 and 18:7 in addition to ch. 21 as a whole. If, however, v. 33 had been added in the period of the still common tradition – and later omitted in the Greek or its *Vorlage* – then the most plausible reason was as a recapitulation of v. 14 following the later insertion of vv. 15–32.

The other divergence relevant to that block of material is at its opening, where this time the LXX alone offers a formal heading:

וזאת הנחלה

אשר נחל משה את-בני-ישראל בערבות מואב מעבר לירדן יריחו

ואלי

Although they reconstruct the first words differently, M. A. Margolis and S. Holmes are in surprising agreement that the Greek renders a Hebrew original and that the MT has suffered loss. This is far from impossible; for the Hebrew, although an expansionist tradition, has suffered manifest loss elsewhere in Joshua. Again literary factors must be taken into account. Verses 15ff. are almost certainly an addition to and not an original continuation of vv. 8ff. No other tribal territory in Joshua is described twice, apart from the areas allotted to Judah and Benjamin whose towns are separately listed. Was this detailed description in ch. 13 felt to be separate, requiring a formal introduction as in the

LXX and the formal conclusion in v. 32? Or was it felt to be a natural expansion or explication of that in vv. 9–12? What then is the function of v. 32? To answer that question we must turn to the opening of ch. 14.

The apparent second introduction to the land-division of the book of Joshua in 14: 1–5 has several puzzling aspects. A change occurs in its verb for assigning territory – from נחל, used five times in vv. 1–3, to חלק, found twice in vv. 4, 5. Then while v. 5 talks of Yahweh commanding Moses, v. 2 talks of his commanding *through* Moses. But, perhaps most important, v. 1 is a very cumbersome sentence:

ואלה אשר־נחלו בני־ישראל בארץ כנען
אשר נחלו אותם אלעזר הכהן ויהושע בן־נון
וראשי אבות המטות לבני ישראל
‎²(MT) נחלתם / ‎(LXX) נחלו אותם . בגורל נחלתם / כאשר צוה יהוה ...

The Hebrew, especially if read in an unvocalized text, is more awkward than any translation, the main difficulty being the formal identity of the verbal forms interpreted as 'received allotments' in v. 1a and 'gave allotments' in 1b. That the traditional interpretation of the verse *as it stands* is the most reasonable is clear. But there must be a strong suspicion that 14:1a once stood on its own and stated: 'And these are the inheritances which the people of Israel gave in the land of Canaan' – the verb being understood as a Pi'el. Being formally ambiguous, this brief heading was 'corrected' by an editor who 'knew' that it was more specifically a commission headed by Eleazar and Joshua who *gave* the inheritances, while Israel *received* them. The most ready explanation of all these phenomena is that three editorial strata are represented in this passage: (1) v. 1a – an introduction to the west-Jordan distribution corresponding to the east-Jordan conclusion in 13:32; (2) an expansion and correction of this in vv. 1b–3; and (3) a further explanation and final rounding off in vv. 4–5.

If this analysis holds, there are three corollaries. The first is that neither 14:1–5 nor even its core in 1a was composed as the main introduction to the account of the west-Jordan land-division. It serves rather as a recapitulation of an account already introduced at the beginning of ch. 13 but broken off when new details on Transjordan were added. The second is that it is in 14:1a that 13:32 finds its original counterpart, not in the LXX's formal heading to 13:15. And, if both 13:32 and 14:1a were prompted by the addition of 13:15–31, then thirdly it is unlikely that the Masoretic repetition of the note on Levi in 13:33 also served an originally recapitulatory function. We should

---

‎² The combination (ב)גורל נחלתם) is unique; its closest parallel is מגרל נחלתנו in Num 36:3, itself a very difficult verse.

conclude then that neither 13:33 nor the heading in 13:15 was part of the tradition common to MT and LXX.

The growth of the first verses of ch. 14 helps to explain a discrepancy between Hebrew and Greek in the first verse of each of ch. 15, 16 and 17 – where MT reads גורל and LXX attests גבול. These verses introduce the descriptions of the territories of Judah, Joseph, and Manasseh. In each case the divergence between MT and LXX is not confined to that over גבול/גורל. Each verse differs also over how the tribe in question was styled, and this makes any theory of accidental alteration unlikely. Each verse in the Greek states that the territory (גבול) of the tribe in question was *from* such and such a place, a form of territorial description found in 13:16, 30 and 19:33. (Admittedly 17:1 does not exactly state this; but 17:7 does: it spells out what 17:1 would have said had it not been interrupted by the genealogical material in vv. 1–6.) Our versions also differ over the same pair of words twice in ch. 21 (vv. 20, 40). In 21:20 the LXX's testimony to גבול is supported by the parallel Hebrew account of Levitical and priestly cites in 1 Chron 6:51 – the Chronicler has no parallel to 21:40.

These observations suggest that it was only in that re-edition of the book of Joshua which we find in the MT, and *not* in the 'original' compilation of the book, that it was made explicit in 15:1 and 16:1 and 17:1 that the holdings of Judah, Joseph, and Manasseh were granted by lot. גורל is used in the tradition common to LXX and MT in the intro-ductory passage 14:1–5 and the concluding 19:51. It is used in the new introduction in 18:1–10 and in the introductory formula of each of the seven notes in ch. 18–19 detailing the allotment to the seven remaining tribes. We find it in ch. 21 about the Levitical allotments. In each case it clearly means 'lot' not 'allotment'. Taking these observations along with our earlier suggestion that the kernel of Josh 14:1–5 is just v. 1a (a verse which itself presupposes the following territorial descriptions in ch. 15ff.) we may deduce that ch. 13–17 of Joshua were without mention of גורל or 'lot' until a very late stage in their development. Even then, the only mention of גורל in the common tradition occurs in our second stratum of 14:1–5, vv. 1b–3, which has several affinities with ch. 21 (especially with 21:1–4, which are the introduction to the Levitical material by its Joshua editor – see further chapter 3).

These few details of the textual history of Joshua define limits within which literary solutions must be found to the problems of the book's growth. They attest a process of composition by means of progressive supplementation. Two literary solutions are apparently excluded. The one: J. Wellhausen's often endorsed theory that the core of 18:1–10 once stood before ch. 13 or ch. 14, at the head of an account of a grant *by lot* to *all* of the tribes. The other: that 13:15, and even more certainly 14:1, marks the start of the contribution to Joshua from the 'P'-document of the 'Hexateuch'.

3

THE 'LEVITICAL CITIES': TEXTS AND HISTORY*

Any fresh appraisal of the history of the 'Levitical Cities' must take as its starting-point a renewed evaluation of our main sources, in practice a comparison of two *texts* (not *lists*): Josh 21:1–42 and 1 Chron 6:39–66. Such a re-evaluation has been offered in recent Edinburgh dissertations by J. P. Ross (1973) and the present author (Auld 1976). The purpose of this paper is two-fold: to present the results of these studies of the texts together with a sample of their arguments; and to re-open the discussion of their historical evaluation.

Part 1

(a) THE ARRANGEMENT OF THE TEXTS

If the shorter text in Chronicles is taken as the basis for comparison, then the correspondence between these quite differently arranged texts is as follows – 1 Chron 6:39b–45[1] is represented in Joshua 21 by 10–19; 46–49 by 5–8a; 50 by 9; and 51–66 by 20–40. The introduction in 1 Chron 6:39a is unlike anything in the Joshua text; while, on the other side, Joshua has substantial additional material in 21:1–4, 8a, 41–42. However, even with all that said, the correspondences between the texts are by no means complete – in fact the Joshua text is considerably fuller than its counterpart, partly because it offers totals at every possible point and partly because of small but seemingly important differences in terminology.

The Chronicler gives much greater prominence than Joshua to the Aaronites. The detailed description of their allotment is given in the very first place, this being concluded by a summarizing total (45b). There follows in summary form information about allotments to the three Levitical groups (46–48). It may be worth emphasizing at this point that nowhere in 1 Chron 6:39–66 are the Aaronites said to be either priests or Levites. This silence is quite remarkable in view both of the explicit assertions in Joshua 21 and of regular scholarly references to the two forms of 'the list of Levitic cities'. There follows an apparent

* Published in *Zeitschrift für die Alttestamentliche Wissenschaft* **91** (1979), 194–206.
[1] The verse numeration used here is that of the MT; most versions of the LXX, as well as most English versions, have our passage beginning with v. 54, not v. 39

25

conclusion in v. 49, and then a clumsy continuation (50) which refers back to the allotment from the tribes of Judah, Simeon and Benjamin. There follow finally the full descriptions of the allotments to the three Levitical groups – with no summarizing totals. It should be noted that while these full descriptions follow the same order of Levitical families as the earlier summary section and while each family is allotted cities from the same tribes, the actual order in which the tribes are detailed differs in two cases: in the Gershonite section, half Manasseh appears last in the summary but first in the detailed allotment; and the same is true of Zebulun in the Merarite section.

The Joshua material is even more obviously a text than a list. It is cast in narrative form – this being found especially in the outer casing (1–3, 41–42). Next, the summary information is offered (4–8), with that on the southern group taking its appropriate first place. Verse 8 appears to function as a transitional verse that could look forwards or backwards or both; while the following two verses give a rather clumsy introduction to the first main section. This feeling of clumsiness arises in two quite different ways. Verse 9 draws our attention back to the southern tribes, but with two differences: the tribes are styled differently; and Benjamin is treated differently from Judah and Simeon. Secondly, v. 10 treats the Aaronites almost as independently as does the Chronicler, whereas v. 4 has talked of the lot coming out for the Kohathite families.

The text in Joshua 21 is more regular than that in 1 Chronicles 6 – indeed, if it was the only one we possessed, only two elements in it would awaken comment: the tension between v. 4 and vv. 9–10; and the inconsistency between the summaries and the full descriptions over the order of the tribes. What has hindered many scholars from taking seriously the tradition of the Chronicler is first of all the less ordered structure of the whole, and secondly the fact of the thoroughgoing discrepancies between the totals in the summary sections and the numbers of city names actually found in the full descriptions. And of course this tradition too is inconsistent over the order of the tribes.

However, once the Chronicler's tradition is perceived for what it is, its own coherence is much more readily apparent. It must not be judged on the basis of Joshua 21 – it did not start as a list of Levitic cities (and is arguably *still* not such a list). Its rationale is one of growth and not of structure. Any assessment of 6:39–66 must take account of three factors: (1) vv. 39–45 follow immediately on the *Aaronite* genealogy in 6:35–38, which itself follows the functional differentiation between the Levites (6:33) and the Aaronites (6:34). (2) That passage, v. 39ff., comes to a natural conclusion in v. 45b. (3) There is a further conclusion at the end of the summary section (v. 49). In short 6:39–66 is a very arbitrarily defined text, and any comparison between it and Joshua 21 must bear this in mind.

Preliminary observations suggest then that we are dealing with two texts that have quite different aims but whose individual contents almost completely overlap. That material common to the texts has links with both Joshua and Chronicles only confirms how closely they are interwoven: (1) The provision of cities of refuge and the special grant of Hebron to Caleb links them with Joshua (and Numbers). (2) The arrangement of Aaronite and Levitic families they manifest has precise parallels only in the books of Chronicles.

After close examination, it is unthinkable that 1 Chron 6:39–66 is a rearranged abridgement (subsequently damaged by several losses) of Josh 21:1–42. J. P. Ross and the present writer arrived independently at one vital conclusion: the result of almost every examination of comparable details in the two texts is that the relevant detail in the Chronicles text is prior to that in the Joshua one. But enough general comment!

(b) THE DEVELOPMENT OF 1 CHRON 6:39–66

If we had to analyse 1 Chron 6:39–66 without any knowledge of a parallel in Joshua 21, and if we paid attention to its general context, the simplest solution we could offer would be that it had *just grown*. It is made up of four parts, (a) an Aaronite list, (b) a Levitic summary, (c) an Aaronite summary, and (d) a Levitic list – and the end of each part makes a good conclusion. Each part depends on what has gone before, but what has gone before is complete in itself.

The summary material is widely regarded as one of the latest elements in the development of the text – and so too J. P. Ross regards it. Indeed, it is the placing of this 'late' element in second position that may have prompted the different two-source or two-stage theories for the composition of our text. But why not accept the challenge of the most straightforward approach to the Chronicler's text and context, and consider the Levitic summary not as a *deduction* from the arrangement of the full list but as its *programme*? What follows in vv. 51–66 is an early attempt at a list of Levitic cities conforming to the summaries.

The following tentative account may be offered of the development of the Chronicler's text:

(1) A list of Aaronite cities (so obviously in and from Judah – the area or state – that no comment was required).

(2) A summary of the tribes which made allotments to the three Levitic families. (The number of cities in each holding had not been specified at this stage, only tribal affiliations.) Contemporaneous with this, the addition in v. 45 of 'from the tribe of Benjamin' – the assumption still being that the others in the list were from Judah (now the tribe).

(3) A pedantic note (v. 50), using different terminology for 'tribe', setting straight the record as to which tribes had allocated cities to the Aaronites.

(4) A list of Levitic cities, arranged by families and the relevant allocating tribes.

(5) The addition of the totals, using as close an approximation to regularity as was possible given the presence of 13 names in the first section.

(c) THE EDITION OF JOSH 21:1–42

Granted the above, the present text of Joshua 21, in its main essentials, represents but three further steps, possibly achieved in one editorial stage: (a) the *logical* rearrangement of all the above material, (b) the achievement of a list corresponding numerically to the summary, and (c) the setting of the whole in a narrative framework which explained the editor's intentions.

The attractions of this hypothesis are several and various. It has permitted a straightforward approach to the Chronicler's text on its *own* merits. It provides us with a source for one of the chapters of Joshua – and the result of this 'find' is that we can observe the editor of Joshua 21 at work, and plot his own contribution quite accurately. This in turn renders more comprehensible two linguistic irregularities and peculiarities of Joshua 21. On the one side the predominant use of *mṭh* for 'tribe'(as distinct from *mṭh bny*), which is regular only in Joshua 20 (3 times) and if found nowhere else in the tradition common to MT and LXX in Joshua, is to be attributed to the source of the chapter. And on the other hand, the two exceptions to this otherwise regular usage in Joshua 21 can be more readily explained in the light of 1 Chronicles 6. (1) It is easier in 6:50, a verse which may represent on its own one stratum in the Chronicler's text, to explain the irregular *mṭh bny*, than in 21:9. (2) The even more striking use of *šbṭ* in the phrase that concludes 21:16b (unparalleled in Chronicles) is part of a tidy afterthought provoked by the use of the material in v. 9 as part of a more elaborate heading to the account of the allocation to the Aaronites than is found in the Chronicler. The hypothesis, then, has seductive advantages; but can it be further grounded?

(d) COMPARATIVE DETAILS

(1) At first sight, the Joshua text appears *preferable* to the Chronicler's (is that a good criterion for *prior*?) in the matter of the summaries. It deals together in similar terms with all four 'Levitical' clans in 21:4–7, while the other deals separately and in different terms with the Levites (6:46–48) and Aaronites (6:50). Yet we have noted already that Josh 21:4 harmonizes well with vv. 9–10 – the latter, like the corresponding

material in the Chronicler (6:50), emphasize the distinctiveness of the Aaronites. Then 21:4 follows immediately on Joshua's special introductory material in vv. 1–3. And so the possibility must be taken into account that v. 4 is part of that introduction. If that is the case, then neither of our texts preserves evidence of an original *four*-sentence summary paragraph.

(2) In the matter of the introductory and concluding formulae in both texts it may be sufficient to recall J. P. Ross's *reductio ad absurdum*: were Joshua deemed prior,

> we should have to suppose that the general tendency of texts to grow and accrete had here been reversed; that the compiler of Ch had such an objection to the term 'Levites' that he removed it from all the introductions – although this whole major section of his work is devoted to their cites and genealogies; and that, for obscure reasons, he had set his face against concluding formulae (except in the case of the Aaronites). (1973: 126)

(3) The treatment of the 'pasture-lands' leads one to the same conclusion. Mention is even more repeated in Joshua than Chronicles; and the greater concern with this matter of the Joshua editor is underscored by his concluding v. 42, which only repeats what we have already been told *ad nauseam*. If the reconstruction of the original opening proposed below is accurate, then the first edition made this same point much more economically. Given all this interest, it is the more noteworthy that they are not mentioned at all in the summary paragraphs (21:4–7 and 6:46–48).

(4) A host of interlocking problems besets any discussion of Josh 21:9–10 and their parallels in Chronicles. In both books, the passages are uncertain textually. It would be attractive simply to shrug off the problem with the assertion that no challenge to an otherwise good theory could possibly be based on a foundation so precarious! A full treatment would sidetrack us too far; but some details may be noted in the light of the hypothesis already set out.

The first has already been suggested above: that 1 Chron 6:50 occasions no great surprise in its own context. Its use of *mṭh bny* for 'tribe' certainly marks it out – but that linguistic feature only serves to underline what is already clear from the content of the verse: that it is an afterthought that supplies a summary statement about the tribal connections of the Aaronites. A case can be made for the originality of either the MT, which details Judah, Simeon and Benjamin, or the LXX which mentions only the first two. The MT may be making good a need created by vv. 46–48 which mention nine other tribes. On the other hand it may be held that the LXX did not mention Benjamin because that tribe's holding had been specified in v. 45 – all that needed to be made clear in v. 50 was that the hitherto unattributed cities in vv. 42–44 were from Judah and Simeon.

Then in some respects, both MT and LXX in Joshua appear decidedly inferior:

(a) The use of *wytnw* within 1 Chron 6:39–66 is remarkably orderly. In vv. 40, 52 it heads the actual allocations to Aaronites and Levites. In v. 49 (the once concluding statement), it corresponds to *wytnw* in v. 40. And its fourth appearance is in our v. 50, which resumes and complements vv. 46–49. In Joshua 21, the verb is found in the four verses (8, 9, 11, 21) whose counterparts in the Chronicler use it, and also in the additional v. 3. This provides a much less orderly schema in a seemingly much more orderly chapter which purports to offer four coordinate summary statements followed by four coordinate full accounts. Why the double use of the verb in the heading to the Aaronite account (vv. 9, 11), and the single use in the heading to the non-Aaronite Kohathite account, and the non-use in the two remaining headings? Presumably this lack of pattern was a consequence of the use made of the source-material – the Chronicler's text.

(b) *bgwrl* in 6:50 links both with *ky lhm hyh hgwrl* at the end of v. 39 and with *bgwrl* in both vv. 46 and 48. On the other hand it is absent from Josh 21:9. Yet it is not, in 6:50, a rare 'plus' to the Chronicler's text after that text had served as the source for Joshua 21. *bgwrl* is in fact found at the end of 21:8b, a part verse without parallel in Chronicles, where it is unnecessary – it appears that once Joshua 21 assumed much its present form there occurred in vv. 8–9 the simple transposition of *wytnw* and *bgwrl*.

If anything, then, our hypothesis assists the interpretation of these verses.

(5) In what concerns Caleb and Hebron, several differences between Josh 21:11–13 and 1 Chron 6:40–42 are better explained as the work of Joshua editors than vice versa. The Joshua form of the material is divergent in four ways: (i) In v. 11, instead of the Chronicler's simple *ḥbrwn*, Joshua offers *qryt ʾrbʿ ʾby hʿnwq hyʾ ḥbrwn* – this has an exact parallel in Josh 15:13 and nowhere else. (ii) Immediately following, instead of the Chronicler's *bʾrṣ yhwdh*, Joshua offers *bhr yhwdh* (doubtless influenced by Josh 20:7, where *hr* is demanded by the parallelism with Ephraim and Naphtali). (iii) The final word of v. 12, *bʾḥztw*, is not represented in the text of Chronicles. (iv) The Chronicler does not read the usual *wʾt-mgršh* after *ḥbrwn*, as in the Joshua recapitulation in v. 13. In none of these cases is there a good motive for the Chronicler to have a deletion – on the other hand, all are consistent with additions made elsewhere in the Joshua text. This is a striking result because it must be a late insert to the text – such a note can only have been contrived because of the need to reconcile two conflicting pieces of information.

Yet there is evidence to suggest that in these verses we are dealing with an exceptional case of influence on the Chronicler's text from the traditions of Joshua. But not from the present state of Joshua 21 – in this respect our hypothesis is sound. In fact the simplest explanation is one which allows us to plot even more exactly the development of Joshua 21. 1 Chron 6:39b–41 represents an insert inspired by an earlier edition of Joshua 21 than is now available to us – not a simple insert, but one which demanded a certain recasting of the material. The original may be assumed to have read: To the sons of Aaron they gave Hebron in the land of Judah and its pasture-lands round about it, and Libnah and its pasture-lands ... This conclusion invites us to distinguish in principle, even where our tools are insufficient in practice, between the work of the main editor of Joshua 21 who used the Chronicler's text as his main source, and the efforts of subsequent expanders and glossators of this text.

(e) THE TEXTUAL SITUATION

What has been offered in the foregoing pages is but a very brief sample of the much greater weight of evidence and argumentation marshalled elsewhere by the present author (Auld 1976). In itself this sample can only constitute an invitation to consider favourably the literary hypothesis proposed: that in virtually every detail 1 Chron 6:39–66 is prior to Joshua 21; that the Chronicler's text is something of a 'collage' fashioned only gradually; that in Joshua we see the logical rearrangement of this source material and its expansion in narrative form.

One further result emerged from this renewed scrutiny of the two texts. It confirmed, and was itself confirmed by, another element in the present author's studies in Joshua – that the Septuagint tradition (especially LXX[B]) is witness to a Hebrew tradition preferable in many respects to that of the Masoretic text. At several points in Joshua 21 it is shorter than or different from the MT; and in almost every one of these details it is closer to the source in Chronicles. It is therefore witness to an earlier stage in an already expansionist tradition which has expanded still further to produce the Hebrew text familiar to us. A single example may serve to suggest that our MT is a deliberate re-edition of the earlier text witnessed to by the LXX. LXX attests gbwlm for MT gwrlm in both v. 20 and v. 40 of Joshua 21. The latter verse has no parallel in Chronicles; however, the parallel to the former, 6:51, reads gbwlm – and that this is original is confirmed by the use of the same term in the Chronicler's distinctive brief introduction in v. 39a. The situation then is quite in line with our proposed hypothesis. That the small textual alteration in the MT of our chapter is no isolated 'mistake' is clear from three further examples in Josh 15:1, 16:1 and 17:1. One last point: that the Greek text of Joshua 21 supplies the link between the widely divergent Hebrew texts of that chapter and 1 Chronicles 6 was already deduced by W. F.

Albright in his programmatic comparison of the actual city-lists in 1945. This new study, which thanks to his efforts has not required to reopen the discussion of the actual city names, serves to put this result of his in a wider context.

Yet it must also be clear that the above results demand a thorough reappraisal of the historical context for the lists proposed by W. F. Albright in this essay – proposals that have been particularly influential as developed by B. Mazar (1960).

Part 2

(a) SURVEY OF SCHOLARSHIP

It is never amiss to begin a review of modern scholarship on the book of Joshua with a mention of the first edition of M. Noth's commentary of 1938. His historical assessment of the list is based on a literary observation: that the list of Levitic cities has been secondarily expanded by the insertion into it of the list of asylum cities. Hebron is mentioned twice (Josh 21:11, 13); its presence in both lists may have prompted their merger. Then Shechem, qualified as being in the hill country of Ephraim (21:21), is attributed to the tribe of that name and not to Manasseh. That the others are also secondary M. Noth argues from the following observation: that elsewhere in Joshua names are quoted from Joshua 21 *before* the asylum cities were added (cf. 13:18 with 21:36f., 19:35b with 21:32). In fact it was argued above that the double mention of Hebron was influenced not by the tradition of the cities of asylum but by that on Caleb and Hebron (Josh 15:13). One the other hand, 'the hill country of Ephraim' in 21:21 is no mark of the dependence of that verse on 20:7 – the phrase is absent from the generally preferable LXX, as is 'the hill country of Naphtali' from both MT and LXX in 21:32 (cf. 20:7). However, these eliminations leave M. Noth with a list containing no mention of Hebron, Shechem or Jerusalem, and indeed with no city from the heartlands of the hill country of Judah or Ephraim. He deduced it was a list of Levitical families living outside the bounds of the post-exilic community, a list moreover that ignored the province of Samaria.

W. F. Albright's fruitful essay studied the transmission in many versions of the text of both Joshua 21 and 1 Chronicles 6. He noted the importance of LXX[B] in Joshua 21 as a mediator between the rather different Hebrew lists, and deduced it was witness to the parent list from which our familiar Hebrew texts were derived. The present paper has sought to explain the 'mid-way' situation of the Greek version rather differently. W. F. Albright was equally convinced that Hebron and Shechem were additions to his parent list of 48 names. For him their presence in the lists familiar to us helps to explain the slight numerical asymmetry of these lists. The addition of Hebron has resulted in Judah and Simeon having one more than their fair share of eight cities. That of Shechem (to the wrong tribe) has been compensated for accidentally but happily by the loss of a name from Ephraim's original four – a similar accident explaining the presence of only three names for Naphtali (but equally happy because it restores the total from the expanded 50 to the original 48!). The stumbling-block to W. F. Albright's hypothesis is that different names have been dropped from the 'original' four each of Ephraim and Naphtali in Joshua from the Chronicler. W. F. Albright asks us to believe that parallel and convenient 'accidents' have occurred at identical points in two now separate texts. And many have believed him! The regularity of four cities from each tribe restored to the original of the list, W. F. Albright makes two final points: that only under the united monarchy were all the cities under Israelite control, and that all those whose sites were reasonably identified were occupied in that period. The dating, shape and contents of the original were accordingly assured.

In a paper of 1950 largely devoted to a critique of S. Mowinckel's views on Joshua 13–19, M. Noth observed, against W. F. Albright's insistence that all the cities must have originally shared the same political authority, that this was less than obvious for a list of *Levitic* cities which were concerned with cultic rather than political realities. As to historical assessment, he was content to repeat his 1938 opinion. In the second edition of his commentary (1953), while repeating this view, he quoted with approval A. Alt's thesis of 1946 (1953[2]: 281–305): this linked the list with Josiah's policies – his bringing all the priests out of all the cities of Judah (2 Kings 23:8), and his killing all the priests of the high places in Samaria (23:19, 20). M. Noth appears not to have discussed W. F. Albright's *archaeological* criterion for dating the list.

B. Mazar's already noted contribution to this problem dates from 1959. He concedes that there are of course schematic or formal elements in our information about the Levitic cities; 'yet behind this veil lies an indisputable tradition, a tradition that Levitic cities did exist at some time in the history of Israel'. Among those who agree with that general thesis he notes that M. Löhr, S. Klein and W. F. Albright prefer a date in the united monarchy, A. Alt under Joshua. While the proposals of W. F. Albright are accepted by B. Mazar in general,

> it must be said that in certain cases the discrepancies between place-names can be explained in a different way. ... In my opinion, it is clear that the original text (copied in the two books in their respective versions) was an official document, possibly from the archives of the Jerusalem priesthood.

Basing himself on a number of passages in Chronicles, to which he gives greater than customary credence, he deduces that we are dealing with a list of those cities in which Solomon settled Levites as specially loyal to his religion and administration. The cities were largely in border areas or less than reliable (recently Canaanite) enclaves – hence the virtual absence of names from the Judahite and Ephraimite heartlands.

Y. Aharoni's *The Land of the Bible*, published in Hebrew in 1962 (ET 1967; 1979²), embraces the textual reconstruction of W. F. Albright *and* the historical explanation of B. Mazar with the small difference that the measure belongs to the period of David not Solomon (1979: 301–305). In disposing of any other type of account of the list, he adds brusquely: 'There is no justification for interpreting a geographical list in the Bible as utopian when it is possible to associate it with a real situation in some particular period.' Z. Kallai's even more detailed work on the tribal allotments gives further support to this position, assigning the date to somewhere from the last years of David to the first half of Solomon's reign (ET 1986: 447–76).

The latest and perhaps most confident word on this apparently established consensus was recently stated by Y. Tsafrir in a note within the *Nelson Glueck Memorial Volume* of 1975 (Eng. Sum. 119):

> Since Mazar's exposition ... doubts concerning the reality of the list of Levitic cities have been dispelled .... Based on Albright's textual analysis, the reconstruction of the original list is now made possible. There is no doubt that the aim of the list's author was to show the formal equality existing among the twelve tribes of Israel. Each tribe, whether large or small, was allotted four Levitic cities; this quota stood even if the tribe itself had in reality disappeared.

Y. Tsafrir is sympathetic to B. Mazar's refusal to concede W. F. Albright's exclusion of Hebron and Shechem from the original list – the reason for the presence of Kibzaim after Gezer in Joshua 21 but Jokmean in 1 Chronicles 6 is not that both were original and one dropped from each list to compensate for Shechem, but that the one town changed its name.

His solution is ingenious: that the Beth-shemesh of the original list was that in Naphtali, which has now but three names, not in Judah, which with Simeon has nine. The argument is as follows. Beth-shemesh (presumably – it is in fact listed as 'yr šmš) is claimed as Dunilu in the list of Dan's cities in Josh 19:40–47, 'which is close in time and function to the list of Levitic cities'. It was only in a later phase that it became a city of Judah. On the other hand it may be deduced from its mention in Judg 1:33 that northern Beth-shemesh, situated at the centre of a Canaanite region, was captured by Israel only during the days of David. It was then a likely candidate for inclusion within the list of Levitic cities, 'as Mazar has demonstrated'.

(b) THE STATE OF THE QUESTION

If the proposal made in the first part of this essay is found acceptable, that the tradition of the cities of Aaronites and Levites was a stage by stage growth within the context if not of the present book of Chronicles then at least of the source material on the Levites and Aaronites now in 1 Chronicles 6, then many will deduce that the end of that process of growth was not accomplished until a late stage in Israel's history, a stage at which they would be happy also to locate the present edition/ insertion of Joshua 21 into that book. Yet even if that conclusion is acceptable, nothing is yet said about the dating of the first stage in the tradition: the information about the 13 cities of the Aaronites in the 'Land of Judah'.

Some conclusions are however appropriate. Further discussion can be freed of the numerical incubus of 48 and also of its close associate, the principle of tribal equality. The brilliance of W. F. Albright's textual studies need no longer be marred by gross assumptions of series of lucky accidents. Then new criteria will require to be found for isolating the sources of the various strata and dating them: the 13 Aaronite cities, the first draft of Levitic cities, and the additions to round that total up to the ideal figure of 48. Thirdly it will have to be decided whether it is still proper to invoke B. Mazar's theory, unless in very reduced form. The dating becomes very problematic. It is doubtful how far the Chronicler's narratives about *Levitic* dispositions should be cited to illustrate a list in Chronicles of *Aaronite* cities. And a higher degree of plausibility attaches only to the comparison of the Transjordanian section of the Levitic list with 1 Chron 26:29–32: David's disposition of Levites 'to have the oversight of the Reubenites, the Gadites, and the half-tribe of the Manassites for everything pertaining to God and for the affairs of the king'. (It is surprising that among the passages from Chronicles discussed by B. Mazar is not included 2 Chron 31:11–21, where Hezekiah's arrangements for the 'cities of the priests' and for the care of the Aaronites and Levites are recounted in some detail.) And fourthly it will have to be considered whether the theories of A. Alt and M. Noth can survive the rejection of the case against Hebron and Shechem. A. Alt saw Hebron as original but Shechem as an import from Josh 20:7, so agreeing with M. Noth about the complete absence of 'Samaria' (1953^2: 294–5).

Y. Tsafrir's contribution, lastly, is the more difficult to deal with, because it is more limited – and at the same time rather attractive. It would be unanswerable were Beth-Anath, the other city which caused problems for Naphtali (Judg 1:33), one of the Levitic cities granted by that tribe. Its presence and the absence of Beth-Shemesh would be very striking. And yet it is remarkable that we do know of two cities called Beth-shemesh (how many more bore that name?) – and precisely in the areas where there is numerical discrepancy in our two texts. Some of Y. Tsafrir's observations rest on conclusions by others which we have seen to be less than well founded, and others beg some further questions (such as the dating of the Danite list and of the material in Judges 1). Yet his central point does demand an answer in terms of the hypothesis advanced in this paper, or else that hypothesis is somewhat weakened.

I have argued elsewhere (Auld 1976) that the division is so nearly regular that one suspects there must have been a very strong factor preventing total regularity. The givenness of a list of thirteen names in the oldest part of the source material may be just this factor. Irregularity has a ring of authenticity.

Can our hypothesis accommodate Y. Tsafrir's observation? The transposition of Beth-shemesh must have occurred after the achievement of regularity. It was suggested above that the addition to the summaries (and to the Aaronite list) of the numerical totals was prior to, and even an encouragement towards, the achievement of an actual list of 48 names. That is not *necessary*, although the presence in 1 Chronicles 6 of both totals and actual irregularity made it *likely*. In fact the theory, familiar to us from Numbers 35, of a regular distribution may have been sufficient impetus to the achievement of the full list. In passing it should be noted that the problem does not consist in conceiving of the alteration of a list once a total had been appended. Differences over lists and their relevant totals between MT and LXX in Joshua 15 make it plain that totals were regularly revised to conform to alterations in the preceding text. What is at stake is Y. Tsafrir's invitation to believe that a transposition occurred in an otherwise regular common (or source) text.

If the text of 1 Chronicles 6 once contained 48 names, then it has suffered much distortion in all its versions. If the transposition of Beth-shemesh occurred first of all in Joshua 21, then we are dealing with a second exceptional piece of influence from that text to the Chronicler's, like that involved in the verses about Caleb and Hebron. Accommodation of this attractive theory is then possible. Others must judge whether it is necessary, or whether we are dealing with a coincidence.

The reflections in this paper overlap at some points with the concerns of M. Haran's interesting essay on the Levitical cities (1961). To use his terminology· if it has not yet succeeded in clarifying the 'historical realities', it may have illuminated some of the path taken to the 'utopian reflection' of the authors of Joshua 21. Whether they were the authors of the Pentateuchal 'P', as M. Haran thinks, is quite another matter!

4

CITIES OF REFUGE IN ISRAELITE TRADITION*

The purpose of this essay is to re-examine the relationships of the biblical texts dealing with refuge for the accidental killer, with special reference to Joshua 20. The composition of that chapter will be discussed and our evidence mentioned for the meaning of the noun *mqlṭ*.

In both language and thought the texts on refuge in the Book of the Covenant and in Deuteronomy are similar: Exod 21:13 appoints for the killer a *mqwm ʾšr ynws šmh*. And the fact that the following verse provides that the deliberate killer may be taken away even from Yahweh's altar makes it likely that the *mqwm* is a sanctuary. Be that as it may, Deuteronomy provides more explicitly for *ʿrym lnws šmh hrṣḥ*. Deut 19:1–7 calls for the threefold division of the land west of the Jordan and the selection of cities of ready access. The following two verses provide for the addition of three further cities should Israel be granted the whole promised land. None of the cities in question is named; and the question must remain open whether the two later verses provide for an expansion of territory to the Euphrates, or merely include Transjordan which is dealt with explicitly in Deut 4:41–43 – earlier in the present book, but possibly from a later stratum than ch. 19 (Noth 1943: 14, n. 1; Mittmann 1975: 131). This note on the Transjordanian situation makes the only mention in any book of the law of actual city names:

> bṣr bmdbr bʾrṣ hmyšr lrʾwbny
> rʾmt bglʿd   lgdy
> gwln bbšn   lmnšy.

One is left wondering whether three double-barrelled names have been chosen by chance each to represent a tribe; or whether behind the present tribal arrangement there lurks an earlier geographical one: Bezer, in the desert on the tableland; Ramoth, in Gilead; and Golan, in Bashan. Unhappily only Ramoth is known outside the lists of refuge and related cities to be discussed in this paper; it is regularly specified as the one in Gilead. And a southern Bezer may well have required to be distinguished from the Edomite *bṣrh*.

Over against those texts which talk of a place, or cities, whither one may flee, stand the similar accounts in Joshua 21 and 1 Chronicles 6 of

* This is a revision of a paper read in March 1977 to the Glasgow University Oriental Society; published in *Journal for the Study of the Old Testament* 10 (1978), 26–40.

37

the cities of priests and Levites. The Chronicler terms all these cities ʿry *hmqlṭ*, the cities of refuge (1 Chron 6:42, 52); while Joshua 21 marks out six of them, three on each side of the Jordan, labelling each as it is mentioned ʿyr *mqlṭ hrṣḥ*, the city of refuge for the killer (Josh 21:13, 21, 27, 32, 36 (LXX), 38 – MT lacks the two verses that list Reuben's four cities).

It is only in the two remaining texts, Numbers 35 and Joshua 20, that the terms ʿrym *lnws šmh hrṣḥ* are used interchangeably. Numbers 35 divides readily into three sections: vv. 1–8 command the institution of 48 Levitical cities; vv. 9–15 the denomination of 6 of these as refuge cities; while vv. 16–34 offer a definition of different kinds of killing. It is easier to agree with Martin Noth's observation that the casuistic directions in the third section for the use of the asylum provision are a secondary addition to vv. 9–15 than with his further argument that the first eight verses are also later than the central section of the chapter (1943: 192, n. 2, 195–6). Indeed, if the chapter is assessed on its own merits it is hard to support any opinion other than the simplest one: that it has just grown by progressive supplementation.

Closer scrutiny of the opening section itself confirms this opinion. Verse 6 is heavy in its present context, and almost certainly intrusive. The first five verses have recorded the general disposition of the Levitical cities, each in the midst of its pasturage. Verse 7 notes that the total will be 48, and v. 8 that grants to the Levites will be proportionate to tribal size. Verse 6, with its comment that the cities for the Levites will be the 6 cities of refuge plus 42 others, both assumes the total of 48 given first in the following verse, and anticipates the second section of the chapter. It has apparently been drafted, in its opening at least, on the model of the following two verses – to aid the introduction of the new material in vv. 9–15. It can be argued, then, that the part of Numbers 35 which most concerns the topic of this essay – vv. 9–15 – is a supplement to an appointment of Levitical cities which was itself drafted without mention of refuge cities.

The view is widely held that an earlier version of Joshua 21 on the Levitical cities has been supplemented on the basis of the previous chapter's treatment of refuge cities. Details of this general view vary; but it is often held that the original list of six refuge cities did not completely overlap with the longer Levitical list; and that it was their fusion that led to some of the 'irregularities' of the latter (Albright 1945: 52–3; Noth 1953: 127). The intrusion of Hebron or Qiriath-Arba into the longer list is held to explain why Judah and Simeon have one more than their fair share of eight Levitical cities.

Now it is hard to deny that any supplementation of the longer chapter has taken place on the basis of Joshua 20; and some details will be noted shortly. However, one of the contentions of this essay is that our conclusions about the growth of Numbers 35 assist our understanding of

Joshua 20. It is also true of that chapter that its six cities have been excerpted from the longer list of Levitical cities. If it can be sustained that the traditions about priests and Levites are a source for those about cities of refuge, it will become all the more important to establish in what sense the Chronicler labelled all the names listed in 1 Chronicles 6 'cities of *mqlṭ*'.

Our next task, then, must be to compare what Josh 20:7–8 has to say about the names of the refuge cities with the corresponding entries in both Joshua 21 and 1 Chronicles 6. In the four columns of the facing pages overleaf are the text of Deut 4:43 and Josh 20:7–8; and excerpts from Joshua 21 and 1 Chronicles 6. Anything underlined in either of the centre columns is a special reading of the Hebrew Masoretic text – either a plus or a variant.

JOSH 20:7–8

Several differences should first be noted between these two verses. They open with different verbs: whichever we settle on for v. 7, it is resumed by the colourless *ntnw* in v. 8. Verse 7 moves from north to south, v. 8 from south to north. The cities in v. 7 are plotted geographically, by the main mountain ranges of western Palestine; those in v. 8, tribally.

Next, if we recall our earlier discussion of whether we are dealing in v. 8 with double names or whether there lurks evidence of an earlier geographical arrangement in the east too, the first western name is also – and necessarily – one particular *qdš*, the one in Galilee.

Then *mʿbr lyrdn* is found only in a small number of once so-called 'priestly' passages at the end of Numbers and in the second half of Joshua, and in Chronicles (Num 22:1; 32:19, 32; 34:15; 35:14; Josh 13:32; 14:3; 17:5; 18:7; 20:8; 21:36 (LXX); 1 Chron 6:63; 12:37; 26:30 – the sole exception is Judg 7:25). And *mṭh* with a tribal name – as opposed to either, e.g., *bny rʾwbn* or *mṭh bny rʾwbn* – is not certainly attested in Joshua outside Joshua 21 and this verse of Joshua 20 (MT has *mṭh* alone in 13:24; 17:1; while LXX attests it in 13:15; 15:1; 16:8). It seems then that the expressions for 'tribe' and 'across the Jordan' tell us something about the affinities of v. 8.

Given that the opening of Joshua 20 says nothing about the total number of cities envisaged, and nothing about their disposition on both sides of the Jordan, we have seen enough evidence to make us consider whether our two verses 7 and 8 were not drafted separately. They do not *obviously* derive from some archival list of six cities.

JOSH 20:8 AND DEUT 4:43

These two verses are clearly very closely related. The names appear in the same order. Each is assigned to a tribe. The patronymic *mnšy* is very

Deuteronomy 4	Joshua 20
	7 וַיַּקְדִּשׁוּ (ויקדשו)
	את־קדש בגליל בהר נפתלי
	ואת־שכם בהר אפרים
	ואת־קרית ארבע היא חברון בהר יהודה
43	8 ומעבר לירדן יריחו מזרחה
	נתנו
את־בצר במדבר בארץ המישר לראובני	את־בצר במדבר במישר ממטה ראובן
ואת־ראמת בגלעד לגדי	ואת־ראמת בגלעד ממטה גד
ואת־גולן בבשן למנשי	ואת־גלון בבשן ממטה מנשה

rare (Deut 4:43; 29:7; 2 Kings 10:33; 1 Chron 26:32). Of its four appearances only that in 2 Kings 10:33 parallels its use for the *half*-tribe of Manasseh. Talk of *mṭh mnšh* in 20:8 for the half-tribe is as unusual (elsewhere only in Josh 17:1 and 1 Chron 6:47).

The direction of their dependence, one on the other, must be a very open question. Deut 4:41–43 does not appear well anchored in its context, and could well represent a late addition to a late chapter. Yet, all that granted, it may be a response to the talk we noted in Deuteronomy 19 about the possible provision of three further cities.

Joshua 21	1 Chronicles 6

Joshua 21

32 וממטה נפתלי
את־עיר מקלט הרצח
את־קדש בגליל ואת־מגרשה

20/21 ויהי ערי גורלם ממטה
אפרים: ויתנו להם
את־עיר מקלט הרצח
את־שכם ואת־מגרשה
בהר אפרים

11 ויתנו להם
את־קרית ארבע אבי הענוק
היא חברון בהר יהודה
ואת־מגרשה סביבתיה
12 ואת־שדה העיר ואת־חצריה
נתנו לכלב בן־יפנה באחזתו
13 ולבני אהרן הכהן נתנו
את־עיר מקלט הרצח את־חברון
ואת־מגרשה ואת־לבנה ...

36 ומעבר לירדן יריחו
ממטה ראובן
את־עיר מקלט הרצח
את־בצר במדבר במישר
ואת־מגרשה

38 וממטה גד
את־עיר מקלט הרצח
את־רמת בגלעד ואת־מגרשה

27 ממשפחת הלוים מחצי מטה
מנשה את־עיר מקלט הרצח
את־גלון בבשן ואת־מגרשה

1 Chronicles 6

61 וממטה נפתלי
את־קדש בגליל ואת־מגרשיה

51/52 ויהי ערי גבולם ממטה
אפרים: ויתנו להם
את־ערי המקלט
את־שכם ואת־מגרשיה
בהר אפרים

40 ויתנו להם
את־
חברון בארץ יהודה
ואת־מגרשיה סביבתיה
41 ואת־שדה העיר ואת־חצריה
נתנו לכלב בן־יפנה
42 ולבני אהרן   נתנו
את־ערי המקלט   את־חברון
ואת־לבנה ...

63 ומעבר לירדן למזרח הירדן
ממטה ראובן

את־בצר במדבר
ואת־מגרשיה

65 וממטה גד
את־ראמות בגלעד ואת־מגרשיה

56 ממשפחת חצי מטה מנשה
את־גולן בבשן ואת־מגרשיה

MT/LXX IN JOSHUA

The studies republished as chapters 1 and 2 of this volume have convinced me in general that the Septuagint of Joshua, especially as found in the Vaticanus text, is witness to a Hebrew text shorter, earlier and better than that preserved by the Masoretic tradition. The divergences noted in the few verses reproduced above provide no exceptions to this general rule. *yryḥw mzrḥh*, or at least *mzrḥh* in 20:8, is a typical expansion; as is the MT's pedantic note in 21:13 that Aaron was *hkhn* – here the shorter LXX is supported by the parallel from the Chronicler (6:42).

The LXX is preferable not just when shorter, but also when different. In the opening verb of 20:7, the Greek *diesteilan* can hardly represent the Hebrew *wyqdšw*. Yet the latter could well be a corruption inspired by the following name of the not dissimilar *wyqrw* (cf. *BHS, ad loc.*) – the same unusual hiph'il as is used in Num 35:11 of appointing refuge cities: *whqrytm lkm 'rym*.

Then in 21:20 we meet just one of five instances in the book of Joshua in which a form of *gwrl* is found in the MT while the LXX attests the corresponding form of *gbwl*. However, it has some importance as being the only one of the five where the LXX finds independent Hebrew corroboration – from the Chronicler. Recognition of the worth of the LXX in three other cases – the opening verses of chapters 15, 16 and 17 – helps our appreciation of the literary growth of these chapters. Furthermore, the five instances in question furnish the only evidence in the Hebrew book of Joshua for 'something allotted' as the sense of *gwrl*; elsewhere it means only 'a lot cast' – and this will have been the only sense in the original book.

The last textual point concerns *bhr 'prym* in 21:21. If it is really a Greek minus rather than a Hebrew plus, then it may be a unique case of simple carelessness in the LXX tradition (as the following section notes, 1 Chron 6:52 agrees here with the MT). However, two considerations support the shorter text here as well: in v. 11 *bhr yhwdh* appears before *w't-mgršh*, but in v. 21 our phrase has been tacked on as an afterthought; then v. 32 has no mention of *bhr nptly*. Perhaps Shechem, as a simple unqualified name, was felt in the Masoretic tradition to require support.

THE CHRONICLER ON THE RELEVANT VERSES

Even if we decide to follow the LXX tradition in Joshua 21, there are still a number of differences between it and 1 Chronicles 6. It was noted earlier that Joshua 21 specifies six cities as *'yr mqlt hrsh*, while the Chronicler suggests in two omnibus headings that all the following cities are *'ry hmqlt*. This important divergence calls for further discussion later; but it can be noted immediately that the Chronicler's two headings appear immediately before mention of Hebron and Shechem – just where we find the relevant Joshua phrases.

Next, its mention of *bhr 'prym* in v. 52 could be either an import from the expanded MT of Josh 21:21, or its inspiration.

Three discrepancies in vv. 40–42 will also require scrutiny later: the non-mention of Qiriath-Arba, the use of *'rs* not *hr yhwdh*, and the absence at the end – after the second *hbrwn* – of *w't-mgršh*.

Finally, v. 63 lacks *bmyšr*, and the opening phrase of v. 56 has suffered manifest corruption.

After close examination, the common scholarly viewpoint becomes untenable that 1 Chron 6:39–66 is a rearranged abridgement of Josh 21:1–42, subsequently damaged by several losses (cf. chapters 3 and 5; and, in greater detail, Auld 1976: 235–80). Once the Chronicler's tradition is perceived for what it is, its own coherence is much more readily apparent. It must not be judged on the basis of Joshua 21 – it did not start as a list of *Levitic* cities, and is arguably still not such a list. What is most obvious is that its material appears in a different order from that in Joshua; but when like is compared with like, it is apparent that it is considerably shorter and in many ways preferable. If we had to analyse it without knowledge of its parallel in Joshua 21, but paying attention to its general context in Chronicles, our simplest solution would be that it had just grown. It is made up of four parts: (a) an Aaronite list of cities, vv. 39–45; (b) a summary of the Levitic allocations, vv. 46–49; (c) a summary of the Aaronite situation, v. 50; and (d) a Levitic list of cities, vv. 51–66. The end of each of these parts makes a good conclusion. Each successive part depends on what has gone before; but what goes before is complete in itself. What we meet in Joshua 21 is the orderly and logical rearrangement of material whose gradual and haphazard growth is documented by the untidy situation in 1 Chronicles 6. This re-edition has three main facets: (1) the provision of an introductory narrative to set the scene, vv. 1–4; (2) the supplementation of the main body of the text with a series of notes, in particular the addition of subtotals to make explicit the relationship between the numerical system and the list of cities; (3) the rounding-off of the whole with two notes.

Albright's important analysis in 1945 of the actual city-names in our two chapters had noted that the LXX of Joshua 21 offered a middle link between the surprisingly divergent Hebrew lists. The analysis proposed here offers an explanation of this: the Chronicler's text is the source of Joshua 21; and the Greek of Joshua 21, being as usual witness to an earlier edition of Joshua, is closer to its source-material than the familiar Hebrew.

Could the Chronicler's text be derived from an earlier edition of Joshua 21 than that available to the LXX translators? Two observations tell against this: it has already been suggested that it grew gradually by supplementation. The probability must be that this occurred in its present context. Verses 39ff. follow immediately on the Aaronite genealogy in 6:35–38, and that itself follows the functional differentiation between the Levites (v. 33) serving the tabernacle and the Aaronites (v. 34) making offerings and atonement – and these two groups are even more strongly contrasted in vv. 39–66 than in the parallel Joshua 21. Then secondly: the precise arrangement of Aaronite and Levitical clans reflected in our two chapters is paralleled only elsewhere in Chronicles. This reinforces our conclusion that the Chronicler's version is at home, while Joshua 21 is derived from it.

Yet two outstanding problems confront us. What prompted the discussion of the Calebite claim to Hebron? And why did the Chronicler label all these cities 'cities of refuge'?

HEBRON IN JOSH 21:11–13/1 CHRON 6:40–42

There are several differences between these passages which are better explained as the work of Joshua editors than *vice versa*. The Joshua form of this material is fuller in four ways: (1) In v. 11, instead of the Chronicler's simple *ḥbrwn*, Joshua offers *qryt ʾrbʿ ʾby hʿnwq hyʾ ḥbrwn* – this has an exact parallel in Josh 15:13 and nowhere else. (2) Immediately following, instead of the Chronicler's *bʾrṣ yhwdh*, Joshua offers *bhr yhwdh* – a phrase which occurs elsewhere only in Josh 11:21; 20:7 and in 2 Chron 27:4. (3) The final word of v. 12, *bʾhztw*, is not reflected in the Chronicler's text. And (4) the Chronicler did not read the usual *wʾt mgršh* after *ḥbrwn* as in the Joshua recapitulation in v. 13. In none of these cases is there a good motive for the Chronicler to have made a deletion or alteration. On the other hand, as Joshua additions they are quite in harmony with many others.

It appears then that the relationship of 1 Chron 6:40–42 with Josh 21:11–13 is perfectly consistent with the general relationship between these chapters. Yet this is a striking result. The close link between Caleb and Hebron is only obliquely alluded to elsewhere in Chronicles – but it is a significant element in the later Deuteronomistic or post-Deuteronomistic material in Joshua (14:6–15 and 15:13–19). And so it is a case where we might have expected an exception to our developing hypothesis: an isolated example of a late insertion into the Chronicler's text to bring it into line with a natural development within the Joshua tradition. Yet the details just quoted tell against such a conclusion.

But an insert it is. Such a note can only have been contrived because of the need to reconcile two conflicting pieces of information. And if *here too* the present text of Chronicles is preferable to that of Joshua, further study of the note should be based on the former.

Apparently *wlbny ʾhrn ntnw* at the beginning of v. 42 resumes the longer *lbny ʾhrn ... wytnw lhm* in v. 39b and the beginning of v. 40. But which is prior in the growth of the material? Is the latter, as might seem more likely, a brief recapitulation of the former after an insert; or is the former an expansion of the originally brief heading, made when a suitable opportunity was given? Three comments are appropriate:

(a) In 1 Chron 6:39–66, it is only in v. 39b that it is made explicit – in the phrase *lmšpḥt hqhty* – that the Aaronites are Kohathite Levites. This is made much clearer in Joshua 21.

(b) The phrase *lmšpḥt hqhty* also embodies an element unique in the Chronicler's text. All other references to the Kohathites use the form *bny qht*. However, in Joshua 21 the phrase is found not only in the parallel v. 10, but also within the special Joshua introduction in v. 4a. Perhaps this distinctive form is the one preferred by the Joshua editor (*bny hqty* is used in 1 Chron 6:18; 9:32; 2 Chron 29:12; but *mšpḥt hqty* – outside the verses in question – only in Num 3:27, 30; 4:18; 37; 26:57).

(c) The concluding words of v. 39b, *ky lhm hyh hgwrl*, are reminiscent of Josh 18:11 and may be inspired by it.

These three features of v. 39b suggest that our earlier suspicion was not so far wide of the mark – we may be dealing in these verses with an exceptional case of influence on the Chronicler's text from the traditions of Joshua. But not from the present state of Joshua 21 (even in the LXX) – in this respect at least our general hypothesis appears sound. When the first editor of Joshua 21 rearranged and expanded 1 Chron 6:39–66, the ascription of Hebron to the Aaronites conflicted with information already in chapters 14 or 15 about its grant to Caleb. This conflict either the first editor of Joshua 21 or another resolved by giving the city itself and the immediately adjoining grazing lands to the Aaronites, and the farmland and all the dependent villages to Caleb.

In short, then, the double mention of Hebron is caused by the inserted note on Caleb. But the drafting of this note is also influenced by the wish of the Joshua editor to make clear that the Aaronites were a sub-group of the Kohathites. We may deduce that the Chronicler's original text contained at least *lbny ʾhrn ntnw ʾt-ḥbrwn bʾrṣ yhwdh wʾt-mgršyh sbybtyh wʾt-lbnh wʾt-mgršyh* ... The implication of this heading was that all the following Aaronite cities were in the *land* of Judah and all had grazing land round about them. It was from this kernel, as was suggested above, that the following 20 verses on the Levitical cities developed.

The way is now open to ask whether the phrase that most concerns this paper, *ʿry hmqlṭ*, was also part of this more original heading. Did the specification of Hebron and the others as cities of *mqlṭ* occur before or after the insert on Caleb?

Either is of course possible. But it may be slightly in favour of the phrase's greater originality to suggest that a later editor might have been more likely to insert the phrase at the first mention of Hebron than the second. But this is too fragile a case to bear any further argument about a Chronicler's theory of 13 Aaronite cities of refuge. Yet, as we shall see immediately, our phrase may have greater claim to priority than Joshua's six-fold alternative, *ʿyr mqlṭ hrṣḥ*.

LEVITE CITIES AND REFUGE CITIES

Now that the development of the lists of Aaronite and Levitic cities in Chronicles and Joshua 21 has been more closely plotted, it is appropriate to turn our attention again to a comparison of them with the names in Joshua 20. Five of the six names in that chapter are identical to names from the longer lists. Only Qiriath-Arba differs from the Chronicler's text. Then, even if we exclude the Chronicler from our considerations for a moment, 21:11 as it stands is hardly dependent on 20:7 as it stands – if it were, we should expect the first, or more strictly only, mention of Qiriath-Arba to be labelled ʿyr mqlṭ hrṣh, like Shechem in v. 21. The fact that Hebron's alternative name, even if a later addition to Joshua 20 and 21 from the traditions on that town in chapters 14 and 15, was added in 21:11 to the *first* mention of Hebron only underscores that it is in connection with the *second* mention of the name two verses later that its status as a refuge-city is affirmed – that second mention which appears to have a greater claim to originality than the first. It would seem that the concept of *mqlṭ* and the name *qryt-ʾrbʿ* did not *always* go hand in hand.

Each of the six names in Joshua 20 heads the relevant sub-section of the longer list. Indeed, that may be the reason why *these* names were quarried from the longer list by an editor who wanted to report, after Joshua's account of the land-division, that effect had been *given* to the legislation on refuge in Deuteronomy 19.

One further consideration may sustain the hypothesis that the names in Joshua 20 were taken from the following chapter. It is possible that the qualifications *bmdbr*, *bglʿd*, and *bbšn* appended to *bṣr*, *rʾmt*, and *gwln* were not originally inseparable from these names, and were intended in the Levitical lists to do double duty – to specify the location not just of the names they followed but also the remaining names in the relevant (tribal) subsection. If they functioned like the Chronicler's *bʾrṣ yhwdh* after *ḥbrwn* in our reconstruction of v. 40, then they stated that Reuben allocated Bezer and three other cities in the desert; Gad, Ramoth and three others in Gilead; and Manasseh, Golan and one other in Bashan (this may be a preferable alternative to viewing these three cities as a special group just *because* their names were double-barrelled). Of course, if this argument holds, and Josh 20:8 was compiled rather unintelligently from the following chapter, then *it* must be the source of Deut 4:43 – a question which earlier we left open.

Our main conclusions so far may be summarized as follows:

1. Num 35:9–15, on the six cities of refuge, is secondary to 35:1–5, 7–8 on the Levitic cities.
2. Josh 20:7–8, the only text that actually names all six cities, is not obviously drafted as one piece – and v. 8 has clear affinities with late strata in Numbers and Joshua.

3. The relationship between the almost identical Josh 20:8 and Deut 4:43 is a very open question.

4. The shorter LXX in Josh 21:21 is to be followed in not reading *bhr ʾprym*.

5. Joshua 21 is based on the parallel material on Chronicles – and most of that material developed in its present context, and was not imported into 1 Chronicles 6 from elsewhere.

6. Exceptionally, 1 Chron 6:39–40 embodies material drafted by an earlier editor of Joshua than was responsible for the present form of that chapter.

7. The possibility cannot be excluded that the cities granted to Aaronites in the land of Judah were originally styled 'cities of *mqlṭ*'.

8. The names in Joshua 20 are derived from the following chapter, not *vice versa* – and it may be that Deut 4:43, in its turn, depends on Josh 20:8.

THE MEANING OF *mqlṭ*

It is hard to avoid the conclusion that the phrase *ʿry hmqlṭ*, whether or not part of the kernel of 1 Chron 6:40–45, was part of the Chronicler's text taken over by the first editor of Joshua 21. This is the earliest biblical use of the term *mqlṭ*, and the use from which all the others derive. Either *mqlṭ* meant something other than refuge when first used, or the Chronicler (or his source) had a different conception of refuge from Deuteronomy, whose theories are given expression in Joshua and Numbers.

Perhaps this question too must be left open. Post-biblical Hebrew usage of a verb *qlṭ* (to absorb, receive) may be derived from the final meaning of the biblical noun. And no satisfactory link has been made, to my knowledge, between biblical *mqlṭ* and the unique participle in Lev 22:23 – *qlwṭ*, which describes some irregularity or deformity in a sacrificial animal.

What is clear now is that Joshua 20 marks the reconciliation of once diverse traditions. The original meaning of *ʿry hmqlṭ* is no longer certain. But apparently it overlapped sufficiently with the Deuteronomic legislation for *ʿrym lnws šmh hrṣḥ* to cause a problem for a body of material (Joshua 21) now embedded in the Deuteronomistic corpus. Joshua 20 represents the solution to the problem: it is now to *ʿry hmqlṭ* (the Chronicler's phrase) mentioned in v. 2 that the killer is to flee (so v. 3, using the Deuteronomic terminology). Names are abstracted from Joshua 21 – hence their precise equivalence with the names in that chapter; and Joshua 21 is altered to agree with the new conception – the two original occurrences of *ʿry hmqlṭ*, appearing before Hebron and Shechem, are deftly altered to read *ʿyr mqlṭ hrṣḥ* and this new coinage is added where necessary. This demonstration that both 20:7 and 20:8 have been quarried from Joshua 21 *may* modify our earlier tentative conclusion that these verses were drafted separately.

One final observation about Joshua 20 suggests that we are dealing here with a redefinition (perhaps polemical) of *mqlṭ*, and that even the equation of *ʿry hmqlṭ* and *ʿrym lnws šmh hrṣḥ* was not felt adequate to secure the point. The chapter concludes: *ʾlh hyw ʿry hmwʿdh* ... Unhappily, *mwʿdh* is a hapax – uncertainty dogs our quest! But its cognates are sufficiently familiar to justify rendering, 'These are the appointed cities ... ', even if some more precise original nuance may escape us. The function of this variation in the closing v. 9 is surely to make abundantly clear the new accepted sense of *ʿry hmqlṭ*.

The list of refuge cities is not a source for the modern historian, but the solution of his ancient counterpart.

5

THE CITIES IN JOSHUA 21: THE CONTRIBUTION OF TEXTUAL CRITICISM*

Several branches of biblical scholarship have offered contributions to our understanding of Joshua 21: commentators on the book of Joshua, students of the ancient versions, researchers into the riddles of the literary history of Torah and Former Prophets, and historians – whether of early Israel's tribal geography, or of her priestly and Levitical institutions. Each of these pursuits is complex enough on its own. When they are combined, they appear unmanageable. And yet, combined the right way, they may offer us more definite answers than we could expect if each were kept separate.

In a series of studies published between 1975 and 1980 (Auld 1980: 121f.) I discussed the literary history of the second half of the book of Joshua in the light of two overlapping sets of relationships: between the Hebrew and Greek texts of Joshua, and between material in Joshua and clearly related material in other books (especially Judges 1 and within 1 Chronicles 1–9). Quite the most complex issues to be faced were those presented by the Hebrew and Greek texts of Josh 21:1–42 and of 1 Chron 6:39–66 on the cities for the Aaronites and (other?) Levites. The consensus opinion has long been that the Chronicler's text results from a reshaping and shortening of Joshua. At that time, I argued for the opposite case: that for the most part 1 Chron 6:39–66 was the source which a late editor of Joshua had reshaped and expanded to produce Josh 21:1–42. Reasons of space and time precluded publication in that period of all the relevant evidence.

Albright's acute study of the place-names on their own demonstrated that the city names as attested in the B text of Joshua (LXX) occupied a middle position between the remarkably different names preserved in the Hebrew texts of Joshua 21 and 1 Chronicles 6. The conclusion has naturally been drawn that the Chronicler had as source a Hebrew text much closer to the *Vorlage* of Codex Vaticanus than to the Masoretic text of Joshua 21; and this view is widely held. My own studies paid more attention to the whole texts, and less to the lists of city names

* A first draft of this paper was read to and helpfully discussed in a meeting of Professor E. Tov's Septuagint Seminar in the Hebrew University. This fresh version, and especially the discussion of משפחה, has benefited from my reading of Professor J. Barr's Schweich Lectures, further aspects of which I hope to discuss elsewhere. Published in *Textus* **XV** (1990), 141–52.

extracted from them. These studies amply confirmed Albright's view that the Hebrew text witnessed to by the Greek of Joshua is in an intermediate position between the Hebrew texts of Joshua and of Chronicles; but they argued that the main direction of influence was from 1 Chronicles 6 to Joshua 21 rather than the other way round. It seemed to me that the order of the Chronicler's material (the details of the grant from 'greater' Judah to Aaron, then a summary of the situation elsewhere, then a summary of the southern situation, and, only after all these, the details from the rest of the country) was more likely to have arisen from gradual growth and supplementation rather than from an author's planning. Disordered growth also helped to explain the puzzling variation in terminology, which was harder to explain in the context of the otherwise more orderly Joshua 21. Joshua 21 had been produced by reshaping, expanding, and bringing more logical order to the disparate materials found in 1 Chron 6:39–66. The firstfruits of that rewriting of the material can be sampled in Joshua 21 (LXX); and still further supplementation is apparent in MT. Of course, at this stage in the argument, it would have been possible to claim that a common source had been available to the editors of both Joshua and Chronicles, and that this source was much more extensively reworked in Joshua than in Chronicles. However, not just the prominence of Aaron (which is less marked in Joshua 21) but also the unusual order of the Levitical clans, Kohath–Gershon–Merari, find their closest parallels in the books of Chronicles. And this suggests influence from Chronicles on the longer Joshua version of the tradition.

The intervening years have seen further discussion of Joshua 21 and 1 Chronicles 6, including some interesting engagement with the issues I raised. It may be useful to distinguish between three different sorts of response.

EXEGETICAL AND TEXTUAL

Butler pays scrupulous and often sympathetic attention to textual proposals, accepts the evidence of deliberate adjustment by later scribes to the textual traditions represented by MT and LXX, and notes that some of my 'conclusions depend upon larger literary presuppositions'(1983: 179). Boling's commentary (Boling and Wright 1982), by contrast, did not have my work available, but this was not still true of Boling (1985).

I should have preferred Butler to note that some of my textual proposals had led to larger literary conclusions (spelled out subsequently in Auld 1980); however, he may be correct! Williamson, while not committing himself, notes that the consensus has been 'forcefully challenged' (1982: 68). Then Greenspoon's only relevant note is his refusal to accept the priority of LXX גבול, even though this is supported by 1 Chron 6:51, over MT גורל in Josh 21:20, 40 (1983: 168).

HISTORICO–GEOGRAPHICAL

Many of Na'aman's observations are in fact of a text-critical nature, and some of these will be discussed below. He holds to the priority of Joshua 21, but without the summaries of the tribes which had been added after the Chronicler had copied the list (1986: 209). He also suggests that vv. 4–7 might have been a later addition – with 8a (*sic*) an example of *Wieder-aufnahme* of 3a – but an addition before the Chronicler's re-edition of the material. Against my suggestion that the Chronicler's text had grown in stages, he argues that the material fitted the time of the monarchy but not of the Chronicler (212). I find this a very strange comment, for Na'aman himself goes on to argue (216) that 'a writer living in a late period could have made use of an early, authentic document'; and to admit to being convinced by my suggestion that the thirteen Aaronite cities reflect the original part of the document. Surely if one later writer could have used earlier documents, so also could a series of compilers.

Kallai responds briefly to some of my remarks in the English edition of his Hebrew *magnum opus* of 1967. It is clear to him (1986: 463, n. 41) that the lack of the usual introductory remark from 1 Chron 6:39f. to the effect that the following cities were from Judah and Simeon is a mark of the dislocation caused by the Chronicler's rearrangement of Joshua 21. He will not allow that בארץ יהודה in 6:40 originally served this function: it simply distorts the more accurate notation in Josh 20:7; 21:11, that defined Hebron as the city of refuge בהר יהודה.

LITERARY–CRITICAL

Two different responses belong to this category. Kartveit (1989: 69–77) offers a number of well-stated points of criticism. Some of these draw renewed attention to questions which must remain open; others do not show sufficient awareness of wider textual and literary evidence. Much of the discussion relates to Josh 21:3–4, 8–10. He argues (71) against my view that Josh 21:3 was drafted on the basis of Josh 21:8/1 Chron 6:49 with the claim that 21:8 was drafted more recently than 21:3. This he 'demonstrates' with the assertion that אל־פי יהוה in v. 3 is more archaic than כאשר צוה יהוה ביד משה in v. 8. Suffice it to say that both appear in a single verse, Josh 17:4, which I have argued (Auld 1980: 94f.) was a source for the terminology of the redactor of Joshua 21. Then the very important issue of the presence or absence of Benjamin in 1 Chron 6:50/Josh 21:9 (Kartveit 1989: 76) is much more complicated than he acknowledges: when he notes that it is read in Chronicles but

not in Joshua, he is describing correctly the MT – however, the LXX
evidence is the direct opposite. During his discussion of whether
'Levites' has been added to a shorter text or deleted from a longer one
(75), he asserts rightly that 'die übrigen Merari-Söhne' (1 Chron 6:62) is
a senseless expression, but wrongly that this can be explained only by
reference to a mutilation of Josh 21:34. It seems to me that the
Chronicler's בני מררי הנותרים does make sense: context precludes 'to the
rest of the Merarites', for none have yet been mentioned – but it allows
'to the Merarites who remained', that is, who were the only group
detailed in vv. 46–48 but remained to be dealt with in detail. The final
question I quote from Kartveit (75f.) is why a recent and political
expression ארץ יהודה ('land of Judah') in 1 Chron 6:40 should
have been replaced in Josh 21:11 by the more ancient and geographical
הר יהודה ('hill-country of Judah'). Here again he is surely guilty of
persuasive definition. ארץ יהודה is attested in a wider spread of texts
than those from Jeremiah to which he draws attention. On the other hand
הר יהודה is restricted to the four passages he quotes, which are in fact
three late elements in the book of Joshua and a single reference in
2 Chronicles – hardly good evidence for an ancient phrase.

Next, the importance of my case, if valid, for Pentateuchal criticism
was recognized by Cortese, from whom it has also elicited a detailed
attempt at rebuttal. This, however, also includes much erroneous
parody. Yet, as I shall attempt to demonstrate below, even if Cortese,
Kallai, and Na'aman are correct in continuing to claim that the
Chronicler depended on Joshua for his information on these cities, it
may still be the case – to a much greater extent than even Na'aman
concedes – that the text of Joshua the Chronicler used was considerably
shorter than the one we know. The material in the related Joshua 21 and
1 Chronicles 6 which provides the closest links with Num 35:1–8 is
precisely the material we do find in Joshua but do not find in Chronicles.
Cortese, in order to satisfy his wider Pentateuchal/Hexateuchal purposes, needs to show not simply that the order of the material in Joshua
is more original than that in Chronicles, but also that the longer text is
prior to the shorter. Admittedly, on issues relating to the 'original'
ordering of the material, he does raise interesting questions, but not on
the more vital issue of the relative length of the two forms of the
tradition. The Chronicler may have wanted to highlight the role of the
Aaronites, and may have ineptly reorganized the material from Joshua
21 (although I still require persuasion on both these points); but no good
reason has been advanced why he should so successfully, even if not
deliberately, have purged that text of links with the Torah.

Some of the criticisms directed in these studies against my proposals
are well taken; others might not have been made had I published the
fuller evidence of which I was aware. The further discussion necessary
admittedly still transcends the proper limits of a single article.

It is appropriate here to concentrate on textual rather than historical issues. However, such study is also the necessary precursor of any historical evaluation. Rofé's study of the neighbouring and related Joshua 20 (1985) has tellingly displayed the logical priority and crucial importance of text-critical work. Na'aman has observed (1986: 216f) that (almost) all of the names listed for the (non-Aaronite) Levites appear elsewhere and could in fact have been transcribed from earlier parts of the book of Joshua: the cities of refuge (ch. 20), the Transjordanian cities (ch. 13), and the cities from northern Israel (ch. 19). Whether the details of his own proposals are right or wrong, his wider remarks ought to have precluded any further (apparently straightforward) approach to these texts by historians of realia, who start by noting that all the cities in question were in territory controlled by Israel only during the United Monarchy, and may continue by means of archaeological survey to consider in which periods each city was in fact occupied. It is not sufficient for historical geographers to admit that some of their source materials have suffered corruption, distortion, or alteration. In an area where so little is known or knowable, textual history and literary history may be the most reliable of the histories we can write.

The received Hebrew text of Joshua 21 is apparently a mostly orderly text. Historians eager to use its information easily accommodate its few obvious oddities as minor adjustments to a sound source, or accidents of textual transmission. However, comparisons with the related texts make us face the question whether order has not been brought out of more disordered beginnings, in each text in different ways. If this were the case, such less ordered beginnings would of course be of no less interest historically.

There are at least three puzzling features of the interrelationships which may have been noted, but have not been explored in recent published discussion: (1) the much greater agreement between all the texts in their transmission of the city names from Transjordan; (2) the odd feature of Greek Joshua, which renders מגרש by a form of περισπορια at the beginning and end of the chapter, but by a form of αφορισμενα in the middle; (3) the widely divergent attestation of forms of משפחה in the various texts.

(1) Of the four names listed for each of Reuben and Gad at the end of the relevant Hebrew texts in Joshua 21 and 1 Chronicles 6, three are identical and one differs only over a vowel letter. Earlier in the texts only 15 names are identical, and only 7 more very similar, while in some 20 cases the names attested are much less alike, or are apparently incompatible, or are simply absent. Such virtual agreement over Reuben and Gad is remarkable; it is only remotely approached at the beginning of the texts, in the cities granted from Judah, Simeon, and Benjamin, where 6 names are identical and 5 exhibit minor differences. The major discrepancies relate to the half of the material which deals with the

centre and north of the country west of the Jordan. (The details can be
assimilated at a glance from the tables in Albright 1945: 61–65.)

(2) The different renderings of מגרש within Joshua LXX were noted
by Holmes (1914: 72): that περισπορια is used in vv. 2, 3, 8,11 and
then in vv. 34–42 (×13); but αφορισμενα in vv.13–33 (×35) –
περισπορια is the only rendering used in 1 Chronicles 6. Delekat
observed (1964: 22) that the implications of this for the textual history
of the material had never been assessed. Ross was later to use this
feature in his remarks (1973: 148–52), but not quite accurately. Butler
records Delekat's suggestion that Josh 21:2–11, 34–42 must not have
appeared originally in the Greek; but does not take up his challenge
(1983: 221). Barr (1989: 133) mentions the spelling of מגרשה.

Do these two features belong together? They could certainly be
integrated with other possibly relevant details:

(a) Na'aman's observation has already been noted, that the names
assigned to the Merarites from Reuben and Gad are all found in Joshua
13.

(b) The information about Transjordanian settlements in Josh
13:7b-13, 15–32 has been added clumsily and apparently in stages
(Auld 1980: 57, 67). It is interesting that it is precisely in this context
that we find appended, in 13:14 (and also 13:33 in MT), a note about the
different status of Levi.

(c) The institution of refuge was secondarily extended, as the books
of Deuteronomy and Joshua developed, from west of the Jordan to the
east. This is attested by the wording or placing of each of the texts which
deals with the issue – by the addition of vv. 8–9 to the basic legislation
in Deut 19:1–7, 10; by the addition of Deut 4:41–43 to an already late
chapter in that book; and by the fact that v. 8 of Joshua 20 describes the
allocation of Transjordanian cities in different terms from those used by
the original v. 7 about the three cities from west of the Jordan.

If the information about Transjordan represented a later addition to
the tradition of Levitic cities, then the prior version of that material had
nothing to do with the ideal of 48 = 4 × 12 which was so nearly
achieved in Joshua 21. I say nearly. Although Joshua 21 talks of 12
tribes, not all provide 4 cities; and although it talks of 4 Levitical
families, not all receive 12 cities. The total suggests that the details
conform better to an ideal than in fact they do.

And the shape of that earlier draft may have been closer to the
disorderly situation we still find in 1 Chronicles 6 than to the more
regular Joshua 21. (Was the prior version composed of something like
1 Chron 6:39–45 (Aaronites) and 49, 51–55, 57–62 (West of Jordan
Levites)? Wherever that shorter and simpler version originated, the
structure of Levitic clans belongs best to Chronicles, while the demands

of numerical balance require Golan in Bashan and Ashtaroth to be attributed to a different Levitic group from their eastern cousins.)

(3) Forms of משפחה are used less in Joshua 21 (LXX) and in 1 Chron 6 (although not always in the same verses) than in Joshua 21 (MT). And in some cases the discrepancies over the usage of this word overlap with other textual problems. The very complex situation can be summarized in five stages as follows:

(a) The noun occurs, in both MT and LXX, in eight verses of Joshua 21. In five of these (vv. 7, 20, 26, 33, 40), LXX attests the forms found in the MT; while in the other three (vv. 4, 10, 34) LXX attests a singular form and MT the corresponding plural. Only in vv. 10 and 34 is the plene spelling used; while, in v. 4, the consonantal Hebrew text is in fact ambiguous and has been read differently by the Masoretes and by the LXX translators.

(b) Joshua 21 (MT) provides a further four instances: two in the form ממשפחת pointed as plural (vv. 5, 27); two in the form ממשפחות (vv. 6, 40). The latter form is also used in the MT in v. 10, where LXX offers a singular.

(c) The parallel tradition in 1 Chronicles 6 uses the term eight times also, like the Greek in Joshua 21. Here too LXX attests the forms found in the MT in five instances: singular in vv. 39, 55 and plural in vv. 47, 48, 51. Then in vv. 46 and 56 MT is singular while LXX is plural, and in v. 45 LXX appears to reflect the more regular למשפחתם for MT's exceptional במשפחותיהם.

(d) However, despite the relative homogeneity of each tradition (Joshua 21 and 1 Chronicles 6) within itself, it is actually only in four verses (7/48, 10/39, 20/51, 26/55) that instances of the noun משפחה overlap in both MT and LXX of both Joshua 21 and 1 Chronicles 6. And only in the first of these is the actual form used (למשפחתם) attested in all the versions of both accounts being surveyed. And even that statement depends on reading 1 Chron 6:48 with Mandelkern's *Concordance* – BHS offers the less usual plene spelling למשפחותם, as in v. 47 (Barr 1989: 52f.).

(e) Of the four pluses in the MT of Joshua 21 with respect to the LXX (see (b) above), the first three are shared with 1 Chronicles 6 (vv. 5/46, 6/47, and 27/56). However, before this fact is seized on by partisans of the received Hebrew text, it is important to note that the Hebrew texts of our two chapters differ over the exact form of משפחה used in each of these three 'shared' cases: 21:5, 27 – ממשפחת (pl) correspond to 6:46, 56 – ממשפחת (singular, but translated as plural in LXX). Then 21:6 – ממשפחות corresponds to 6:47 למשפחותם (למשפחתם in *BHS*).

How should this head-breaking variety be assessed? The unusual, though limited, agreement just noted at (e) above between 1 Chronicles 6 and Joshua 21 (MT) against Joshua 21 (LXX) ought to give pause to

any sufferers from the disease of *Settantamania* (Septuagint madness)
diagnosed in me by E. Cortese (1985: 384, 391). Only Joshua (MT)
offers anything approaching a regular usage of משפחה; it uses the noun
in each of the summary verses (5/46, 6/47, 7/48), here supported by
Chronicles; and it uses the noun at head and tail of each of the detailed
lists of towns, here largely supported by Joshua (LXX). The usage of
this noun may offer a good test-case for the larger question already
posed: is Joshua 21 (MT) a good witness to an ordered and regular text
other versions of which have suffered in transmission and/or translation
(Joshua 21 (LXX) and when being altered by the Chronicler for his own
purposes? Or is it witness to a tradition to which only a semblance of
regularity has been lately brought, and whose prior stages (or elements
in them) can still be detected in Joshua 21 (LXX) and 1 Chronicles 6?

My own preference, in this as so many textual issues in Joshua, is to
follow the lead given by Holmes. Within the summarizing verses
5–7/46–48, it is only in 7/48 that all versions agree in detail (see (d)
above). The use of למשפחתם in this verse will have been simply stylistic
– as English might use 'in their turn' in the concluding member of a list.
That its presence in 5–6/46–47 results from later standardization can be
deduced from the reference of this noun in these two verses: only there
within Joshua 21 is משפחה used to refer to groups of the regular non-
Levitical twelve tribes of Israel (or, in the case of the MT of 1 Chron
6:46 to refer simply to a single tribe); elsewhere in this material, except
for 1 Chron 6:56, משפחה refers only to the Levitical families or their
sub-clans.

The other three passages in which some form of משפחה occurs in both
versions of both texts share a significant common feature: they are used
in headings (10/39, 20/51) or conclusions (26/55) to the sections on the
two subgroups of the Kohathites: there a further technical term is
appropriate, even if not absolutely necessary. In 10/39, the Chronicler's
למשפחת is likely to have been the original form of the word used: it is
identical to the form found in Josh 21:4 (LXX) – plural in MT – a verse
which by any account of the production of Joshua 21 is a foreshadowing
of v. 10. The alteration of למשפחת in 21:10 into ממשפחת – plural again in
MT – is readily understandable given its proximity in that verse to the
following מבני לוי.

These four common occurrences of משפחה, even if in somewhat
different forms, can be taken as witnesses to an assured minimal usage
of this word. However, an even more reasonable pattern of 'original'
usage would be achieved if we accepted the Chronicler's attestation of
במשפחותיהם at the end of the Aaronite listing in 6:45. Josh 21:19 (MT)
offers instead ומגרשיהן. (LXX is shorter, and attests neither.) Williamson
(1982: 75) wisely notes that neither text should be emended to agree
with the other, for each alternative is part of a wider pattern in its own
context. Yet, once we move beyond commentary on either book in its

own terms to the historical question about the development of this tradition, a choice can no longer be avoided.

If those five instances reflect the 'original' usage of משפחה, then the expansions and alterations and regularizations we find in the different extant versions can be readily understood. Whether they have taken place independently and naturally, or whether one or other of the expanded traditions influenced the expansion of another, is hard to pronounce on. What is worth noting, however, is this: if it is the case that only the four occurrences of משפחה common to both versions of both traditions are original, then there is a high probability that only the למשפחת forms and למשפחתם are original, and that the ממשפחת/ממשפחות forms are secondary.

If the shorter text is also the more original, at least in terms of length, then we have a choice between two options. Either we accept some elements of the old consensus, and admit at least that the ordering of the materials is more primitive in Joshua. In this case, the Joshua we know has been thoroughly expanded since an earlier draft served as the source for 1 Chronicles 6. Or we maintain the principal elements of the case for which I argued some ten years ago. I suspect that neither option will give any comfort to E. Cortese.

As a general rule, we expect the Chronicles version of any tradition to be later than any material it shares with Torah or Former Prophets. Even if this is a good rule, and I have some doubts about that (Auld 1983: 14–16), it can only be a general rule. We ought not to exclude *a priori* the possibility of at least isolated additions being made to Torah and Former Prophets in a period as late as the compilation of Chronicles. It may be that Numbers 35 and Joshua 21 are just such exceptions which prove the general rule just stated. Certainly, if we were on the look-out for late supplements in the books of Numbers and Joshua, then these chapters would be prime candidates.

Most of the terminology which Joshua 21 shares with Num 35:1–8 and Josh 14:1–5, and which could be significant for plotting wider literary relationships, is in fact found in the opening and closing verses of Joshua 21, namely vv.1–3 and 40–42 (Auld 1980: 65–67). And these verses of course have no counterpart in 1 Chronicles 6. The absence of all Torah or 'Priestly' terminology from the Chronicles version could be an accidental result of its abbreviation. However, there is one interesting counter-indication. The noun אחזה, often labelled 'Priestly', is used in Josh 21:12, 41; and to the former of these verses there exists a counterpart in 1 Chron 6:41. The Chronicler's text is identical to Josh 21:12 except that it lacks the final באחזתו. There appears to be no motive for its deletion. This may be the single vital indicator that 1 Chron 6:39–66 is related to a stage in the development of Joshua 21 which had not yet undergone editing from hands that are known as 'Priestly', in the widest sense of that term.

WORDS

6

A JUDEAN SANCTUARY OF 'ANAT (JOSH 15:59)?*

Enjoying protected status in a canonized tradition, בית ענות of Josh 15:59 has achieved a modest importance in some studies of the recent past. It has been described (*Enc. Miqr. II*:95–96) as a dialectal by-form of בית ענת found in Josh 19:38 and Judg 1:33. With the added observation that this by-form shows a vocalic shift more familiar in Phoenician than Hebrew, it is cited to justify the interpretation – and even the reading! – of an Aramaic inscription from Memphis (Dupont-Sommer 1956: 84). Its authority thus strengthened, it supports the intrusion of Lady 'Anat into a cryptic utterance of Moses in place of the troublesome *pi'el* in Exod 32:18 (Whybray 1967). And finally, a large-scale historical geography (Kallai 1967: 330) has been deterred from adopting the widely accepted identification of the site.

All the information relevant to this unique occurrence of the name in Josh 15:59 is cited, but I believe wrongly assessed, in Loewenstamm's article (*Enc. Miqr. II*:95–96). It makes six points: (1) בית ענות is perhaps also Βαιτανη of Judith 1:9; (2) Eusebius (*Onomasticon* 24, 15–17; 94, 20–21) sets Βηθανιν or Βηθενιμ two miles from Abraham's tere-binths, and apparently this too is the biblical בית ענות; (3) בית ענת is identified with Beit 'Ainûn, which is 3 km. east of the Abrahamic site; (4) Βαιτανων in LXX^A of Josh 15:59, being similar to the Arabic name, has inspired the 'correction' of the biblical text to בית ענון; (5) LXX^B's Βαιταναμ, a typical degeneration from Βαιθαναθ, i.e. בית ענת, has supported an alteration of the Masoretic text in that direction; (6) ענות is but a secondary form of the name of the Canaanite goddess whose sanctuary has given the site its name.

Kallai's Hebrew original covers much the same ground. His distinctive observations are: (1) the accuracy of Eusebius's specifications leaves no doubt but that he was referring to Kh. Beit 'Ainûn; (2) it is more difficult to conclude that the place he viewed was identical with בית ענות; (3) Avi-Yonah (1951: 170) is probably correct in stating that the original form of the name cited in the *Onomasticon* was בית עינים. His English translation (1986: 391) supports the main thrust of the present paper.

It has been recognized by some scholars that the Septuagint's witness to textual history is particularly important in the book of Joshua. In recent studies of that book (Auld 1976), I have argued that this

* Published in *Tel Aviv* 4 (1977), 85 6.

translation reflects a Hebrew tradition more archaic than the Masoretic text at most points of difference. Now it may fairly be assumed that the lists of tribal allocations (Joshua 13–21) might mark an exception to this rule: that less help might be forthcoming from the LXX in our study of the many proper names in Joshua than in other details of that book. Since there are several difficulties inherent in rendering Hebrew proper name into Greek, the Greek evidence might be considered less trust-worthy. In any case, one hardly expects editorial concern to alter such proper names, so the Greek evidence should be of lesser significance. And yet it is a fact that the LXX preserves two blocks of names lost in MT – Judah's tenth district around Bethlehem, after Josh 15:59; and the Levitical cities from Reuben, after 21:35. Further, the existence of a parallel Hebrew witness to Joshua 21 in 1 Chronicles 6 has encouraged the acceptance of LXX readings such as עשו for עין in 21:16.

In the case under scrutiny it is also preferable to assume an original בית ענן(ו) or בית ענם than to accept either the MT or follow Margolis (1931–38: 316) in reconstructing the first LXX rendering as Βαιθ Αναθ. Such an original – and final 'm' and 'n' are readily confused in Hebrew and Greek (which final consonant should be given the priority in 15:51, גשן or Γοσομ?) – corresponds better with Βαιτανη in Judith 1:9, where Brooke and McLean (1940:44) note some support for an even closer link: Βατανην in f, and Βατανων in dgps. It can readily be associated with either alternative of Eusebius. And corresponds well, if not perfectly, with the location and name of the contemporary Beit 'Ainûn.

Kochavi's survey of the site (1972: 57–58, No. 118) detected remains of the Chalcolithic, Iron Age II, Byzantine, and Ottoman periods. Our first paragraph, if reread in the light of what follows, hints at the danger in *preferring* linguistics to good textual criticism. Should future excava-tions confirm the absence of Late Bronze Age and Iron Age I remains, it is important that the name בית ענות – whose authority is no greater than a scribal error – should not give rise to a theory of a flourishing sanctuary of 'Anat deep in monarchical Judah.

Two footnotes: Prof. Aharoni, to whose memory this note is grate-fully offered, observed briefly (1967: 97) that this toponym was one of those containing a divine name; however, he did not discuss the site further except to agree with the conventional identification with Beit 'Ainûn. Secondly, בית ענים would have two possible parallels in the Hebrew Bible, although more apparent than real: ענם in Josh 15:50, where the first radical may be cognate with Arabic g, not '; and ענם in 1 Chron 6:58, which may be a corruption of עין גנים (cf. Josh 21:29).

7

CREATION AND LAND: SOURCES AND EXEGESIS*

This essay attempts a contribution to the interpretation of one verse in the opening chapter of the Bible. I invite you to view it again in both ancient and very modern perspective.

The new vantage point from which I suggest that we look at Gen 1:28 has been located in two quite independent studies. They have appeared only this year; and they complement each other remarkably.

Deuteronomist und Jahwist by Martin Rose (1981) is a rich study which illuminates many more parts of the Bible than the following account can suggest. In a series of detailed and methodical probes, Rose scrutinizes anew several so-called 'Yahwistic' passages in Genesis, Exodus, and Numbers which have long been linked with elements of the narrative in the first half of Joshua and the beginning of Deuteronomy. A very few of his discussions are inconclusive; however, in almost every case he demonstrates (1) that the J-passages are dependent from a literary point of view on the related material in Joshua or Deuteronomy; and (2) that the parent material either clearly belongs to, or has a close affinity with, the first main Deuteronomistic stratum. Rose deduces that Deuteronomy and Joshua – or at least earlier but still recognizably Deuteronomistic drafts of them – were available to and were utilized by some of those responsible for the so-called J stratum of the Pentateuch. Another nail in the coffin of a J-document from the time of David and Solomon.

My own *Joshua, Moses and the Land* (1980) deals with quite different texts. It proposes new solutions to the vexed problems of the literary development of both the second half of Joshua and the final chapters of Numbers. Comparing these, it seeks to demonstrate that as Joshua 13–22 was gradually drafted and redrafted, so – stage by stage – the end of Numbers was rewritten to make it conform. As the account of what Joshua (and his colleagues) achieved in the land grew more detailed and more complex, so Moses' instructions were gradually made fuller. My study only seeks to demonstrate what was the source from which some of the latest additions to the Torah were drawn. Rose's demonstration that earlier texts in Joshua had also inspired earlier elements of the Moses story has only confirmed my suspicion that several of the 'sources' of the Pentateuch are indeed 'documentary' –

* Published in *Proceedings of the 8th World Congress of Jewish Studies* (Jerusalem: 1982), 7–13.

and are freely available for our scrutiny without having first to be hypothetically reconstructed.

Both our books conclude with the same invitation: to start looking at problems in the Pentateuch from its end, not its beginning. To begin 'in the beginning' has proved a trap. Two stories of creation laid side by side and two accounts of Noah brilliantly combined almost without remainder have created expectations of a Pentateuch composed of parallel and once separately existing sources. Over a century of brilliant expertise has been unable to satisfy these expectations – and just as unable to release us from them. And if, in this essay, I too move straight to the beginning, it is to suggest how some aspects of the exegesis of God's blessing of humanity may be clarified by a view from the end.

> And God blessed them, and God said to them, 'Be fruitful and multiply and fill the earth and subdue it; and have dominion over the fish of the sea and over the birds of the air and over every thing that moves upon the earth'.

I have chosen Gen 1:28 because a series of important articles have found in it programmatic significance for the 'Priestly Source' of the Pentateuch, and have seen in it a clue to the vexed question of the extent of P.

Brueggemann (1972), seeking to locate the kerygma of the 'Priestly' tradition, suggested that a suitable focus was provided by the 'formidable blessing declaration in Gen 1:28' and that in fact its five verbs 'are the central thrust of the faith of the priestly circle'. While 'the full form of the blessing occurs only in Gen 1', Brueggemann claims that 'it reverberates throughout the P narratives'. The full formula is given to Adam, then partial forms in turn to Noah, Abraham, Jacob, Joseph, and the generation of Moses. Some of these partial forms are linked to a promise of land to the patriarchs. And this helps Brueggemann to circumvent what would otherwise be a problem for his thesis: of the verbs in his 'full formula' *kbš* and *rdh* never reappear in Genesis – and, of these, *kbš* will reappear only in Numbers 32 and Joshua 18, neither of which he is happy to ascribe to P. While admitting that these two terms 'are not derived in any convincing way from specific use in the older tradition', he still claims that 'they surely reflect the intention and mindset of the land taking tradition' and so suggests that in this respect the language of Gen 1:28 'is reminiscent of the *old conquest traditions*'.

Next Blenkinsopp (1976), seeking to define 'The structure of P', while referring favourably to Brueggemann's discussion of recurrent expressions related to the language of Gen 1:28, found firmer ground elsewhere. He drew attention first to the three solemn conclusion formulae which give special structural prominence to the creation of the world (Genesis 2), the construction of the sanctuary (Exodus 40), and the establishment of the sanctuary in the land and the land's division between the tribes (Joshua 18–19). He then reminded us of P's

frequently repeated 'execution formulae' – X did according to all God
had commanded him, etc. In fact he suggests that conclusion and
execution formulae are intertwined at the beginning and end of P. Just
before mention of God finishing his work (Gen 2:2) comes the
command to subdue the earth (*kbš/'rṣ* – Gen 1:28). Similarly, not long
before the report that Israel had finished dividing the land (Josh 19:51),
comes the note that the land was subdued before them (*'rṣ/nkbš* – Josh
18:1).

> Use of the same verb (*kbš*), by no means a commonly attested one, suggests
> that with the allotment of the land the command given at creation to fill the
> earth and subdue it has now been fulfilled; hence once again the pattern of
> command and execution. It is also noteworthy that the word *'rṣ* stands for
> both the created world and the land of promise, the usage strongly suggesting
> symbolic association between them. (290)

Then thirdly, Lohfink (1978) drew on both these studies. Approving
both of the prominence ascribed by Brueggemann to Gen 1:28 and of
Blenkinsopp's structural defence of the position that the conclusion of P
is to be found in Joshua, he returned to the old question: what sort of a
historian was P? He describes in detail how the gradual fulfilment of the
first three terms of the divine blessing *(prw wrbw wml'w 't-h'rṣ)* is noted
again and again throughout Genesis and in Exodus 1. He finds that the
appearance again in Josh 18:1 of *kbš* (which has been absent from P
since Genesis 1!) represents no less than the literary bracket round the
entire work of P. Finally, the absence of any note describing the
fulfilment of man's peaceful lordship over animals hints that that
belongs only to a future paradise.

Viewed from the beginning of the Pentateuch this whole case has
certain attractions. It is natural as one reads on from Genesis 1 to hear –
and even listen for – echoes of notes struck at the outset. But even
considered in these terms, the argument does involve some special
pleading. It is a rather odd sort of literary structure if only three out of
the five elements of its programme are repeated frequently, one only
once, and the final term not at all. Lohfink too is straining at the
evidence when he claims Josh 18:1 for P, but denies P those elements of
Numbers 32 which use *kbš* – and all the more, when he does assign to
that source the neighbouring Num 34:1–18. However, I want to suggest
now that what has been taken as an opportunity in these articles is really
a problem. Viewed from the study of Joshua and the end of the
Pentateuch, the case is much less attractive. And moreover, the studies
we have just reviewed represent something of a novelty in the long
history of interpretation of Genesis 1.

Gen 1:28 – now so important – has been described as the least
commented-on verse in the first chapter of the Bible. Cassuto, for
example, passes over it in silence. Where it was discussed in early and

medieval Jewish authorities, it was to remark on an oddity about *kbšh* which more recent studies appear to have ignored. Genesis Rabbah (cited in the Soncino *Midrash* I, 1939: 62–3) and Rashi (Rosenbaum and Silbermann 1929) both observe that what is *read* as a plural imperative is *written* without *waw*, and so might be rendered 'subdue her'. They explain that it was to man that the command to have issue was given and not to woman – and that in fact it is part of a man's business to control his wife lest she become a gadabout and come to grief. It is not my concern to add support to this medieval interpretation of our verse – it seems to me to evade the sexual partnership of vv. 26ff. by grasping at an orthographic irregularity. Yet it remains true that it was by paying closer attention than the moderns to the form of the word itself that the ancients were afforded their exegetical opportunity. I note in passing a second aspect in which Rashi's exegesis is more scrupulous than some recent comments on our verse: *kbšh* is the final word of the first half of v. 28, and so more naturally relates to what has gone before than to the following grant of dominion over the animal kingdom.

Yet, as a deliberate element in a programmatic 'Priestly' formula, *kbšh* is odd – and its defective written form is only the first of its oddities. It is also the only element of v. 28 not repeated in Genesis 1. And grammatically, it provides the only example of a suffixed object within the whole chapter – *br'm* in 5:2 being the other exception in the primeval history. (P prefers to mark the object with *'t*.) It might be added that the *qal* theme of *kbš* nowhere else in the Bible has *'rṣ* as its stated or implied object. No wonder that it was this word rather than the rest of the verse that drew the comments of the ancients.

By contrast to this, *wh'rṣ nkbšh lpnyhm* of Josh 18:1 is much more secure in its context. To be sure, that verse is a new introduction to a passage (vv. 2–10) that had originally been drafted without it. But it is one of a series of late additions to the end of Joshua and Numbers which are related to each other in language and ideas. If we find space to scrutinize their terminology carefully, we should find it more closely linked to material in Chronicles than to 'Priestly' strata in the Pentateuch. In our case the link is with 1 Chron 22:18f. (Auld 1980: 63).

I should prefer to conclude that if use of the same terminology to talk of subduing the earth (or land) in both Genesis 1 and Joshua 18 is more than accidental, then *kbšh* in Gen 1:28 may represent an adjustment to the creator's original blessing to make it conform with what Joshua (or even Chronicles) had reported as having happened. In fact this explanation of the relationship of the texts may serve to make less surprising the unique construction in Genesis 1 of *kbš* (*qal*) with *'rṣ*. It is intended to anticipate the more familiar passive construction elsewhere.

However, the reconstruction of the history of one word in Genesis 1 will carry more authority if the interpretation of the chapter is thereby facilitated. In the heady days of economic expansion, colonialism, industrialization, few would have questioned that subduing the earth and the animal kingdom was a God-given right. Benno Jacob's commentary here (1974: 11) is doubly typical: (1) it is only on *kbšh* within v. 28 that he offers any comment; (2) all he has to say is that 'man is given unlimited power over the earth. No human work on it can be called a violation of God's will.'

Many recent exegetes have recoiled from such unfettered comment. Nehama Leibowitz writes (1976: 4–6):

> The phrase 'subdue it' ... is rather puzzling at first glance, bearing as it does a bellicose significance which is at variance with the peaceful ideals that our sages considered to be the goal of mankind. ... The blessing ... cannot refer to man being bidden to make war on his neighbours. ... The phrase refers rather to man's conquest of the desert and his constructive and civilising endeavours to build and inhabit the world, harness the forces of nature for his own good and exploit the mineral wealth around him. ... Man is not subservient to the world. The forces of nature are not supernatural ones that are superior to him. But he stands on the side of God against Nature.

Good practical Zionism – but is it good exegesis of *kbšh*? Steck has certainly reached an overlapping conclusion by a rather different route (1978: 107): 'The subjection and harnessing of the earth for man's use ... points to man's tilling of the soil with the aim of winning food from seed and his growing of useful plants. This is mentioned immediately afterward in verse 29.' Yet v. 30 makes plain that God's offer of food is to all animals as well as man – to my mind that makes it less likely that v. 29 has cultivation of crops in prospect. And if so, then *kbšh* is still not clarified.

I hinted earlier at another contemporary exegetical approach. Westermann (1974: 220, 222) Lohfink (1978: 156–71), and Vawter (1977: 57–61) have all in different ways attempted to clarify *kbš* in Genesis 1 in the light of the following half-verse, and in particular of its verb *rdh*. This is all the more easily achieved in that the sense of *rdh*, which makes an earlier appearance in v. 26b, has already been clarified in most discussions before *kbšh* is reached. For Vawter, 'subdue' is but 'part of the same uncompromising rhetoric within which "have dominion" falls ... Probably no distinction is intended between the two terms.' Westermann and Lohfink actually describe *kbšh* as part of v. 28b. *rdh* is now widely held to be an image of royal power – an interpretation reinforced by Wildberger's now classical discussion of 'Das Abbild Gottes' (1965). Yet Westermann (1965), though willing to explain *kbš* by the same royal image, has to admit that the Bible never attests the verb in a kingly context.

But should *kbš* be so tamed? It appears to me that Benno Jacob was franker than all the other commentators I have mentioned when he noted that the verb implies 'unlimited power'. The Bible uses the verb of military conquest, enslavement and rape. If the opening chapter of the Bible did have the paradise myths in mind, then it is unlikely that *kbšh* was an original part of its text.

Both ancient and modern commentators have resorted to stratagems to explain *kbšh*. Its form is rather odd in the context of Genesis 1. If it is derived from the book of Joshua, then its presence within the Torah may be part of a larger pattern. But why did an editor add it to Gen 1:28?

To answer that question would be the business of another paper. All I can do here is note that *prh* and *rbh* occur together outside Genesis in Jer 3:16 and 23:3 (and in Ezek 26:11 – MT, but not LXX) in talk of return to the land; and that in two Pentateuchal passages (Exod 23:29–30 and Lev 36:3–13) they are linked with talk of warfare in the land. These sections of Prophets and Torah may have facilitated the intrusion of *kbšh* into God's blessing.

8

TRIBAL TERMINOLOGY IN JOSHUA AND JUDGES*

The thinking behind this paper had several starting points.

One was my work on the Hebrew and Greek texts in the book of Joshua. Masoretic Text and Septuagint in that book represent quite divergent textual traditions: these frequently differ, especially in the geographical chapters 14–19, over how a tribe is introduced. In MT, for example, Josh 17:1 mentions *mṭh mnšh*, 19:1 talks simply of *šmʿwn*, 19:10 speaks of *bny zbwln*, while 19:24 uses the longest formula – *mṭh bny 'šr*. In each of these verses, LXX attests a different style of naming the tribe in question: *mṭh bny mnšh* in 17:1; *bny šmʿwn* in 19:1; and simply *zbwln* and *'šr* in 19:10 and 24.

There are thirteen more examples of such variation in these chapters (Josh 13:15, 24; 15:1; 16:8; 17:7; 18:11 (×2), 21; 19:9 (×2), 16, 32, 40). In general the Greek text attests a shorter formula than the Hebrew, and less use of the noun *mṭh*. This corresponds well with the general differences between MT and LXX in Joshua. My suggestion (Auld 1979a: 1–4) was that this special noun for 'tribe' (*mṭh*) had been used originally only in the secondary framework passages Josh 14:1–5 and 19:51. Subsequent scribes within the already diverging traditions had intruded the term piecemeal into the intervening lists so framed.

A second impulse was provided by several works from the later 1970s which attempted to engage rigorously with Social Anthropology: I mention in particular the work published in English by de Geus (1976), Rogerson (1978), and Gottwald (1980). The demise of Noth's amphictyony thesis, which has been amply documented over the last 20 years, has in no way lessened scholarly interest in pre-monarchic Israel as a tribal society. The observations of social anthropologists have been assiduously and ingeniously compared with biblical materials in the quest for a more suitable model for pre-state Israel.

The most ambitious and detailed such attempt is Gottwald's *The Tribes of Yahweh* (1980). In general I welcome warmly his attempt to bring more reality and scientific rigour into the working language of biblical scholars. Yet I have doubts whether he himself is sufficiently rigorous in his criticism of the biblical texts.

Gottwald admits some fluidity in the biblical terminology for tribes and their sub-divisions. And he concedes 'that in customary speech the technical terms were not required (we commonly say New York or

* Published in *Le Origini di Israele* (Rome: 1987), 87 98.

California instead of the State of New York and the State of California)'
(246). But he is quite clear that *šbṭ* and *mṭh* are the *regular* biblical terms
for the *primary* social/structural subdivisions of Israel.

My third point of reference is the *History of Israel* by Professor
Soggin (1984). He too is impressed by the sociological contribution of
our American colleagues (157), and recognizes that their work may
have implications for the normal translation of *šbṭ* and *mṭh* as 'tribe'
(167). However, I find particularly interesting his suggestion (30, 171)
that it is to the post-exilic hierocracy that we should look for the
situation in which the idea of a pre-monarchical tribal structure
developed. I think that I can provide in this essay some of the evidence
to support his proposal.

One of the interesting features of biblical Hebrew is that the two quite
distinct words, *šbṭ* and *mṭh*, both span the same semantic range: from
'stock/rod/staff/sceptre' to 'tribe'.

It is widely supposed that *šbṭ*/*mṭh* came to designate a 'tribe' because
the leader or elder of that tribe had a rod/sceptre as a personal badge of
office. This is a perfectly possible point of view: the words for the
symbol of leadership had first been extended to mean leadership itself,
and then finally the group that was led. Greek αρχη and Latin *imperium*
are familiar examples of terms which first denoted authority itself, and
only afterwards the area or group over which that authority was
exercised. However, one of the purposes of this essay is to urge that the
primary sense of *šbṭ*/*mṭh* is much more often to the fore in biblical texts
than translators and interpreters allow. In fact I want to test on you the
hypothesis that *šbṭ*/*mṭh* came to denote 'tribe' (whatever precise
sociological definition we give to that term) only in later biblical texts.
What Gottwald would have us believe – that, say, *nptly* was only a
popular abbreviation of the formal and proper *šbṭ nptly* – is simply not
true.

In order that we may obtain some external leverage on the meanings
of *šbṭ* and *mṭh* in Joshua and Judges, we should first review the usage of
these nouns elsewhere in biblical Hebrew (a full conventional account
of *mṭh* is available in Simian-Yofre 1984; cf. also the brief but useful
discussion in Umhau Wolf 1946).

It is manifest that *šbṭ* is used in its primary sense in Gen 49:10—
l' yswr šbṭ myhwdh, and in Zech 10:11 – *šbṭ mṣrym yswr*. Then, at the
end of Psalm 78, where the *'hl* of Joseph and *šbṭ* of Ephraim (v. 67) are
rejected in favour of the *šbṭ* of Judah and Mount Zion (v. 68), LXX
rightly translates *šbṭ* by σκηπτρον, as it does also in Zechariah 10 (it
uses αρχων in Genesis 49).

We might usefully review next the use of *šbṭ* in relatively late
passages within Isaiah, Jeremiah and Ezekiel.

The symbolic joining of the 'rods' or 'staffs' of north and south in
Ezek 37:15–23 shows that the primary sense of *šbṭ* as 'staff (of

authority)' still operates as late as the Exile, even in connection with names like Judah and Joseph/Ephraim.

We need to look rather more closely at Jer 10:16 (= 51:19). There God is contrasted with idols in the following terms (at least in MT):

> Not like these is *ḥlq y'qb*
> for he is the one who formed all things,
> and Israel is *šbṭ nḥltw*.

What *šbṭ* means here may be clarified by reading the verses that follow this passage within Jeremiah 51:

> You are my hammer and weapon of war:
> with you I break nations in pieces;
>   with you I destroy kingdoms;
>   . . . .
>   with you I break in pieces governors and
> commanders. (Jer 51:20–23)

According to the received Hebrew text, Israel is a 'rod' wielded by Yahweh – just as Yahweh called Assyria *šbṭ 'py* according to Isaiah of Jerusalem (Isa 10:5–15). This almost certainly does not represent the original text of Jeremiah; for in both passages LXX attests a shorter text that lacks the word *šbṭ*. However, this evidence from MT 'pluses' in the later Jeremiah tradition strengthens my case. For it demonstrates that *šbṭ* continued until late biblical times to be used in its primary sense, even when it was combined with names like 'Israel'.

Isa 63:17 uses in parallel 'your servants' and *šbṭy nḥltk*. This suggests to me that these *šbṭym*, like God's 'servants', are the agents or sub-authorities through whom he rules.

Of course Hebrew literature took a special delight in *double entendre*. In Isa 10:5, for example, which I have just quoted, *šbṭ 'py* suggests both the royal sceptre of Assyria and the fact that he was a rod for beating Israel. It could be true that these verses in Jeremiah and Isaiah intended to convey both the privilege of Israel (that she was a treasured possession of her God) and the responsibility of Israel (that she was the tool of her God). Perhaps! – but I would like to have more evidence that *šbṭ* did mean 'tribe'.

Even in the book of Numbers, where the familiar twelve-tribal *systems* are universal and regular, there is still clear evidence that the *words mṭh* and *šbṭ* do not (always) mean 'tribe'.

In chapters 2 and 10, we find Israel in the desert, grouped in four bands of three. Each principal 'force' (*ṣb'*) or 'camp' (*mḥnh*) possesses a *dgl* ('standard'), while each of the other eight has a *mṭh* – the connection *dgl mṭh* is never found. That suggests to me that *mṭh* here still refers to some sort of insignia.

The narrative in Numbers 17 about the collection of twelve 'rods', one from each *byt 'b* in Israel, and the sprouting of the *mṭh 'hrn* is reminiscent of Ezekiel 37 discussed above. It also helps to explain the phrase *mṭh lwy šbṭ 'byk* in Num 18:2, which might otherwise appear pleonastic.

Finally, the command in Num 4:18 – *'l-tkrytw 't-šbṭ mšpḥt hqhty mtwk hlwym* is surely designed to preserve the authority and pre-eminence of that Levitical family. It does not provide any evidence of the 'fluid usage of the term "tribe"' detected by Gottwald and many others.

We can very quickly review the few remaining biblical texts outside the Pentateuch and Former Prophets, in which the meaning 'tribe' is usually attributed to *šbṭ* or *mṭh*.

Isa 49:6 talks of the mission of the 'servant of the Lord' to the *šbṭy y'qb* and the obscure *nṣwry yśr'l*.

The closing chapters of Ezekiel (45–48) use *šbṭym* ten times.

Then, if we render *mṭh* in Mic 6:9 by 'authority' or 'leader', rather than the conventional 'tribe', we may restore sense to a verse which has often been considered corrupt.

In Ps 74:2, *g'lt šbṭ nḥltk* is often rendered 'the tribe of your possession which you have redeemed'. However, Dahood offered instead, 'redeem *with your club* your patrimony' (1968: 200).

Ps 105:37, talking of the exodus, may be rendered 'Then he led them forth with silver and gold, and there was none among his tribes who stumbled.' Yet the previous verse has spoken of Yahweh's assault on Egypt's *bkwr* and *r'šyt*; and so it may be that by using *šbṭyw* verse 37 draws attention to Israel's 'leadership' too, and not simply her 'tribes'.

Finally, and significantly, we have Ps 122:4 – whose standard translation has provided Gottwald with the title for his *magnum opus*:

> where the tribes go up,
>   the tribes of Yahweh,
> as was decreed for Israel,
>   to give thanks to the name of the Lord.

Yet, when the immediately following verse reads 'There thrones for judgement were set, the thrones of the house of David', I wonder whether the meaning of *šbṭy-yh* is not rather less egalitarian than Gottwald would wish.

Armed and forewarned by this reconnaissance of the whole biblical field, we can turn now to the books of Joshua and Judges. For it is in them that we might expect to find the best historical evidence for Israel's pre-monarchical tribalism.

The scanty evidence in the book of Judges is almost deafening in its near silence – at least as far as terminology is concerned. The main body of the book (chapters 1–16) uses the noun *šbṭ* once only – and there in the sense of 'staff' or 'sceptre' (5:14)! Indeed, it is very sparing in its use of terms for social structure and organization. *mšphh* is found in Judg 1:25; 9:1; and 13:2. In the last of these cases it denotes the Danites, yet not necessarily as an independent 'clan' or 'tribe'. For the role of Judah in Judg 15:9ff. may suggest that Dan was simply reckoned part of Judah by this narrator (full accounts of *mšphh* are available in Liver 1950: 582–8 and Zobel 1986: 86–93).

The series of later appendices in chapters 17–21 do use *šbt* more often. The brilliant story-telling in these five chapters is effective propaganda on behalf of Judah, the Jerusalem cult, and the Davidic line. However, these narratives are hardly of prime worth as a source of information about pre-monarchic Israel.

It is all the more striking that precisely in these later biblical stories about a time 'when there was no king is Israel', *šbt* does not always denote one of the twelve familiar 'tribes' of Israel. On the one side, Judah is termed a *mšphh* in Judg 17:7 – as are the Danites in 18:2, 11 (compare the opening of the Samson story in 13:2 noted above). On the other, the Benjaminites have several *šbtym* (20:12). In that chapter, Benjamin and Israel are rival forces, each with subsidiary authorities. The commentaries of Gray, Boling and Soggin should not be followed here in preferring the *apparently* easier singular *šbt* of LXX to MT's plural *šbty*. Only in chapter 21, after punishment is over, is Benjamin as a whole considered to be one *šbt* missing from the totality of Israel. Then, as if this argument were not enough, we find Benjamin said to have several *šbtym* again in 1 Sam 9:21 (where Saul protests the insignificance of his family). Finally, at the end of these appendices (21:24), *šbt* and *mšphh* are used in parallel.

In the main body of the book of Judges, where the narrative *may* be historically more authentic, there is but one occurrence of *šbt*, but not meaning 'tribe' – and none of *mth*. And even in the supplements to the book *šbt* does not correspond to 'tribe' as we usually understand that term.

The situation in the book of Joshua is much more complex. However, the terms *šbt* and *mth* are used in a series of fairly distinct contexts.

They are used in the plural to denote the totality of Israel – or at least a full representation of her leadership (11:23; 12:7; 22:14; 23:4; 24:1). It is arguable at least in Josh 24:1, where Joshua summons *'t-kl-šbty yśr'l* who are further specified as 'the elders, the heads, the judges, and the officers of Israel', that *šbt* means 'authority' or 'leader'.

Only in the context of the twelve stones from the Jordan (Joshua 3–4) is the number twelve actually mentioned in connection with *šbt*. And, following our discussion above of *dgl* and *mth* in Numbers 2 and 10, we could suggest that the twelve stones set up at Gilgal were intended as more substantial and permanent versions of the twelve 'staffs (of authority)' within Israel.

Both *mṭh* and *šbṭ* are used in the story of the identification by lot of the guilty Achan (Josh 7:1–18). Yet *šbṭ yhwdh* in verse 16 and *mšpḥt yhwdh* in verse 17 (MT) seem to be used interchangeably.

It seems to me that only in the 22 verses that talk of the 'half-''tribe'' of Manasseh' can we be reasonably certain that semantic development is complete for *šbṭ/mṭh* (Josh 1:12; 4:12; 12:6; 13:7, 29–31; 17:1–7; 18:7; 20:8; 21:5, 6, 25, 27; 22:1, 7, 9, 10, 11, 13, 15, 21, 30, 31). Half-'staffs' and half-'authorities' hardly make sense. I have argued in some detail that this very artificial system of 2½ Transjordanian and 9½ Cisjordanian 'tribes' represents one of the latest modifications to the text of the book of Joshua (Auld 1980: 57–9).

And that brings our discussion round full circle to where we began: to the complex and varied attestation of *mṭh* in the framing of the territorial lists in Joshua 14–21. I suspect that *mṭh* has been widely intruded into these texts by copyists. They may well have understood the term to mean 'tribe' – like those who coined the phrase *ḥṣy-šbṭ mnšh*, and like those who translated *šbṭ* and *mṭh* into Greek by φυλη. The standard rendering of both nouns by *šbṭ'* in Aramaic and Syriac does not betray *any* point of view!

So far, we have been concerned only with words, and with their history. Are there wider historical implications? If a term for 'tribe' emerged only in late biblical Hebrew – or, more precisely, if the semantic development of *šbṭ/mṭh* from 'authority (within/over a group)' to 'autonomous group' should be detected only in post-exilic texts – then what are we to say about the 'reality' to which this term refers, and about its history?

It is possible to accept all of the foregoing arguments, and still hold to the traditional view of the tribes. It may be that *mšpḥh* and *byt 'b* are flexible enough terms to fill enough of the gap caused by our removal of *mṭh* and *šbṭ*. It may be that the tribes of Israel were in fact ancient, but were simply not yet *called šbṭ* or *mṭh*. However, is it also possible that the very idea of a tribal system preceding the state, the very thesis of a shift in Israel around 1000 BCE from tribalism to monarchy, was simply a post-monarchical theoretical construct? (The issue have been reviewed again recently, with help from the social sciences, in Frick 1985; and in Mayes 1985.)

We as historians must distinguish very carefully between the sources and the conclusions of our biblical predecessors. When we attempt to reread our sources without tribal assumptions, what do we find?

How many of the individual narratives in the book of Judges are authentically ancient? And what may a social anthropologist deduce from them? Are Manasseh, Asher, Zebulun, and Naphtali, which appear all together in Judg 6:35, social or topographical terms?

Do the arrangements for Solomon's monthly levy represent a harnessing, or a disregarding of Israel's ancient tribal structures? Or, alternatively, does the account of his administrative units in 1 Kings 4:7–19 simply use the most natural topographical terms for economically equivalent geographical units? Far from being a *successor* to Israel's tribal system, is Solomon's structure in fact a *source* for it? (As argued in, for example, Ahlström 1982: 32–4.)

However, this is already the business for another – still unwritten – paper. Yet one last word is appropriate about post-exilic interest in such matters.

It is not easy to decide how much of the detailed material on tribal geography within the present book of Joshua was contained in its principal draft, itself already exilic; and how much was added at a (much) later date. I have argued in a number of studies that the immediate *source* of *some* of the topographical detail in the book of Joshua may even lie in the books of Chronicles.

Common (Deuteronomistic) authorship of Joshua, Judges, and Kings is widely accepted. Yet how much of this 'tribal' material would have been known to the author(s) of Kings?

The books of Kings hardly use these terms – whether *šbṭ* or *mṭh*. As for the actual names of the so-called 'tribes', we have already noted the use of six in Solomon's district lists (1 Kings 4 – Ephraim (v. 8), Naphtali (v. 15), Asher (v. 16), Issachar (v. 17), Benjamin (v. 18) – and Judah (v. 19)). Three of these (Benjamin, Issachar and Naphtali) reappear in a manifestly topographical sense in 1 Kings 15 (*'rṣ nptly* again in 2 Kings 15:29). The formulaic note in 1 Kings 8:1 (= 2 Chron 5:2) about the assembly at the dedication of the temple describes a gathering of representative authorities. And that leaves only two contexts to mention: (a) 2 Kings 10:33, where talk of Gadites, Reubenites, and Manassites will depend on the late formula already discussed from the book of Joshua; (b) the whole issue of the division of Solomon's realm in 1 Kings 11–12 – and the interpretation of those chapters would require a whole paper! Suffice it to say that they are hardly unambiguous evidence for a pre-monarchic system of twelve tribes.

The usage of such 'tribal' names in Chronicles gives quite a different impression from the passages we have just noted in Kings. In fact hardly any of the Kings evidence does reappear in Chronicles. However, there is relevant material among some Chronicler's 'pluses' to the common Kings/Chronicles traditions.

2 Chron 30:10–11 reports some participation from Asher, Manasseh and Zebulun in Hezekiah's great reforming festival – although verse 18 records that some of those northerners (this time from Ephraim, Manasseh, Issachar and Zebulun) did not observe the correct rites. Similarly, in 2 Chron 31:1, Ephraim and Manasseh stand for 'the north'.

The best clue to what the Chronicler is doing is provided in his report of Josiah's destruction of false altars 'in the cities of Manasseh, Ephraim, and Simeon, and as far as Naphtali' (2 Chron 34:6). 2 Kings had specified simply 'the cities of Samaria' (23:19). *šmrwn* the Chronicler uses only for the actual capital city of former Israel. As description of a larger territory, it had pejorative associations for him; and so he replaced it with archaic or at least archaizing 'tribal' names, already familiar from the genealogies at the beginning of his work (1 Chronicles 1–9). It may be to this sort of context that much of the 'tribal' interest of Joshua and Numbers belongs.

CONNECTIONS

9

JUDGES 1 AND HISTORY: A RECONSIDERATION*

With the opening chapter of Judges, as with many other continuing problems of Old Testament studies, it is the case that most of the relevant questions were posed a century ago ('Judges 1' or 'the chapter' will refer to the whole passage 1:1–2:5 unless otherwise clear from the context). And yet it is not the purpose of this article to review the literature on Judges 1 – that in itself would require a lengthy article. Rather this study must go its own way and reconsider the chapter itself in the conviction that several of its long-observed details demand a thoroughly new approach.

The main part of this article will consist of a selective commentary on Judges 1, concentrating on two main concerns: (a) the pinpointing of possible links with material elsewhere in the Old Testament; and (b) an analysis of the structure and development of the passage as a whole. This commentary will be preceded by some more general discussion of the chapter both in itself and in its setting, and will be followed by an attempt to tease out some of its implications.

Tribute must be paid at the outset to the masterly treatment of our chapter by one of last century's masters in particular, Karl Budde (1887: 93–166). It would be tedious in what follows to record each and every agreement and disagreement with his paper. However, this article seeks to be both a response to and a development of his account of the problems of Judges 1.

Introduction

Most scholars of the later nineteenth century – and indeed most since! – would have agreed with Budde that, since only the second introduction to Judges in 2:6ff. finds a continuation in the main substance of the book (3–16), the material in 1:1–2:5 is clearly an insert against the will of the editor of the following (1897: IX); and with Wellhausen that, while Judg 1:1–2:5 appears to be an alternative rather than a successor to Joshua 1–24, it is also the case that not a few passages in our chapter appear identically or similarly in Joshua too – and that it would come as no surprise to see the whole chapter assimilated in it (1889: 213).

Our chapter was viewed as an excerpt from an earlier, 'prophetic'

* Published in *Vetus Testamentum* 25 (1975), 261 85.

account of Israel's settlement in Canaan – an account superseded by the Deuteronomic version in which scattered traces of it survived, and indeed into which this excerpt was subsequently intruded. While there was considerable scholarly consensus about these points of view, there did exist some recognition that some problems and loose ends remained. There was discussion of the raggedness of the chapter, including its self-contradictions (Kuenen for example, answered by Moore 1895: 7) – although these latter could readily be disposed of as later additions to the original text (different scholars made a different selection! See Moore 1895: 5; Wellhausen 1889: 214f.). And it was even noted that parts of our chapter represented a more developed form of the (assumed original) text than their parallels in the book of Joshua (Budde 1887; Kittel 1894: 265). It was observed further that the bulk of the material in 2:1–5 was more expressive of the sentiments of the Deuteronomic redactor than of the earlier 'prophetic' narrative (Bertheau, in his commentary of 1845, had simply assigned 1:1–36 and 2:1–5 to different authors. Wellhausen (1889: 215) extricates 2:1a, 5b as being from the same earlier stratum as the bulk of the first chapter). However, none of these problems was felt to be sufficiently acute to necessitate a radical re-thinking of the approach to the chapter.

Discussion of our chapter then has been something of an appendix to discussion of the book of Joshua – and so also of the problem of the Pentateuch (or 'Hexateuch'). However, given the consensus already described on the relation between Judges 1 and the book of Joshua, its precise 'stratification' in the familiar terminology of Pentateuchal criticism has depended on the 'stratification' arrived at for Joshua. Where an already combined JE was considered to be the principal early source available to the compilers of Joshua (Wellhausen), Judges 1 could be seen to represent the purer, earlier form of J. Where criticism reckoned with two 'Yahwistic' strands (Smend, Eissfeldt, Fohrer), the bulk of our chapter could be assigned to the earlier (J^1, L, N). Where the majority of the earlier traditions in the book of Joshua are assigned to J itself then the bulk of our chapter is deemed pre-Yahwistic (e.g. Rudolph 1938: 272). Accordingly the following reconsideration of the chapter will almost inevitably constitute something of an appendix or detached note to 'The Book of Joshua and the Question "Tetrateuch-Pentateuch-Hexateuch?"' (cf. Auld 1976). However, its principal purpose must be to investigate what can be learned about the edition of our familiar book of Judges from a study of the composition of its opening chapter, and to deduce some of the consequences for the modern historian of early Israel.

Can Judg 1:1–2:5 be termed a unity? And of what significance is it that this chapter appears between the almost identical notes Josh 24:28–31 and Judg 2:6–9? The first of these questions is deceptively simple. Earlier criticism, as we have noted, recovered the unity of the passage by noting a few glosses and elaborations and by rescuing 2:1a, 5b as the original conclusion of the chapter. More recent scholarship has concentrated on how a Deuteronomic editor responsible for this second introduction to the book of Judges has used or misused the early traditions of an only partially successful settlement as an explanation of Israel's subsequent troubles (an element by no means absent from earlier studies). Of course this approach too safeguards the essential unity of the whole chapter as it stands. Nevertheless, just how far 'unity' is an appropriate term for even the bulk of Judg 1:1–36 will be discussed more fully below.

What of the second question – on the setting of our chapter? Smend recently argued in the von Rad Festschrift (Smend 1971: 506) that Judg 2:6–9 is a classic case of recapitulation (in this instance of Josh 24:28–31) on the occasion of a substantial insertion into a passage. His case has several attractions; and his caution in advancing it stems from the cumulative nature of the supporting arguments, which depend largely on the strength of his conclusions about other insertions (most of which, however, fall within the context of the present book of Joshua). These additions he assigns to a 'nomistic' hand that produced a second edition of the Deuteronomistic History (DtrN) (the Joshua passages discussed are 1:7–9; 13:1b–6; and 23). Of course it is more than likely that in the original Deuteronomist's conception his short transitional passage linking his account of Joshua to that of the Judges appeared but once (it is immaterial for our purpose here whether 24:28–31 originally belonged at the end of 24:1–27 or at the end of 23 – Smend argues for the priority of 24 over 23). It follows that one of the notes has been adapted from the other. But it is much less than obvious that 'Josh 24:28–31 is repeated in Judg 2:6–9 with one larger transposition and a few small alterations most of which show the secondary character of Judg 2:6–9' (Smend 1971: 506).

Firstly, the LXX (both A and B) in the Joshua note shares the arrangement of the Judges note. The MT in Joshua mentions first the death of Joshua and then the fidelity of the people during his lifetime and of his contemporaries who outlived him. The LXX and all Judges versions reverse the order. Certainly the one makes a better tailpiece to the story of Joshua, and the other a better introduction to that of the Judges. However, that need only signify that a later editor in the Masoretic tradition of the book of Joshua made a small but relevant transposition in this text. At one other point too Smend (506, n. 45) notes his preference for the testimony of only one tradition – but this time the MT in Judges, which in 2:7 reads ראו for ידעו attested elsewhere. It may be noteworthy that even the MT in Judges continues in v. 10 with לא־ידעו. And where MT and LXX differ in the book of Joshua the latter is generally to be preferred (as argued in chapters 1 and 2 above).

Secondly, it is more likely that the work of secondary edition consisted in the omission at the end of Joshua 24:28 of the words לרשת את־הארץ from the source-material in Judg 2:6 than in their being added to that verse. Within the book of Joshua the phrase appears in the main Deuteronomistic strand in 1:11 (and 18:3?) Not that that demonstrates any more than that the Judges text may be preferable in this detail. On the other hand the attempt is usually made to execute editorial insertions in style. However, our present book of Joshua gives the impression that the settlement is complete before the leader's death – surely sufficient motivation for the omission of the words. (It is important to note that there is considerable variation between the versions of both the Joshua and the Judges texts at this point – indeed it is only over the final phrase in question that the versions of the two texts agree in disagreeing.)

Thirdly, while it is possible that the variety within the versions of Joshua over the name of his inheritance and burial-place (MT: תמנת־סרח; LXX^A: Θαμνασαχαρ; LXX^B: Θαμναθασαχαρα) may simply reflect textual corruption, it is not impossible that it points to deliberate alteration of the original but offensive תמנת־חרס which is the unanimous testimony of the best representatives of the versions of Judg 2:6–9.

If Judg 2:6–9 is a better pointer to the text of the original note than Josh 24:28–31, then what conclusions should be drawn? Perhaps that we have evidence here of the editorial work involved in the creation of our now familiar book division between Joshua and Judges. At least 24:32f. appear to be additions to a once separate 'book' of Joshua – why not the preceding remodelled transitional note also?

The first four words of Judg 1:1, ויהי אחרי מות יהושע, appear to have been modelled on the corresponding words of the book of Joshua. It is likely therefore that they at least belong to this later editorial stage of 'book' division. Furthermore, while there may have been point – granting the hypothesis of recapitulation after insertion – in repeating mention of Joshua's death at the end of the long insert, there seems less cause to repeat it right at the beginning. It has been argued that these words mark an addition later than the insertion of the main part of the chapter. However, great caution must be shown before advancing such a case; as with the discussion about the relationship between 1:1–36 and 2:1–5, so here too one has to be very sure about what constitutes the essential thrust of a passage before one decides which phrases in its received text point towards that and which away from it. It may then be not unreasonable to proceed with the working hypothesis that our chapter is a deliberately contrived introduction to the 'book' of Judges, and turn back to look again at our chapter in itself.

Whatever the reason for one's interest in its content, it must be admitted that it exhibits many marks of untidy, unattractive composition. Indeed it may be helpful to look briefly at the unsatisfactory nature of the chapter under three headings.

Several elements in the chapter are simply ungrammatical, the most frequent type of lapse being (unmotivated?) fluctuation between singular and plural: 1:4, 10f., 16, 17, 34. For the most part this fluctuation is confirmed by the LXX versions. And yet a detailed use of their evidence could only follow a general appraisal of the worth of their testimony to the text of the chapter as a whole. Important in that would be a study of the few substantial variations from the MT, which will be detailed below. Such variation is by no means without parallel in biblical Hebrew – but it appears to a greater extent than usual in this chapter. On occasion an explanation can be plausibly offered. The unexpected singular וילך in v. 11 may not be unrelated to the singular form ויעל in its close parallel in Josh 15:15, despite the change in verb. The singular ויקרא in v. 17 may reflect a return to the original singular subject יהודה; or it may be regarded as having an impersonal subject. But in both cases the change in subject is harsh. On occasion the lack of strict grammar may point to a corruption – a corruption, that is, which had occurred before the separation of the now familiar textual traditions. On occasion, the common tradition in the chapter must be witness either to untidy composition or to early corruption. The addition of את שמעון after the initial ויעל in v. 4 would achieve good grammar in v. 4, sense between vv. 3 and 4, and symmetry between vv. 4 and 17. However, not all the difficulties can be so easily removed; and so it may be bad editing that the chapter suffers from and not faulty transmission.

There are several material contradictions within the chapter. Quite different information about pre-Davidic Jerusalem is given in 1:8 and 21. Of course it should not occasion surprise, given that the city lay on the (Benjaminite side of the) traditional border between Judah and Benjamin (Josh 15:8; 18:16), that there should have been pressure on the city from both sides. Nevertheless, seen from the standpoint of the origin and development of the traditions in this chapter, it is likely that one of these verses was intended as a correction of the other. There is the further contradiction, between vv. 10 and 20, as to whether it was Judah or Caleb that rid Hebron of the three Anaqim. Again it may be that opposing primitive traditions have been harmonized (by implication at least). But we must consider seriously whether one of these verses has become associated with this text later than the other, and is in fact intended to correct the impression given by the other.

There is rapid fluctuation between methods of referring to tribes, the commonest example being the variation between יהודה (in vv. 2, 3, 4,

10, 17, 18, 19) and בני יהודה (in vv. 8, 9, 16). There is variation also
between ישראל and בני ישראל – and indeed tribes mentioned only once
may occur in this form or that. It may be that the difference between the
'simple' names from Manasseh to Naphtali in 1:27–33 and בני דן
in vv. 34f. corresponds to a difference in stratum. However, were
that valid for the whole passage, it would attest a very complicated
development.

Strictures like the above by no means apply to all of the material in
our chapter. Indeed the brief narratives about Adonibezeq (1:5–7),
Othniel (1:12–15), the capture of Bethel (1:22–26) and Yahweh's
messenger (2:1–5) could be likened to gems unhappily displayed in a
poor setting, linked as they are by a narrative which is not infrequently
incoherent and quite ungrammatical.

Nevertheless, despite the considerable untidiness of the chapter
certain structural elements are still apparent:

(1) The mutual assistance pact between Judah and Simeon provides
some sort of framework for the first part of the chapter – it appears
clearly in vv. 3f. and 17.
(2) The opening of v. 22, ויעלו בית־יוסף גם־הם, seems to provide a
counterbalance to either יהודה יעלה in v. 2 or ויעל יהודה in v. 4.
(3) The mention of Josephites in both vv. 22f. and 35 suggests that for
one compiler at least all the northern tribes could be conveniently
subsumed under this name – just as Qenites and Qenizzites are casually
mentioned in the first part of the chapter alongside Judah and Simeon.
(4) The passage opens (1:1) with בני ישראל seeking an oracle from
Yahweh and closes (2:4) with כל־בני ישראל being addressed by his
messenger. These elements need not all have been contemporaneous in
conception or execution; but their presence does suggest that the
development of our passage has not been entirely haphazard. However,
such preliminary generalities require reinforcement and further
exploration.

Commentary

1:1–2 The identity of the opening four words, except for the difference
of name, with the opening words of Josh 1:1 has already been noted (p.
82). There is an extensive parallel between the remainder of the verse
and Judg 20:18. Both use שאל ב־ for oracular consultation – a usage
restricted to Judges and Samuel (and parallels in Chronicles): שאל ביהוה
in Judg 1:1; 20:23, 27; 1 Sam 10:22; 12:10; 23:2, 4; 28:6; 30:8;
2 Sam 2:1; 5:19, 23; שאל באלהים in Judg 18:5; 20:18; 1 Sam 14:37;
22:13, 15; 1 Chr 14:10, 14 (= 2 Sam 5:19, 23 excepting אלהים for יהוה).
Both מי יעלה־לנו and בתחלה are used in a distinctive manner in these two

passages; and, most important, only here is Judah singled out in quite this way. The text of the two part-verses is as follows:

Judg 20:18	Judg 1:1
וישאלו באלהים	וישאלו בני ישראל ביהוה
ויאמרו בני ישראל	לאמר
מי יעלה־לנו	מי יעלה־לנו
בתחלה	אל הכנעני בתחלה
למלחמה עם בני בנימן:	להלחם בו:

Again Yahweh's answer in 1:2 is similar although not identical to that in 20:19. These two Judges passages must either be from the same hand, or else one has been derived from the other. It is certainly not impossible that 1:1–2 is an adaptation of two quotations (Josh 1:1 and Judg 20:18f.) – and if so it is later than both.

1:3–4 That the situation of mutual assistance reappears in v. 17 has already been noted. These verses do not follow on naturally from 1f.: (a) the opening verses appear to envisage Judah's leadership of Israel against the Canaanites over the whole land, whereas this sequel has only Judah's גורל in prospect; (b) the association with Simeon is similarly unmotivated; (c) the Canaanites of vv. 1f. have become, at least by v. 4, Canaanites and Perizzites – although there perhaps under the influence of v. 5. Certainly the move from singular to plural in v. 4 (cf. above p. 83) is also difficult. Within the Greek tradition, LXX[A] (but not B) offers singular forms for both בידם and ויקום, and moves to the plural only in v. 5.

1:5–7 This anecdote follows very heavily after v. 4. Budde and many others treat 1–3 and 4–8 as the sub-units of the first part of the chapter. As will now be apparent, the present approach finds such a division doubly inadequate. In the chapter as it stands, v. 4 functions as an anticipation of the following narrative, or v. 5b as a résumé of v. 4. The subject of the plural verbs in this passage is not specified. Indeed it is not explained just who conveyed the mutilated king to Jerusalem (v. 7b); however, it is very likely that the NEB is correct to treat ויביאהו as impersonal and to render it by an English passive (cf. ויתנו in v. 20). It is possible that in vv. 4 and 5ff. we meet traditions which were originally quite distinct and whose similarity consisted mainly in the fact that both recounted actions at בזק. In fact each could have occurred at a different Bezeq – in a paper read to the SOTS in January 1971, J. D. Martin discussed the localization possibilities; it may turn out unwise to make one firm identification the starting point of one's discussion of these verses. As for links between this passage and material elsewhere in the Old Testament, the only other instances of the duet Canaanite/Perizzite are in Gen 13:7; 34:30 and in the LXX of Josh 16:10.

It is much harder to determine whether there is any link between this

narrative and the narrative in Joshua 10 about Adoni-zedeq. Superficially there is no need to suggest a connection: the kings have different
– even if similar – names; the 'Israelite' assailants are different in each
case; and there is neither mention of an alliance in Judges 1 nor of
mutilation in Joshua 10. And yet, for all that, one suspects that our
narrative is about a king of Jerusalem, and this for two reasons: v. 7b
would appear to relate that the mutilated king was taken *home* to die
(Judah's capture of Jerusalem is not related until the following verse;
and even in such a contorted chapter as this v. 8 can hardly be
understood in a pluperfect sense); and military exploits such as are
claimed by the king can be more readily credited to a king of Jerusalem
than to the king of an otherwise unknown town. Accordingly it appears
not at all unlikely that Judges 1 originally narrated a version of the down
fall of Adoni-*zedeq* of Jerusalem, and that his name was mistakenly
'corrected' to conform to the very similar place-name *Bezeq*. Of course
none of this implies a link between our passage and the actual material
in Joshua 10 – only that it is not impossible that both are about the same
king of Jerusalem.

1:8: Whatever the subject of the plural verbs in 5ff., the subject here is
quite explicitly בני יהודה. And, whatever historical problems may arise,
the verse makes a perfectly passable narrative continuation of the story
in vv. 5–7, especially if we are to accept that the unfortunate king
belonged to Jerusalem.

The final two clauses are closely parallelled by the two last, and rather
fuller, clauses of Judg 20:48. The only other two instances of the phrase
שלח באש are in 2 Kings 8:12 and Ps 74:7. The verbs נלחם and לכד are in
no way remarkable in themselves; nor indeed is the phrase הכה לפי חרב,
although it is found almost exclusively in contexts which are only
Deuteronomistic in the widest sense of that term (in Judges it is found
only in 1 and 18–21). However, all three are found together outside this
verse in only a small number of instances that appear significant for our
purposes. The trio makes its appearance in most of the episodes
described in Josh 10:29–39, where Joshua and all Israel reduce Libnah,
Lachish, Eglon, Hebron and Debir. The text is rather uncertain in this
passage; the LXX attests the trio in vv. 29f. whereas the MT lacks
וילכדו, while in vv. 36 and 38 the LXX appears to attest ויחנו (καὶ
περιεκάθισεν) for וילחמו. And the only other passage is Josh 19:47,
where according to the MT בני דן reduce and rename לשם, and according
to the LXX οἱ υἱοὶ Ἰουδα reduce and rename Lachish (*sic!*). Two
preliminary observations might be made. Firstly, in Josh 19:47 (LXX),
as in our verse, the exploit described is about men of Judah. (It is
particularly interesting to find this mention of Judah in Josh 19; one
suspects that either the information is accurate, or the note late.) And
then, by contrast with the situation in Joshua, it is intriguing that after
vv. 5–7 have offered us details about Adoni-zedeq (if indeed that may

be granted) different from those given in Joshua 10, our verse follows this by recording the destruction of the one city of the Joshua 10 alliance – its head, no less! – which does not figure in 10:29–39. (This statement is not completely accurate, if the text of Joshua 10 is to be trusted. While Libnah is detailed in v. 29 as one of the five cities destroyed, it is Jarmuth which is listed in v. 3 with the other four as cities whose kings made a league with Adoni-zedeq of Jerusalem.)

1:9 The connection between our chapter and Joshua 10 is maintained here too. The trio ההר והנגב והשפלה reappears only in Josh 10:40, although there with the addition of והאשדות. That verse is part of a concluding formula about exploits of Joshua and all Israel; whereas our verse functions rather as an anticipation of the exploits in Hebron and Debir recorded in vv. 10ff. about Judah.

1:10 Two details in the first clause of this verse mark it off from the preceding one: it is in the singular, with יהודה and not בני יהודה as the subject; and the Canaanite is specified not as יושב followed directly by the noun, but as היושב ב. The note about the former name of Hebron reappears in identical form in the opening words of Josh 14:15. (In our verse they are separated from the first clause in the LXX by its additional phrase καὶ ἐξῆλθεν Χεβρων ἐξ ἐναντίας.) There seems to be no motivation for the move to the plural ויכו in MT and LXX[B] – LXX[A] represents a singular form. The name of these three original Hebronites are quoted again in Num 13:22 and Josh 15:14. (In Numbers, in the MT in Joshua and in the LXX in our verse, the names are followed by ילידי הענק.)

1:11–15 This passage is virtually identical to Josh 15:15–19; and it is noteworthy that our version, especially in the MT, agrees with the LXX tradition in Joshua 15 where that differs from the MT.

11 The greatest difference between the versions is over the first word. In face of the united tradition of the versions of Josh 15:15 that the verse should open with the singular ויעל, MT here has וילך, LXX[A] renders the plural וילכו and LXX[B] the plural form ויעלו. Furthermore there is a major material question at stake over who is the subject of this first verb. In Joshua the position is clear; the LXX specifies Caleb as subject in 15:15, however, even in the MT there can be no doubt; for there too he is the stated subject of the actions in vv. 14 and 16. In our Judges passage, Caleb is not mentioned till v. 12 – and in the Greek tradition of v. 11 he is explicitly excluded by the plural forms of the verbs. Indeed in this verse it is hard to conceive of any subject other than Judah or men of Judah being appropriate.

The formula … לפנים … ושם is found only in vv. 10, 11 (and their parallels in Josh 14:15; 15:15) and in v. 23. And indeed the name קרית־ספר is known to us only through this narrative. The equation of Hebron with Qiriath-Arba is made in Gen 23:2; 35:27; Josh 14:15; 15:13, 54; 20:7; 21:11; and Judg 1:10 – in fact at each occurrence of the latter except for Neh 11:25. Similarly Bethel and Luz are identified in Gen 28:19; 35:6 (although not in 48:3) and Josh 18:13 as well as here in Judg 1:23 – however, they appear to be distinguished in Josh 16:2.

13 The words הקטן ממנו are common to the Judges versions of this anecdote but are not part of the mainstream of the Joshua tradition in 15:17. (The words are attested in LXX[A] – one of the very rare occasions on which that version does not agree with either MT or LXX[B]: here it even differs from their combined testimony.) However, the complete phrase עתניאל . . . ממנו does reappear in Judg 3:9, where we encounter Othniel in another role as the first of the Judges.

14 There is considerable variation among the versions of this verse and its parallel in Josh 15:18. In the Hebrew tradition the two verses differ only over whether the word 'field' is definite or not. The Greek tradition in Joshua appears to render not לשאול מאת־אביה (ה)שדה but rather לאמר אשאול מאת־אבי שדה. And again in our verse in Judges, LXX[A] and LXX[B], while differing from each other in two or three smaller points of detail, agree against the other versions so far mentioned in the following three ways:

(a) for ותסיתהו they have καὶ ἐπέσεισεν αὐτήν – B removing all doubt about the gender of the subject by specifying Γοθονιηλ;
(b) for ותצנח they offer two verbs;
(c) they detail the complaint shouted from the donkey, in anticipation of what, with all other versions, they quote in the following verse.

Given the evidence of all the other versions, it is hard not to conclude that the LXX in Judges 1 has gone its own expansionist way. What is more intriguing, however, is to find the LXX in Joshua offering a text longer than the MT. A tentative defence of this reading might be offered on two grounds:

(i) It is not at all impossible that לשאול is an abbreviated corruption of לאמר אשאול.
(ii) Whatever the meaning of the verb in ותסיתהו, this longer LXX text makes more sense of the pronominal suffix. Soggin (1988. 166) follows Noth's suggestion (1953: 86) to ignore the suffix and offer the quite hypothetical translation 'she decided'; both admit that the verb has a pejorative sense elsewhere in the Old Testament. In fact any suggestion that Othniel should take the initiative would make a strange introduction to the following clauses in which his new wife does all the asking and receiving. Of course, if that were granted, then the conclusion would be likely that it was from the proto-Masoretic corruption of the Joshua text that the version in Judges was first taken and then, at least in the Greek tradition, expanded.

15 In this verse, however, the MT has closer affinities to the LXX in Josh 15:19 – cf. in particular the use of לך after the initial ותאמר; the specification of כלב as subject of ויתן; and, in the Kᵉthibh at least, the use of the singular forms גלת עלית/תחתית. (At this point, the LXX's rather strange λύτρωσιν μετεώρων/ταπεινῶν may well render what we find in the Kᵉthibh of Josh 15:19 – גלת עליות/תחתיות. In this verse too the LXX appears expansionist, and an unsatisfactory witness to the primitive text: it adds ᾿Ασχα, although it is already clear she is subject; and adds after כלב the phrase κατὰ τὴν καρδίαν αὐτῆς.) There is one point of difference between the two Hebrew verses over which the Greek versions can offer no assistance: הבה־לי in Judges for תנה־לי in Joshua. Both can be readily parallelled in Joshua and Judges, and so a decision on priority is hard to make.

1:16 The LXX versions each supply a different proper name (᾿Ιωβαβ in A, and ᾿Ιοθορ in B) after the initial ובני and also make קיני definite. However, in so doing they remove only one of the ungrammatical features of the verse. The difficult move from plural to singular was already noted above on p. 83, and is confirmed by LXXᴬ (B's κατῴκησαν represents only the second of the two final verbs – and in the plural).

1:17 The counterpart to vv. 3ff. The use of שם העיר in both vv. 17 and 23 may be a pointer to deliberate editing. The return at the end of the verse to the singular is harsh (A offers a plural form).

1:18 The most remarkable textual point in this verse is that it is negative in the Greek versions (BHS notes the possible parallel with the negative phrase in v. 19b). The MT appears to be in keeping with those parts of this chapter which have been told 'ad maiorem Judaeae gloriam'. The LXX is again also longer, apparently representing a text with the concluding words ואת אשדוד וסביבותיה. It is hard not to associate this verse with the problematic note in Josh 15:45–47. And yet even with the LXX's addition here of Ashdod, the lists are the same neither in order nor in total.

1:19 The actor is again יהודה, as in vv. 17 and 18. The MT's use of לא or אין with an infinitive is certainly not without analogy – the usage is discussed in GK 1141; however, the passages quoted there appear to imply some impropriety. It seems best to accept the testimony of the LXX that the original text included יכלו, and so was closely parallel to Josh 17:12. This would involve a marked difference from the notes on Benjamin (v. 21) and Manasseh (vv. 27f). where it appears that the יכלו of the source has been removed – see below. Yet whatever the precise meaning this verse does give the first clear testimony, common to both MT and LXX, to any limitation or even reversal of Judah's fortunes. If the positive claim in the MT in v. 18 is accepted as original, then that claim is flatly contradicted in our verse. If the LXX's negative in v. 18 is felt more acceptable, then a compiler had doubtless considered that in v. 19 he was spelling out the consequence of the failure in v. 18. It is arguable that העמק is odd Hebrew for the coastal strip, or even for the gentle uplands (generally described as השפלה) into which that passes.

Josh 17:16 makes a somewhat similar point about the difficulties of the
Josephites in the עמק יזרעאל where the Canaanites had the advantage of
רכב ברזל.

ההר appears nowhere else as object of the verb הוריש; but perhaps it is
not impossible – the object is generally explicitly human, but הארץ, העיר
and הערים האלה are all used. Mention of רכב ברזל is made elsewhere in
the Old Testament only in Josh 17:16, 18 and Judg 4:3, 13.

1:20 Whatever our judgement on the relationship between the pieces of
information given in the previous two verses, there can be no doubt that
v. 20 does run counter to an impression already given in our chapter in
v. 10. Our verse reflects more closely the letter and the spirit of Josh
15:13–19 than does v. 10 – indeed v. 20b is identical to Josh 15:14a
(apart from the 'omission' of the subject 'Caleb').

The phrase כאשר דבר משה is found only in Lev 10:5; Num 17:12 and
(with אליהם) in Josh 4:12. In Deuteronomistic contexts (in the broadest
sense) a ... כאשר דבר clause regularly has Yahweh as subject, and
indeed is relatively common. In Josh 15:13 it is specifically stated to
have been at Yahweh's initiative that Caleb was granted Hebron. Indeed
that idea is not excluded in our verse, for the opening ויתנו must surely
have an impersonal subject. The nearest specific candidate would be
בני יהודה, already quite distant in v. 16.

1:21 The proper interpretation of this verse in its development and setting
is quite crucial for our understanding of the whole passage. It clearly
must be studied in close association with Josh 15:63, where similar
information is given – but about Judah not Benjamin. It has often been
claimed that with this verse, if not already with v. 19, we reach the list of
notes which place on record the failures of the (northern) tribes of Israel
in their attempts to settle Canaan. Further, it has often been noted with
surprise that this list in vv. (19) 21, 27–35 has been interrupted so near its
beginning by the narrative in vv. 22–26 – not that such interruption is
foreign to our chapter! It was suggested above (p. 84) that v. 22 marks the
beginning of a new section. That of course cannot be used as evidence in
a discussion of v. 21 – it itself requires proof. However, two formal points
should be noted straightaway:

(i) vv. 21, 27–35 are only superficially a unity – vv. 21 and 34f. differ
from vv. 27–33 in their use of בני בנימן and בני דן;
(ii) in the phrase את בני בנימן, v. 21 seems linked in form not with vv.
27–33, where בקרב־ is used to express the same idea, but with the first
part of the chapter where not only is את the only word used for 'with'
(את is also used in 2:1; but עם in 1:22) but there is also a direct parallel
in v. 16: וישב את־העם.

Accordingly, if v. 21 should be viewed as the final verse of the first part
of the chapter, then it becomes increasingly likely that in vv. 19–21 (or

even vv. 18–21 according to the LXX) we should recognize a series of 'corrections' of the record in vv. 1–17(18). These had not necessarily been made at the same time. Also it may or may not be that the information in v. 21 is more correct than that in v. 8 – all that is being claimed here is that v. 21 belongs to a later stratum of the chapter. A similar situation obtains for v. 20 and v. 10.

For the next stage of our discussion of this verse we must turn to Josh 15:63, and in particular to the substantial difference between MT and LXX in that verse. I suggest that the LXX's Hebrew original made the following three simple statements:

(1)   והיבוסי יֹשֵׁב (ב)ירושלם
(2)   ולא יכלו בני יהודה להורישׁם
(3)   וישב היבוסי בירושלם עד היום הזה:

It has already been noted that there must be a general predisposition to accept the testimony of LXX in Joshua where that version differs from the MT (see chapters 1 and 2 above; this statement is particularly true of LXX[B]). And there are two good reasons for making no exception here:

(a) It is much easier to understand how the misunderstanding of יֹשֵׁב as a participle necessitated the addition of את at the beginning of the verse (so producing the clumsy sentence found in the MT and in Judg 1:21) than it is to comprehend how the reverse procedure could have taken place.

(b) It appears that the MT's 'addition' of את בני יהודה marks a deliberate moderation of the 'originally' more uncompromising note which had placed on record Judah's complete failure to dislodge the Jebusites – a note perfectly in harmony with Joshua 15 as a whole. Similarly in 16:10 the MT's concluding words ויהי למס־עבד appear to modify the original sense. The longer concluding note in the LXX, giving the information we find in the MT in 1 Kings 9:16, makes its view plain that Gezer remained Canaanite until the Egyptian invasion in Solomon's reign. It appears further that our v. 21 was adapted from the proto-Masoretic tradition of Josh 15:63 (cf. above on v. 14) at some stage after the addition of את בני יהודה but before the alteration of יֹשֵׁב into יושבי. Two additional arguments may serve to clinch this case: (i) The phrase עד היום הזה in v. 21 is unique in Judges 1 but is found in Joshua in three related notes – 13:13; 15:63 and 16:10. (ii) The suggestion made in our verse of a symbiosis of Jebusite and Benjaminite in Jerusalem is quite a novelty; we have no (other) evidence that it either was the case or was even believed to be the case at any stage in Israel's history. That an editor in the Masoretic tradition of the book of Joshua could describe the situation as he appears to have done is much more understandable

What we read then in Judg 1:21 is a rather careless transposition of information found in a particular version of Josh 15:63 by an editor of Judges 1 who knew that two things were wrong with the text before him in v. 8: that no complete victory had ever been won in the early period over Jerusalem; and that, in any case, the pressure on that city in the early period was being applied not by Judah but by Benjamin.

It may be of service at this point to break off the commentary, and summarize our tentative conclusions about the first part of this chapter:

1. The first two verses provide the heading for the whole chapter, and are adapted from the beginning of Joshua and the end of Judges.
2. The basic structure of the first part of the chapter is provided in vv. 3f. and 17, the mutual assistance pact between Judah and Simeon. Certainly vv. 3f. are not a good continuation of v. 1f. – after Judah has been offered victory by Jahweh it is odd to find it seeking assistance from Simeon.
3. The intervening vv. 5–16 represent a variety of southern traditions, drawn in part from the book of Joshua, which are linked with this structure (and to some extent with each other) by the catch-word, or at least 'catch-idea' principle. Some of these individually, and all of them cumulatively correct the emphasis of Joshua 10 that it was Joshua and all Israel that secured the south of Canaan for settlement.
4. On the other hand, vv. 19–21, and perhaps v. 18 too, form a series of corrections – and possibly accurate ones – of the information and impressions offered in vv. 3–17.
5. We are now in a position to see that Judg 1:1–21, far from being an early historical narrative (whether from J or not), is in fact a late composition – itself much supplemented. Its outer framework draws its inspiration from material in Joshua and Judges which seems by no means early. Its main theme is a correction of the book of Joshua. And indeed its concluding verse, often treated as one of its earliest and most authentic contributions to our topographical–historical information, turns out to be based – in form at least – on a supplementary note in that book!

Some of the problems in vv. 22–36 are most extraordinarily complex; and so it is best, in resuming the commentary, not to proceed from verse to verse but rather to orientate ourselves first by those passages where rather firmer conclusions are possible.

1:22–26 This narrative need not long detain us. It was already suggested above (p. 84) that it may have served in one editor's schema as the counterweight to the talk of Judah 'going up' in v. 2 and/or v. 4. The information presented is interesting, but has no clear links with either

Joshua or the rest of Judges. One may assume that the narrative had an independent existence before its incorporation in Judges 1. It would be idle to speculate just how much or how little the editor added to his source – however, he was presumably responsible for at least גַּם־הֵם in v. 22. And that observation may provide confirmation on two other points: that there is in fact a correspondence between this passage and the beginning of the chapter, v. 22 thus marking the opening of the second part of the chapter; and accordingly that the correcting additions to the first part of the chapter conclude with v. 21.

1:34–35 The Josephites of vv. 22–26 reappear at the end of v. 35. Here the versions agree in terming them בֵּית יוֹסֵף – in v. 22 the LXX attests בְּנֵי יוֹסֵף. However, even without this textual uncertainty, it remains unclear what conclusion should be drawn about the editing of the chapter: whether their mention at beginning and end is testimony to some kind of structure in vv. 22–35 as a whole, or whether their reappearance here is due only to a subsequent editor who had adapted to his own purpose some of the material already in the chapter.

The intervening vv. 27–33 are far from uniform (see below); however this section on Dan is quite distinctive: (a) it uses בְּנֵי דָן instead of the 'simple' tribal name; (b) the Amorites rather than the Canaanites are the foe; (c) help is required from a neighbouring Israelite tribe. In the case of Manasseh, v. 28 makes the rather different point that that tribe benefited in time from the improved situation of Israel as a whole.

Our verses on Dan do have their counterpart in the book of Joshua, although not in the Masoretic text. Holmes (1914) has discussed both the relative priority of Josh 19:47f. and Judg 1:34f. and the relative merits of the MT and LXX in the Joshua passage. The comments on this book by Orlinsky (1969) are sympathetic and thoroughly appropriate. To the necessary question why a Hebrew reviser should have omitted the verses from Joshua 19, Holmes suggests that he omitted that part of the narrative which recorded failure and retained the part which recorded conquest. (Cf. above p. 91: over all these passages the MT and LXX in Joshua are consistent in their different outlook.) 'On the other hand', he continues (1914: 70), 'if we take the view that the passages are insertions in the LXX, the difficulties in the way are considerable. First, what necessity was there for transposing the subscription?' (The standard Joshua 19 concluding formula appears in the MT in v. 48, after its short note on Dan's problems and migration; while in the LXX it precedes that version' much longer note on the same.)

> Second, why is the inserted passage, which is continuous in Judges, here divided into two parts, one part before v. 47 MT and the other after it? If the scribe had wished to insert Jud. i 34, 35 we should expect to find the LXX narrative parallel with MT up to the end of v. 47; then the insertion of the undivided passage, the whole being rounded off by the subscription. As it is, the hypothesis of insertion requires us to believe that the LXX translator first

transposed the subscription – a wholly unnecessary proceeding – that he then inserted the first part of Jud. i 34, 35, went on with the MT and finally inserted the second part of the passage.

Holmes's case is unexceptionable as far as it goes. In his Introduction Holmes had already noted that 'the use of ὑπομένω (continue) ... seems decisive for a Hebrew original. The meaning of the word הואיל was not known to the Greek translators. In the passage in Judges and in Jos. xvii 12 it is rendered by ἄρχομαι; in Jos. vii 7 by καταμένω. The only possible inference is that the translator had a Hebrew text before him: that ὑπέμεινεν is his rendering of ויואל and not an inexplicable variant of ἤρξατο in Jud. i 35.' (1914: 16) Of course in itself that does not imply that that Hebrew text was in fact the original one. The following points may serve to remove any lingering doubts about it:

(i) The note in Joshua (LXX) makes the straightforward point that in the original Danite area it was only her powerful neighbours Judah and Ephraim that were able to penetrate the Amorite-held coastal plain.
(ii) Judahite success was of no interest to the compiler of the note at the end of Judges 1 – hence the omitted verse.
(iii) The original 'Ephraim' of Joshua (LXX) was altered to 'house of Joseph', presumably to correspond to v. 22. This would appear to confirm the suggestion made above, that a deliberate connection was made at some stage in the edition of the chapter. Does this imply that mention in vv. 27–33 of Zebulun, Asher and Naphtali, as well as of Manasseh and Ephraim, was considered natural in a context in which talk of the house/people of Joseph predominated – just as is the case with Qenites and Qenizzites in the broadly Judahite context of the first part of the chapter?
(iv) It appears that the MT in Josh 19:47 was produced in three steps: the elimination of the two verses by then in Judges; the alteration of a Judahite success at Lachish to a Danite one in the north, perhaps after the model of Judges 18; and finally the incorporation of this remodelled note within the main Danite section.

Here again then we appear to be dealing with a part of Judges 1 which has been derived from the book of Joshua, and not very well harmonized with its new immediate context.
1:36 This is an odd tail-piece, with probably no relevance to our problem. LXX[A] (but not B) and some presumably related versions mention 'Edomite' in addition to 'Amorite'. This is taken by some, including the editor of BHS, as sufficient warrant for proposing האדמי for האמרי in this verse. Certainly 'Scorpions' Ascent' is found in the southern border description of Judah (Josh 15:3) or Canaan (Num 34:4); and one Sela at least was in Edom. However, we cannot know just what

conception of Amorite territory some late editor of Judges 1 may have held; and indeed it is hard to doubt that the only link between this verse and its context is in fact the link-word 'Amorite'. Accordingly, if our text is mistaken, it is a mistake of the editor who included this verse – and not of a later copyist.

1:27–33 These verses pose very difficult problems for our study. Their manifest lack of symmetry shows them to be no more worthy of J than is the chapter as a whole. No two of these five notes are constructed alike; and so the impression is given that we are dealing not with an author but with a compiler, or even a series of compilers who have rather ineptly presented the evidence available to them. It is the first two notes, on Manasseh and Ephraim, which have undeniable parallels in the book of Joshua; and these it is too that follow immediately after the Josephite narrative in vv. 22–26.

27f What is the relationship between these verses and Josh 17:11–13? Why are two so clearly related texts so different from each other? And how has the variety in the textual tradition of each arisen?

(a) These two texts are more like each other than either is to similar passages in Joshua or Judges: only they talk of 'daughter-villages' and of 'putting' the local indigenous population to forced labour. Both למס ... ויתנו in Joshua and וישם ... למס in Judges happen to be unique phrases. Certainly they share the use of the inf. absol. הורש with Josh 3:10, and some features with the notes in Judges 1 on Asher and Dan. With that on Asher: mention of both cities and inhabitants of cities; with that on Dan: the use of ויואל and the suggestion that the situation of the enclaves was influenced from outside the tribe itself. However, on balance, it is more likely that the notes on Asher and Dan have been influenced by that on Manasseh (see below) than that together with it they represent what is distinctive of Judges 1 or at least the source of this part of it.

(b) We can have greater confidence in the textual reliability of the Judges passage than of its Joshua counterpart.

In Judg 1:28 the LXX seems identical to the MT. In the previous verse it is characteristically fuller, and in two ways:

(i) It offers six city names in place of five – however, one suspects that Ἰεβλααμ in sixth place represents a late 'correction' of an editor who had not realized that Βαλααμ (A)/Βαλαδ (B) in fourth place renders יבלעם in fourth place in the MT.

(ii) It offers (certainly only in B) οὐδὲ τὰ περίοικα αὐτῆς in addition to οὐδὲ τὰς θυγατέρας αὐτῆς after all but the second and third names. (Is this an explanatory comment (by a translator?) like the identification of Beth-Shean with Scythopolis in both A and B? Or is it witness to ואת־חצריה in a branch of the Hebrew tradition (cf. Josh 15:45–47)?)

The textual situation in Josh 17:11–13 is much more complicated – or at least in v. 11, for the tradition appears sound in the latter two verses. And that is important, for it allows us to be quite certain about the distinctiveness of the Joshua and the Judges versions of the tradition – only in Joshua is there talk of the inability of Manasseh (cf. 15:63) to deal with the enclaves; and Josh 17:13a is plural whereas Judg 1:28a is singular. We have already noted that they use different verbs for 'putting' to forced labour (p. 95). Of the six proper names in the MT (the five of Judges MT plus עֵין־דֹּר after דֹּאר), LXX^B renders only three, Beth-Shean, Dor and Megiddo (in positions 1, 3 and 6 in the MT), while LXX^A renders four, appending Taanach to the other three. We shall return to this notable discrepancy; however, at this stage two general comments may be appropriate. Beth-Shean, Dor and Megiddo are common to all versions of both Josh 17:11 and Judg 1:27, and always appear in the same relative order; whereas Ibleam and Taanach appear in positions 2 and 4 in Joshua (MT), but in reverse order in what we have taken above to be the original common tradition in Judges 1. Then the same five names reappear together only once, in 1 Chron 7:29 (LXX – the MT is without Ibleam), but in an order different from either of the texts present in question (the only point common to all texts is Beth-Shean in first place).

(c) There remains sufficient concord within the various versions to permit us to see that our greatest problems are not with the transmission of the text but with the material in it. For while Judg 1:27 reads oddly (although no more so than the note on Asher in vv. 31f.), Josh 17:11 is grammatical nonsense – and that in all its versions! It would appear from the first part of the verse that we are dealing with a continuation of the note on the topography of Manasseh's inheritance in 17:7–10. Verse 10 had already noted in an annoyingly imprecise way that Manasseh's neighbour to the north was Asher and to the east Issachar. (Anyone drawing a map on the basis of other information in Josh 13–21 might wonder how Zebulun fits into this situation; but that is not our concern.) One gets the impression that v. 11 starts by augmenting or qualifying that note – its editor had information that some border cities which a boundary map would have assigned to its northern and eastern neighbours were in fact controlled by Manasseh. It must come as no surprise that if Beth-Shean, lying as it does on the north side of the broad border valley, was in fact Manassite, then it was one of these special cases. However, while that argument could hold, it would be much less easy to apply it to Ibleam, offered in next place by the MT alone. Whatever our judgement on that point, the whole character of the verse changes at the next name in both MT and LXX: from this point we read only of 'inhabitants of cities' and not of the cities themselves; and what is more, the following names bear the marks of being the grammatical predicate and not the subject of their clause. (This is clear in the Greek versions, where all the following names are in the accusative; in the MT the preposition את appears only with the third name, but its effect presumably extends to the end of the list. Such at least had been the assumption of the Greek translators.) The change in the spirit of the passage is made perfectly plain in vv. 12f. If v. 11 opened by stating that Manasseh controlled territory which theoretically belonged to another tribe, these verses now deny Manasseh's ability to control territory which was theoretically its own! If only the evidence of the book of Joshua, MT and versions, were available to us, and we knew nothing of our Judges passage, then the most natural solution would be to suppose that a verse or two had gone missing from our text, and that two originally separate notes had become telescoped. And that may indeed remain the correct solution.

(d) When we turn again to the Judges parallel, we find that the grammar is in order (each name is prefaced with את) but that again the first two names appear alone, while the remainder have יושבי prefaced. (It is intriguing that in both Joshua (MT) and in Judges the second position in the list is held by a simple city name, particularly since (a) the name is different, and (b) the other's name does appear later in the list *with* יושבי!). However, on the evidence so far discussed, it appears that Judg 1:27a only gives the impression of being a better text than Josh 17:11a because in fact it is a deliberate improvement of it. Any theory that the Joshua text was dependent on Judges or that each had been contaminated by the other is excluded on this one ground: while there was no editorial motive for removing את from the names after Dor (or indeed from before בנותיה at each occurrence), there was every reason for the Judges editor to make a difficult text more regular. And so it is not unlikely that these Judges verses too are dependent on a Joshua passage. This solution has the merit (perhaps doubtful in a case of such complexity) of confirming and being confirmed by our general approach to the wider problem. Several ends are left untied: Why does the problematic שלשת הנפת (which reappears in the LXX in the longer form καὶ τὸ τρίτον τῆς Ναφετα καὶ τὰς κώμας αὐτῆς) not appear in Judges? Holmes (1914: 65) suggested attractively that the LXX's misunderstanding of it is clear witness to its presence in the Hebrew text available to it; and that in fact properly understood it may testify to LXX[B]'s own reliability in offering only three names. The phrase could be an addition to the common Joshua tradition made at a stage after the work of the Judges editor. The phrase may have been omitted by a Judges editor after 1:27 had been supplemented to contain more than the three original names witnessed in Joshua (LXX) and common to all versions. It may have been a part of one of the original but now telescoped notes in Joshua 17 which did contain but three names. But the tentative answers which can be offered within the context of this solution are no less plausible than any others.

(e) In conclusion, two details of our passage are worth rather closer scrutiny.

יושבי occurs with a city name more often in Joshua and Judges than elsewhere in the Old Testament, except for Jeremiah in the set phrase יושבי ירושלם (about two dozen instances in Joshua/Judges (but see below) over against four in Samuel/Kings and eighteen in the Prophets, fourteen of these in Jeremiah). In several of the contexts in Joshua and Judges there is textual uncertainty. Of the 23 instances in the LXX and 24 in the MT, only 19 are common to both traditions – and typically more of the MT's 'additions' are in Joshua and more of the LXX's in Judges. Quite apart from the parallel passages in Joshua 15 and 17 and Judges 1 under discussion, the several occurrences in Joshua 8–11 and Judges 20–21 appear to be in passages from later editors, editors who were active just before, and in the very early stages of, textual divergence.

The use of בנות(יה) in the sense of dependent villages or environs is also restricted to a few areas of the Old Testament:

(1) it appears three times in Numbers – 21:25, 32; 32:42;
(2) it is used in Joshua in 15:28 (LXX), 45, 47; and 17:11, 16;
(3) in Judges there are the five cases in 1:27 plus two in 11:26;
(4) the remaining twenty or so instances are all in Nehemiah and Chronicles: Neh 11:25, 27, 28, 30, 31; 1 Chron 2:23; 7:28, 29; 8:12; 18:1; 2 Chron 13:19; 28:18.

Presumably the five or six instances connected with Manasseh which occur three times (in Joshua 17, Judges 1 and 1 Chronicles 7) have a common origin (the near-identity of the names was already noted on p. 96). Once these have been excerpted from the above, we are left with many more comparable instances in the Chronicler than elsewhere. It is interesting too that the associated city names in the Numbers passages, in Judges 11 and in two of the Chronicles passages are all in Transjordan.

A late dating for our passages or their source is not proved by our observations on these two features. Every expression has to be used somewhere first before it becomes current usage; and indeed each is unremarkable in itself, although one could suggest בני or אנשי with a city name as an alternative for the first, and חצריה already common in Joshua for the second. And yet, in the context of all the other arguments adduced, they do at least point to a late dating. (The question of the relative priority of the notes in Joshua 17 and 1 Chronicles 7 is not our concern here.)

29 There is a clear connection between this verse and Josh 16:10. However, by contrast with the fairly clear evidence available on vv. 21, 27f. and their parallels in Joshua, the brevity of this material and its lack of distinctiveness, together with the divergence between MT and LXX in both verses, seem to make impossible any firm decision on dependence. All that may be said is that they offer no evidence *against* our cumulative case.

30–33 Several of the city names in these verses on Zebulun, Asher and Naphtali are identical to, or at least reminiscent of, names in the relevant sections of Joshua 19.

Judg 1:30 details קטרון and נהלל (for which LXX^A offers Ἐνααλα and LXX^B Δωμανα); while קטת and נהלל are the *first* two of the final block of five names in Josh 19:15.

Judg 1:31 details רחב, אפיק, חלבה, אכזיב, אחלב, צידון, עכו in the MT – the LXX adds Dor between Acco and Sidon. While the section in Joshua 19 on Asher makes no mention of either Dor or Acco (in the OT it is only in Judg 1:31 that the name appears), רחב and צידון רבה do appear with other names in v. 28 and the section concludes in vv. 29f. with the names מחבל אכזיבה ועמה ואפק ורחב (at the first name the LXX has translated the initial מ with the preposition ἀπό.

Judg 1:33 details Beth-Shemesh and Beth-Anath which reappear in reverse order as the final names in Josh 19:38.

It is also noteworthy that the three tribes are dealt with in the same order – the only difference being that Joshua 19 mentions Issachar too, between Zebulun and Asher.

However, the brief narrative framework in which we meet these names in our chapter finds no correspondence in the book of Joshua. In Joshua 19, in the cases of Zebulun and Asher, the names in question occur *after* the (concluding?) border-formula . . . (וי)היו תצאתיו; and so it is not implausible to consider them additions to an earlier stage of the text of that chapter – although not necessarily from Judges 1 (the same is true of Josh 15:63 and 16:10 for example). In the case of Naphtali (19:32–39), where that (concluding?) formula appears as early as v. 33 and does not reappear near the end of the main section, the relevant names are the final two. Accordingly, to start with the negative conclusion, if a Joshua editor did cull these names from Judges 1 – or at least from its source – he did not use the same method to insert them in the existing Joshua framework.

But why should an editor of Joshua have repeated evidence from Judges 1 about enclaves when making his additions to Joshua 15–17 and not when working with Joshua 19? Of course this rhetorical question is wrongly stated; we have already determined that Judges 1 was not the source for Josh 15:63, 16:10 and 17:11–13 – rather the other way round!

It is possible that the compiler of Judg 1:30–33 used material gleaned from Joshua 19 to fill out his increasingly critical treatment of the settlement of the northern tribes – or it may only have been material coincidentally reminiscent of it. His information may or may not be true – that is not our problem here; however, it is interesting that it is only in the last two of these notes that he goes as far as to say that, because of their failure to eject the Canaanites, Asher and Naphtali continued to live *amongst them*. Elsewhere it was stated that the original inhabitants continued to live among the Israelite tribe in question. Could it be that in these final verses, where the compiler himself appears to be author and so less bound by the sources, he gives his own rather more extreme view of the situation?

2:1–5 This narrative too need not concern us much here. Its content is distinctive and interesting – and yet for our present purposes its very distinctiveness makes it the more difficult to compare with other texts or to derive from them. However, it is worth noting that מלאך יהוה is found only in certain easily defined contexts in the narrative books of the Old Testament, and very little elsewhere:

In the Pentateuch, in Gen 16:7, 9, 10, 11; 22:11, 15; Exod 3:2; and in Numbers 22 (10x).

Elsewhere in Judges in 5:23; 6:11, 12, 21², 22²; and 13 (10x).

In the other Historical Books in 2 Samuel 24:16; 1 Kings 19:7; 2 Kings 1:3, 15; 19:35.

And elsewhere in the OT in a similarly small scatter of instances. There are differences in our passage between MT and LXX, but they do not bear on our discussion. It has already been noted that this narrative, like 1:1f., concerns the people of Israel (p. 84). And finally, given the apparent date of the preceding material in our passage, there remains no incentive to attempt an isolation of the primitive core of the anecdote.

Conclusions

Despite all the foregoing discussion the ultimate problem of sources remains. To say that Judges 1 is heavily dependent for much of its material on the book of Joshua only postpones the matter until a study is undertaken of the source problems of that book. On the other hand, Joshua has no counterpart to the anecdotes about Adoni-bezeq (even if he is originally the Adoni-zedeq we encounter in Joshua 10), Joseph at Bethel or Yahweh's messenger at Bochim. The editors of Judges 1 had both material and an outlook that were independent of the book of Joshua.

This essay has sought to demonstrate that some parts of Judges 1 (e.g. vv. 20, 21, 34f.) are of the same basic type and function as their parallels in Joshua – editorial notes that correct and supplement a given text. It has sought further to show that this whole preface to the book of Judges – and it has been possible only to hint at what may and what may not have been contained in that! – in fact functions in an analogous way: it too is a late prefatory note to the book of Judges which supplements, corrects and explains the treatment by the Deuteronomistic History of the period of the Judges. Part of it suggests that the troubled history of the northern tribes, about which the body of the book is largely concerned, was due to the failures during their settlement of Canaan. Part of it compensates for the scanty mention of Judah in the remainder of the book – and hints that by contrast that tribe's settlement had been more complete (and incomplete *only* where impossible, v. 19!). It is not unlikely that this new preface is contemporaneous with the division of the long Deuteronomistic History into the now familiar separate books.

There is no room here to draw out all the practical implications for the historian. Clearly it is only *after* the fundamental nature of the chapter as a whole, and of many of its parts, has been grasped that it is in any way appropriate for a student of Israel's early history or political geography to probe this chapter for relevant information.

Such then is the material in the opening chapter of Judges, the chapter whose very distinctiveness over against Joshua permitted a needful critical reappraisal of that book in this last century of scholarship. One must surmise that our forefathers may have been led astray in part by their criteria for isolating J in the Pentateuch (and elsewhere); and in part by not questioning the easy assumption that what inspires criticism of one source is itself a better source – and if better, then also earlier.

One last word. If this essay has removed from the modern historian some 'early' and 'authentic' source-material, it has at least replaced this with a glimpse of one of the biblical historians at work. If he is in any way typical, we may take comfort that as historians of Israel's origins we are *in principle* in a situation no way inferior to that of the biblical editors. They preserved their sources for our inspection, so giving us – who have other sources – a view of the 'events' no more distant than their own. And of their prejudices we may be as aware as we are of our own!

READING JOSHUA AFTER KINGS*

There seem to be at least two questions jostling under the deceptively simple 'What are we reading if we are reading the book of Joshua?' How independent is the book of Joshua? In what sense is it 'a book' in its own right? And in what sense is it merely a part of something bigger – Former Prophets, Deuteronomistic History, Hexateuch, Primary History (from Genesis to Kings)? In asking this question, I am betraying only partially reconstructed interests: beyond *Rezeptionsgeschichte* – and Joshua has been 'received' and studied in all of these contexts – I also want to probe the wider writing context within which Joshua grew, was shaped.

What precisely is the 'book of Joshua' about which we are talking – whether or not it is a part or a whole? What is the extent, shape, and wording of this text? I am drawing attention here to the fact that Joshua is one of the several biblical books where the received (that word again!) Hebrew and Greek texts differ substantially in length, and – though to a lesser extent than some – in order; and where the still scanty evidence from Qumran both illumines and complicates the already familiar relationships. Leonard Greenspoon asked at the 1990 Manchester conference of the Qumran fragments of Joshua: 'Which puzzle are they part of, and where do they fit?' (1992)

In matters of wording and shape and extent, the question of Joshua is the same as the question of Daniel, or Esther, or Jeremiah – yet these three stand more clearly on their own as separate books. In matters of independence or interconnectedness, the question of Joshua is more like the question of Leviticus. In the Pentateuch, a case for at least relative independence within the union has long been more readily urged for Genesis or Deuteronomy. Mary Douglas, in her fascinating account of Numbers, published as *In the Wilderness* (1993), invites us to read *bmdbr* – the book's title in the Hebrew Bible – strongly, and not just as what happens to be the first word of a merely conventionally divided-up portion of the Pentateuch. And I am certainly open to her persuasion that the middle fifths of the Torah also have their own integrity. And yet Leviticus is still the middle of something bigger. How far is that true of Joshua as well?

When the book of Joshua was the main focus of my attention some

* Published in J. Davies, G. Harvey and W. G. E. Watson (eds), *Words Remembered, Texts Renewed: Essays in Honour of John F. A. Sawyer* (JSOTS 195, 1995), 167–81.

fifteen to twenty years ago, I covered some of the necessary groundwork
for a larger commentary. However, quite a lot has happened since; and
the relevant bibliography has swollen. This is nowhere truer than in the
area of text-critical studies. A detailed study of the relationship between
Masoretic text and Septuagint, and especially of Codex Vaticanus,
remains the indispensable investment and has still many rich dividends
to repay. But several new tools have become available in the intervening
period. Kraft and Tov's computer-aligned text is very helpful in
suggesting a retroversion of the LXX into Hebrew, although it is based
on Rahlfs, and so on Alexandrinus rather than the more interesting
Vaticanus. The long-lost fifth and concluding part of Max Margolis'
magisterial edition of the Septuagint of Joshua – believed destroyed
during the Second World War – has come to light, and its publication
been undertaken by Emanuel Tov. Alex Rofé, and Tov and several
others have devoted various papers to particular chapters or issues.
Leonard Greenspoon has published valuable studies of the LXX and of
other ancient Greek versions of Joshua (esp. 1983). The Leiden Peshitta
volume including Joshua has appeared (1991). And fragments from
Qumran have been discussed by Greenspoon (1992), Tov (1992a), and
Kempinski (1993) – and, as I shall shortly indicate, they have still
exciting surprises to spring. Joshua has plenty of stimulus to offer the
textual critic.

Joshua may have rather less to offer the literary critic. Joshua is not
Judges. There are fewer stories and more lists. The humour is, at best,
less obviously omnipresent. And yet the newer literary criticism is
sending out spies; and, who knows, it may be preparing to cross the
river in force. However, I suspect the majority of contemporary readers
will find they are treading less congenial territory than in Judges or
Samuel. Robert Polzin's first volume on *Moses and the Deuteronomist*
(1980) drew our attention to synchronic strategies for coping with
discrepant voices in the narrative; and offers a wealth of suggestive
commentary. And Daniel Hawk's (1991) monograph-length study of
'contesting plots in Joshua', under the title *Every Promise Fulfilled*, has
sought to extend the bridgehead. Well and good. But Polzin and Hawk –
and Hawk as the longer and the more recent is also the more culpable –
remain silent about the conversation between the Hebrew and Greek
texts. This seems to be true also of Mitchell (1993). In a recent SBL
paper, Fewell presented an able deconstructionist reading of Judges,
which reminded her hearers how Achsah, a young bride of the first
generation in the land flowing with milk and honey, had to demand
something as basic as water in her portion of the promised land. Poor
Achsah had to make that disruptive demand not just once in Judges –
she had already made it in Joshua as well. Literary criticism of the Bible
has made resolute strides in the same fifteen year period, even if its
colonization of Joshua is still at a very preliminary stage.

Our historical assumptions – expectations – deductions – perturba-
tions have also altered considerably. After Coote and Whitelam (1987),
Garbini (1988), Lemche (1988), Davies (1992), Thompson (1992), and
Ahlström (1993), some of us like, and some of us dislike, models and
constructs and much denser social-historical theory than we were
accustomed to in the old days of not so long ago, when we simply had to
check not very sophisticated readings of Joshua against the current
views of the archaeologists. But then the archaeologists too are
discoursing in new ways – witness Finkelstein's *The Archaeology of the
Israelite Settlement* (1988). The historian of Israel's origins may have
had to give up on Joshua's spies, and the walls of Jericho. But the town
lists and border descriptions must have some information to impart,
even if not about dispositions made by Moses' successor in his old age.
And the question is still there on the table why it is about Jericho and Ai
and Hazor that Joshua tells its stories. There is no answer to that
question in the most recent monograph to come to my hands: Theodore
Mullen's *Narrative History and Ethnic Boundaries: The Deuteronomistic Historian and the Creation of Israelite National Identity* (1993).
Mullen, like many before him, is interested in the several evidences of
ritual re-enactment within Joshua:

> The compositional style of the deuteronomistic history creates a world of
> dialogue that involves the reader or hearer in the literarily constructed social
> world of the author as though the past were actually the present (or the
> present, past, depending on the perspective of the reader).

There have been several commentaries published since 1980: by
Woudstra (NICOT) in 1981; Boling's completion of George Ernest
Wright's Anchor Bible volume in 1982; Butler (Word) in 1983. John
Gray's New Century commentary appeared in a second edition in 1986,
and the translation of Soggin in a second edition in the Old Testament
Library in 1988. To judge from early reviews by Porter (1992) and
Lemche (1983), Ottosson's novel approach in his Swedish commentary
of 1991 will repay close study   not least because of his fresh attention
to the 'priestly' passages in the book: not inserted into, but taken over by
the Deuteronomist. The latest commentary, from Volkmar Fritz (1994),
is in the same series (HAT) – and indeed in much the same spirit – as
that of Martin Noth. The most obvious advances on Noth's position are
that the *Grundschrift*, behind which no literary history is possible, was
the work of the Deuteronomistic historian; and that that first historian
did include a report of the division of the land.

It is in fact the second edition of Noth's commentary (1953) that has
dominated most academic work for some forty years. That re-edition was
the culmination of some twenty-five years of effort on Joshua and related
issues. His many topographical studies of the late twenties and earlier
thirties, and his long-influential study of the twelve-tribe structure of

early Israel, informed the first edition in 1938. Its publication proved to be a stepping-stone to his magisterial *Überlieferungsgeschichtliche Studien* of 1943. And in the light of that commanding new account of a Deuteronomistic historical work, he produced in 1953 the thoroughly revised second edition of his commentary. Yet his amphictyony thesis is largely discredited. And a series of scholars has successfully contested his reliance on Margolis' resolute preference for the Masoretic text over the *Vorlage* of the Old Greek – that Old Greek which Margolis had laboured so successfully to recover.

But not all things have changed. The thesis of a Deuteronomistic historical work reigns supreme. His impulse. His name for it. But seldom now Noth's thesis. There may be intense debate about whether there was but one Deuteronomistic historian, or two or three or several. There may be deep disagreement whether the foundations of this historical enterprise were laid towards the end of Judah's monarchy, or only after its demise. But Dtr is an internationally traded currency, even if not accepted quite everywhere: most readers know that Joshua is but part of a connected narrative, however often expanded and rewritten, stretching at least from Deuteronomy to Kings. Noth's inheritance and its ongoing significance were explored, mostly sensitively, in several papers offered within interlinked sessions of the 1993 annual meeting of SBL in Washington, fifty years on.

There was of course little talk on that occasion about Pentateuchal matters, although Rendtorff reminded participants of his view that Noth would have done better to go on to treat the Tetrateuch as he had the Deuteronomistic History. However, one of the less stable elements in Noth's position on Joshua, to deduce at least from the *Rezeptionsgeschichte* of his work, is his denial of a Priestly contribution to the book of Joshua. I sought in my *Joshua, Moses and the Land* (1980) to render that denial even more plausible. Quite the most vigorous critique that work has received has been mounted by Enzo Cortese (1985; 1990), with the precise aim of rescuing the Hexateuchal 'Priestly' dimension in Joshua while adhering to Noth's Deuteronomistic thesis. (Not even the more recent work on Exodus by Blum (1990) and Johnstone (1990; 1993), and their view not of a P-source but of a P-rewriting of a D-work, would in my view offer an adequate model for talk of a P-contribution to Joshua.) There is a good deal of name-calling in Cortese's attempt to regain something of Mowinckel's 1964 position. His jibe against me (he would call it diagnosis of me!) which I most enjoy is *Settantamania* (LXX-madness) – I suppose because I feel least vulnerable when arguing on the basis of real differences, objectively there, in a range of ancient texts.

So much for reading or re-reading Joshua. What about 'Reading Joshua after Kings'? My most recent tussle with Kings and Chronicles has persuaded me that Kings must be de-privileged (1994). The books of Kings are not after all the source of Chronicles; they are not the 'text' on which Chronicles is 'commentary'. In fact, exactly like Chronicles, Samuel–Kings are part commentary on, part radical extension of, a pre-existing narrative of the house of David. The material common to Samuel–Kings and Chronicles is an account of David's house, of the monarchy in Jerusalem, from the death of Saul to the fall of Jerusalem. That source document, therefore, must date from after Jerusalem's fall. It tells the story of the schism after Solomon's death, and mentions several of the subsequent kings of Israel who did impinge directly on the story of Judah. But the interleaved continuous, if rather formulaic, story of the kingdom of Israel – that story whose presence in the book makes Kings what it is, and distinguishes it from Chronicles with its (in some respects) more conservative focus on Judah alone – is a later addition. To read Kings this way is certainly to read against the grain of the Deuteronomistic History.

The source which both Samuel–Kings and Chronicles have used for their account of the house of David from the death of Saul to the fall of Jerusalem can be almost entirely recovered: it is more or less the text which Samuel–Kings and Chronicles share. Both successor texts had reproduced the words of their source more or less faithfully. They supplemented these words extensively, and hence often effectively marginalized them; but they hardly ever omitted any of them. The textual evidence for these bold claims and some first corollaries can also be sampled in discussions of the Solomon chapters in articles dedicated to Smend and Malamat (Auld 1992; 1993).

In the remaining pages, I invite readers to curb their impatience to know more about Kings/Chronicles relationships, and/or suspend their disbelief, and consider with me some of the implications for a Deutero-nomistic History and a commentary on Joshua. Have I trapped myself or liberated myself as commentator on Joshua by dealing radically in 2 Samuel and Kings with the Deuteronomistic hypothesis? At the very least I have pushed forward the dating of the earliest edition of Kings: that cannot any longer be late monarchic or early exilic, for it represents a substantial revision of a source which itself cannot be earlier than the Exile at which it ends.

In Noth's classic thesis, the Deuteronomistic History was shaped and informed by a series of chapters penned by the historian himself: some ostensibly his own editorial comment (Joshua 12; Judges 2; 2 Kings 17), some in the form of speeches put into the mouths of the leader of the time (Joshua 23; 1 Samuel 12; 1 Kings 8). Noth rightly – over against many of his successors – reckoned Nathan's dynastic oracle in 2 Samuel 7 as pre-Deuteronomistic. But, in his view, 1 Kings 8 (Solomon's prayer at the dedication of the temple) and 2 Kings 17 (the author's own peroration on the fall of the north) were penned by the same Deuterono-mistic hand. In my view, Solomon's prayer in 1 Kings 8, and his visions at the beginnings of chapters 3 and 9, belong for the most part with

Nathan's oracle. They are all shared by Samuel–Kings and Chronicles, and so derive from the source on which both biblical books have drawn. None of these shared materials can be from the same stratum as special Kings material like 2 Kings 17 on the fall of the north. And of these two strata, only 2 Kings 17 could be considered Deuteronomistic, if it was the Deuteronomists who were responsible for something like the present shape of Kings.

I did not work with Eep Talstra's Dutch thesis on 1 Kings 8 when developing my own views on the Solomon chapters in Kings and Chronicles; and its English translation has become available (1993) only since my work went to the printer. But of course I can now welcome for my own ends Talstra's patient demonstration that Solomon's prayer is far from conforming to Noth's or Weinfeld's (1972) pattern for a Deuteronomistic oration. And, much more important, I salute a study which offers a very attractive model for the integration of synchronic and diachronic approaches to texts. As a bonus, his careful discussion of passages in Deuteronomy and Joshua will greatly benefit any reader who is turning again from Kings to Joshua.

But back to the Deuteronomists: was it they, after all, who were responsible for the shaping of the books of Kings? And my question could be reformulated in two ways:

Was there ever a connected narrative, starting with Israel's beginnings in her land, of which Kings represented the final part?

Granted that there are links in language and thought between Kings and Deuteronomy, in which direction does the influence mainly travel between them? Should we continue to think of a core of Deuteronomy whose standards have become those of a Dtr historian, properly so called? Or should we argue instead, or as well, that many of the principles now enshrined in Deuteronomy were deduced from portions of the story of the nation? Deuteronomy before, or after, or contemporaneous with Kings – and that is a book of Kings rather later than we normally suppose.

Having started at the end, it may be safest if we work backwards. The first story which Samuel and Chronicles share recounts the death of Saul and his sons: those deaths which were the indispensable prelude to the reign of David and the telling of it. The Chronicler preserves a somewhat shorter and more original version of Saul's death; and one of my research students believes he can correlate its emphases with earlier traditions now submerged in 1 Samuel, which of course tells the story of Saul's life and what preceded it before it reports his death (Ho 1995). But are we to continue to believe that the Chronicler knew but chose not to retell the Samuel/Saul story? Or should we begin to reckon with the possibility that 1 Samuel supplied a story which the source common to Samuel–Kings and Chronicles had not told?

It is with the completed books of Kings – not the common source, but the monarchical story including the northern Israel additions – that Judges and Joshua have most in common. In some respects, the issues are clearest with Judges. Close links have been noted, and explored again recently by Eslinger (1989), between the 'Deuteronomistic' preface to Judges in Judg 2:11ff. and the peroration on the fate of northern Israel in 2 Kings 17. And then it is throughout Judges and throughout the Israel supplements to the monarchic story that we find repeatedly a dread pattern of 'doing evil in Yahweh's eyes': always 'evil' and never 'right'. Important editorial elements of Judges are congruent with Kings. But are those sufficient grounds to call Judges and Kings part of the same work? Are their relationships any closer than, say, between Kings and Jeremiah? Judges may even be later than the completed Kings. Several stories within Judges apparently know stories in Kings and offer parable-like commentary on them. I have argued (1989), for example, that a few of the elements in the Gideon-stories depend on Kings and are relatively late.

There are connections between Joshua and different layers of material in Kings.

We have Joshua's curse on any rebuilder of Jericho (Josh 6:26) and the price – the life of his own son – paid by Hiel of Jericho according to 1 Kings 16:34. We have also the note about Gezer and the dowry of the daughter of Pharaoh who became Solomon's wife, which appears in the LXX at the end of Josh 16:10 and in the MT in 1 Kings 9:16. Both of these Kings references are in special Kings material, not shared with Chronicles. But both give the impression of being occasional after-thoughts or cross-references between already completed books of Joshua and Kings, rather than structural links.

Many have noted the similarity in territorial conception between some of the topographical information in the second half of Joshua and the list of Solomon's districts in 1 Kings 4; and have argued for the priority of the much briefer Solomonic arrangement. That list is often claimed to be archival and ancient. Perhaps – but we should note that it is not part of the Solomon story shared between Kings and Chronicles.

Then Joshua 9, like 2 Samuel 21, offers us background information about Gibeon – that sanctuary which, according to the shared source on Solomon, was the great bamah before the temple and altar at Jerusalem were constructed. And in Joshua 22 as well, especially if we are right to detect behind the repeated LXX *bomos* an original Hebrew *bamah* (not מזבח as in MT) of witness between the people east and west of the Jordan, the story of a shrine though not for sacrifice may be making its own contribution to explaining how a *bamah* frequented by Solomon might be legitimate.

The common monarchic tradition and – with somewhat different emphasis from each other – the successor books of Samuel–Kings and

Chronicles associate the divinely granted 'rest' (מנוחה/הניח) with the golden age of David and Solomon: in particular, with the Davidic line and the Jerusalem shrine. But Joshua, and Deuteronomy as well, repeatedly portray the successful occupation of the land as that 'rest' – or at least the first step towards Yahweh's 'rest'.

Closer to Noth's own argument: there are several links between his Deuteronomistic chapters Joshua 23 and 2 Kings 17.

All of these links between Kings and Joshua could be accommodated within a fresh account of a Deuteronomistic History. But should they be? Was it those who rewrote Kings who also wrote Joshua and Judges? The first thing implied by reading Joshua after a deprivileged Kings is no longer being sure that Kings is the destined end of the Joshua story. And that is different from the question: Was Joshua written in the light of Jerusalem's collapse?

At the beginning of this essay, I identified two questions jostling under the deceptively simple 'What are we reading if we are reading the book of Joshua?': How independent is Joshua as a book? And which text of Joshua should we be reading? I want to suggest that the answers to these two questions in fact impinge on each other. But I pause first at the text-critical question.

Josh 8:30–35 (MT) appears two verses later in LXX – after 9:1–2 (MT), rather than before. Which position for this paragraph is original? Possibly neither. Commentators have long remarked that neither the report in 8:30–35 that Joshua had duly performed Moses' instructions in Deuteronomy 27 about setting up plastered stones bearing a copy of the torah nor the observation in 9:1–2 that the kings of the land were now motivated to oppose Israel sits easily or well-connectedly in the book. That in itself might suggest that one or other paragraph is a latecomer – and the suggestion draws support from the different relative position of the paragraphs in MT and LXX.

What provides the old discussion with a new twist is that the end of this report on Joshua's diligence is preserved on a Qumran fragment. This was discussed by Greenspoon (1992: 173), who plausibly recon-structed a reference to the Jordan crossing in a small plus in 8.35; but declared he had 'not been able to identify the source of the longer addition at the close of this section'. That addition has been discussed in some detail by Kempinski (1993), who reconstructs the fragment as part of a text in which Josh 8:34–35 led immediately into the beginning of Josh 5:2. Kempinski's view is that the Qumran fragment preserves the original position within Joshua of the circumcision story – this was subsequently promoted on halakhic grounds to before the story of the first passover in Canaan. It is, however, more natural to assume that in a third version of the book the whole paragraph (8:30–35) appeared much earlier, in fact just after the crossing of the Jordan – so enabling in time the addition of the small plus discussed by Greenspoon within what I shall continue to call 8:35.

The first of two suggestions I want to make is that, if we have three different positions for it, it is in fact not original at all, but a latecomer looking for a suitable home. If Achsah has to campaign twice for water within the promised land of milk and honey, and Dan make two attempts to become settled, here we have a short text making three attempts to win an appropriate context in the book of Joshua. May that not suggest that the rest of the contents of Joshua are already relatively successfully settled?

That is a point worth pausing over. Albrektson (1993) has mentioned Tov with approval in his discussion in the Anderson *Festschrift* of the current official Swedish translation project in which he is involved. He urges that the Hebrew text to be translated should not be any of the received texts, obvious mistakes and all, but a reconstructed text. With Tov, he opts for the 'book' at the stage at which literary development finished and after which textual variation began. He takes as an example Jer 48.4, where צערה (to Zoar) should be read with the LXX, rather than צעיריה (its little ones) of MT. I find it easy to agree that LXX attests an earlier reading. I find it easy to agree that MT should not be translated where late alterations have crept into it. But how do you distinguish between rereadings that became normative within the very period that a shorter text more like the LXX *Vorlage* was being expanded and reshaped to become the proto-Masoretic text from rereadings which later distorted that proto-Masoretic text? Given the presence within the textual tradition common to LXX and MT in Jeremiah of two instances of the construct plural of צעיר and one instance of the plural with suffix, I am far from clear how we exclude the possibility that צערה was already being reread as צעיריה before the longer text of Jeremiah was complete. I have considerable sympathy with my Edinburgh colleague Peter Hayman on the three extended families of copies of the Jewish mystical *Book of Creation* (1993). From that complex textual situation, he finds it hard to sympathize with Emanuel Tov (1992) defining the proto-MT as the stage at which the literary development of biblical books was complete and the textual history began.

But, if the commentator has evidence of an alternative criterion to Tov's, evidence of a book of Joshua already settled and unwelcoming without 8:30–35, should this paragraph be translated within a critical translation of Joshua, at one or other of its three attested positions, just because it is attested in all witnesses? Or should it be omitted, at least from the main text, because literary development had finished before various attempts to insert it were made? Happily it is easier for a large academic commentary to adopt a pluralistic approach than an official translation. And pluralism within a Joshua commentary is both possible, because the divergences are not too bulky; and necessary, because many of them preserve clues to the development of the book. Our most antique textual evidence is bearing increasing witness to textual pluralism. A large commentary has a responsibility to present and comment on the various texts to hand.

In its own way, Josh 8:30–35 also bears on questions of interconnectedness – of Joshua as a Deuteronomic book, or as part of a Dtr History. The paragraph has always been recognized as, in some sense at least, a Deuteronomic text. It obviously recounts the carrying out of the command reported in Deuteronomy 27; though, as Polzin nicely shows (1980), it extends or subverts – we could settle for 'interprets' – it interprets the command quite as much as it carries it out. However, its not-yet-stabilized position within Joshua would remove any or most of its potential value as evidence of a structured relationship between Deuteronomy and Joshua – unless we were to say that it was only within a relationship that such afterthoughts would occur. But I would be very resistant to assigning Josh 8:30–35 to the same stratum as any of the material in Joshua whose attested position was constant according to all our available witnesses.

I mentioned already a LXX plus about Gezer as part of the dowry of the daughter of Pharoah who married Solomon at the end of a note in Josh 16:10 about the relationship of the town of Gezer and its inhabitants to the people of Ephraim. The same information is given in a MT plus in 1 Kings 9:16. Is this another late supplement, like Josh 8:30–35? And, if so, might it suggest that Joshua–Kings, at the time of the supplementing, was regarded as in some sense a single text?

Let me close with an alternative, more speculative account of the Qumran variant – one which tends in a rather different direction from my comments above. If the fragment located the end of 8:30–35 just before the circumcision report beginning in 5:2, then presumably in the complete scroll its opening had immediately followed 5:1. Now several elements of Josh 5:1 are repeated in Josh 9:1–2, the verses which precede our errant paragraph in the LXX. Both open with the identical ויהי כשמע; but, while 5:1 has 'kings of the Amorites beyond the Jordan' and 'kings of the Canaanites by the sea' doing the hearing, 9:1 first offers more generally 'the kings beyond the Jordan' and then supplies detail in a couple of clichéd expressions: 'in the the hill country and in the lowland all along the coast of the Great Sea toward Lebanon', and 'the Hittites, the Amorites, etc' – though in different order in MT and LXX. I suggest that 8:30–35 did appear first at the beginning of chapter 5. But when this paragraph, telling of blessing and cursing at Gerizim and Ebal, was relocated after the campaign at Ai in the central highlands, it brought with it elements of 5:1; and these were rebuilt rather clumsily as 9:1–2 – and are to be found there still in the LXX before 8:30–35, although after it in MT where they function as a somewhat more relevant introduction to chapters 9–11 as a whole.

There are plenty of fresh questions for yet another commentary on Joshua to discuss. Reading Joshua after Kings, indeed reading Joshua after reading Talstra on Solomon's prayer, makes it necessary to re-argue the case for Deuteronomistic origins from the bottom up. It also encourages persevering in one's *Settantamania* – and adding a predilection for Qumran-fragments to the symptoms.

11

JOSHUA AND 1 CHRONICLES*

Within the introduction to her massive and detailed commentary, Sara Japhet surveys the sources of the books of Chronicles and how they are used (1993: 14–23). Her summary conclusions relating to Joshua (16) are brief:

> Of all the potential list material ... only two sections have actually been cited: the Simeonite cities (Josh 19.2–8 // 1 Chron 4.28–33), and the priestly and levitical cities (Josh 21.10–39 // 1 Chron 6.54–81 (MT 39–66)). The book of Joshua is, however, also represented by polemic references, such as to the cities of Manasseh (1 Chron 7.29–Josh 17.11–12) and 'the land that remained' (1 Chron 13.5–Josh 13.2–5), and allusions such as 1 Chron 2.7 to Josh 7.1ff.

Citations – polemic references – and allusions offer an interesting classification to muse over. Another example of linkage between these books will be discussed later – this one from the end of 1 Chronicles. However, it is convenient if I start with the one allusion Japhet has actually cited. Within the genealogy of Judah, 1 Chron 2:7 offers 'And the family of Carmi: Trouble, troubler of Israel, who sinned/broke faith over the ban'. A note like this assumes either that the reader must know a story or that the narrator would be willing on another occasion to tell it. And each element of the brief note (עכר עוכר ישראל אשר מעל בחרם) is also a key element of Joshua 7. Do these together constitute proof that the note in Chronicles alludes to the story as we find it in Joshua? What should cause 'trouble' about such a solution is (a) that מעל is a favourite term of the Chronicler and is used also in Ezra, Nehemiah, Ezekiel, and Daniel (admittedly it is also found several times in Leviticus/Numbers, but in very few contexts – Lev 5:15, 21; 26:40; Num 5:6, 12, 27; 31:16); and (b) that the opening clause of Josh 7:1, with its sole mention in Joshua 7 of this key term, looks very like an addition to an already adequate opening to the story – and, if an addition, then surely one inspired by 1 Chron 2:7. There is no intention to argue here that the terse formulation within the Chronicler's genealogy of Judah was pregnant with the as yet unborn story in Joshua 7, though such a case could be considered. But the claim is being made that we should at least be open to seeing mutual influence between Joshua and Chronicles – in this

* Paper read at the SBL Annual Meeting in Chicago, November 1994. To be published in a *Festschrift* for Professor Z. Kallai.

case: from the story in Joshua 7 to the summary in 1 Chronicles 2 and back to the new title for the story in Josh 7:1a.

On the relationship between Joshua 21 and 1 Chronicles 6, quite the longest instance of shared material in these books, I hope that the jury is still out – I advanced my heretical case for the priority of Chronicles first in 1979, but surveyed the arguments again in a Jerusalem article Japhet does not cite (Auld 1990). Since that was prepared, Kartveit (1989) and Ben Zvi (1992) have added cautionary words. However, I do wonder in passing if there is some tension in what she writes about 1 Chronicles 6: she claims on the one hand that Joshua 21 is the source for the Chronicler on the Levitical and priestly cities, and asserts on the other that 'for all their differences, the versions of Chronicles and Joshua preserve two readings of the same document: while the Joshua text is the more dependable, Chronicles may in fact retain specific details of an original nature' (147). Albright had argued in an influential article (1945) that the connections and differences between Joshua 21 and 1 Chronicles 6 were best explained by reconstructing the common source which both had modified. Albright's 'source' had been a simple list of forty-eight cities, four per tribe, with little or no connecting text. Is this the 'document' Japhet mentions? I had hoped I had shown (1979b) that he had been misled by his interest in history and historical geography into concentrating almost exclusively on the place names within the texts, and failing to explore the puzzling links and differences between the texts as wholes. But Japhet still seems to be hovering uncomfortably between arguing on the one side for the priority of just one of the texts and, on the other, comparing each with a source-list, to which it presumably had had independent access. In any case, I wonder whether 'citation' is the appropriate term for the sort of substantial rewriting we find – whether of Joshua in Chronicles or of Chronicles in Joshua. By 1990 I was more open than I had been in 1979 to admitting mutual influence on the development of these two texts: some features of both are more at home in Joshua and some in Chronicles.

Japhet's other 'citation' is 1 Chron 4:28–33, which is certainly closely related to the account of Simeon's territory in Josh 19:1–9. What interests the reader of Joshua is that this area to the south of Judah has already been described – and somewhat differently – within Joshua 15, as the first district of Judah's towns. Where did Joshua find its alternative listing for Joshua 19? Was it freely or inexpertly copied from Joshua 15? Whatever its source, Joshua 19 is certainly closer in detail to 1 Chronicles 4 than to the relevant verses in Joshua 15 (26–32). The punctuation of 1 Chron 4:28–33 is puzzling, both in MT and to a somewhat lesser extent in LXX. I should be inclined to agree with *BHS* that the first word of 32 should end the report in 28–31 – it had become detached because of the parenthetical אלה עריהם עד־מלך דויד ('these were their cities till David ruled') at the end of v. 31. These words are widely held to be an addition to the text copied from Joshua 19, if not a corruption of the sub-total presently in 19:6b. However, they do offer a reason for the otherwise unexplained existence of two districts: the pre-Davidic nucleus, then an additional few towns. Japhet's observation about משבותם being used within 1 Chronicles 1–9 only at the three points where Joshua is cited (4:33; 6:39; 7:28) offers strong support to the regular view – but only if we know in advance that Joshua is earlier than 1 Chronicles. It could be argued in the opposite direction that the Chronicler brings 'settlements' into his genealogies not where he is drawing on Joshua, but where settlement patterns are unusual. Simeon within Judah, priests and Levites scattered within Israel as a whole, and a blurred demarcation between Manasseh and Ephraim are all good examples of special cases. Her linked observation (122) about זאת in 4:33 would be strengthened if the concluding two words of that verse 'and their registration' (or 'enrolment') were also detached to become the subject of a nominal clause, whose predicate would be the personal names listed in the following verses – 'And this was where they settled and were enrolled: ...'

'Citations' and 'polemic references', in Japhet's book, apparently differentiate not degrees of literalness of quotation, but varied attitudes of the Chronicler to his source. Even what she calls 'citation' allows for much reworking: a clearer distinction in Chronicles between priests and Levites, refuge differently understood, cities that were Simeon's 'till David reigned'. If this is citation, what then is 'polemic'?

Once we free ourselves of the predisposition to view Joshua in its entirety as earlier than Chronicles in its entirety, we are able to compare and contrast the details of their presentations of tribal geography more sympathetically. The basic structural comparisons are striking. For the area west of the Jordan, both deal quite separately with Judah (and Simeon) in some detail first, and then the rest of the western tribes more briefly. Both make a special feature of the Transjordanian tribes and of Levi – in Joshua, their treatment brackets the handling of the rest (Transjordan in chapters 13 and 22; Levi in chapter 21, with an anticipatory note in 13:13); in Chronicles, these groups separate Judah (and Simeon) from the north (Transjordan again first in chapter 5, then Levi in chapter 6).

To continue with contrasts: a further striking difference between these two presentations of tribal geography is that Joshua is very interested and Chronicles studiously uninterested over the number twelve.

There are many approximate tribal dozens throughout the books of Chronicles; but the number twelve never appears in connection with them. The actual lists within 1 Chronicles 2–7 do not include Zebulun or Dan, although both are mentioned among the sons of Israel in 2:1–2, and again in 12:24–37. The latter list of David's armed forces does include twelve 'tribal' divisions (though typically of Chronicles it does not count them), but the twelfth is made up of Reuben, Gad, and half-Manasseh. Then 1 Chron 27:16–22 lists thirteen officers over the tribes: this time the tribes include Aaron as well as Levi, and count both halves of Manasseh separately, but have no mention of Gad or Asher.

By contrast, the second half of the book of Joshua is almost fixated on twelve, cf. Josh 13:7–8, 14; 14:2b–4; 16:4; 17:14–18; 18:2–10 (especially v. 7) – and this interest of the geographical chapters is anticipated in the report of the Jordan crossing (Joshua 3–4) by the twelve men, one from each tribe, carrying the twelve ceremonial stones.

The well-known differences between the two books over the Levitical cities, forty-eight in Joshua 21 from each of the twelve tribes but less than forty-eight names in 1 Chronicles 6 and no mention of Dan, seems to be part of a wider pattern. It could be that the text of Chronicles is defective or that Chronicles plays down the tradition of the twelve tribes here and elsewhere by deliberate omissions and silences. Either is possible. But it must rank as certain that Joshua takes pains to accentuate a twelve-tribe scheme – to demonstrate again and again that there is no conflict between its topographical information and the twelve-tribe structure.

To help understand both the similarities and the differences over shape and structure, we might turn to the different ways our Hebrew and Greek versions of the book of Jeremiah handle Babylon within the section on oracles concerning foreign nations. In the Masoretic Text, these oracles are found at the end of the book (46–51) with the Babylon chapters at their very end (50–51). In the Septuagint, the foreign nation materials are in the middle of the book (26–31) with the chapters on Babylon in their midst (27–28). The structures of the two versions of Jeremiah are different but the aim is the same: whether it appears in the middle of the middle or at the end of the end, our particular attention is directed at what is said about Babylon. If we view the tribal materials in Joshua and Chronicles with the same synoptic eye, we may fairly conclude that both books have a special concern with Transjordan and with the Levites and priests – right in the middle of Chronicles' treatment of the tribal genealogies, but at the end of Joshua's tribal geography (although also more briefly anticipated at the beginning). I am not concerned here with the priority of either version of Jeremiah; but I do want to suggest arguments for the priority of Chronicles over Joshua in spotlighting Transjordan and priests and Levites.

The Chronicler's chapter on the Transjordanian tribes concludes with an apparently matter-of-fact note in 1 Chron 5:25–26, reporting that they were taken captive by the king of Assyria. Though this passage is brief, its key word 'exile' (גלה) has been twice anticipated within chapter 5 (vv. 6, 22 – Japhet 140). This two-verse climax to the report on the eastern tribes helps explain the prominent position of the Transjordanians within the Chronicler's review of the tribes: these eastern tribes are the only section of Israel – I mean the so-called northern kingdom – whose 'exile' the Chronicler actually reports. גלה is very sparingly used in Chronicles, and elsewhere only of Judah (1 Chron 5:41; 9:1; 2 Chron 36:20) or Benjamin (1 Chron 8:6).

This end-of-chapter note begins with a key word of the Chronicler which we have already discussed: they 'broke faith (מעל) with the god of their fathers, and whored after the gods of the peoples of the earth'. Now Joshua 22 takes pains to deny exactly that charge – and so it must already have known the accusation: it elaborates in a long story (vv. 10–34) that the altar which the returning eastern tribes built near the Jordan was precisely not a further example of מעל: it was built to remind them of the central altar; it was *not* built for sacrifice. (It is worth asking whether the oddly drafted note in 2 Kings 10:32–33 – the only mention together of Gad, Reuben, and Manasseh in all of Judges, Samuel, and Kings – is not another polemical response to the Chronicler's note about the exile of the Transjordanians.)

As for the Levitic cities: Joshua 21 – even more than 1 Chronicles 6 – gives the impression from a literary perspective of being secondary, an appendix, an import from elsewhere. Two other considerations point to the priority of 1 Chronicles 6.

Priests and Levites are a very important theme throughout Chronicles. It is rather more of a surprise that the long chapter 21 should occupy such a large space within Joshua.

Priests and Levites are always clearly distinguished throughout Chronicles. Joshua 21 in its 'pluses' over against 1 Chronicles 6 emphasizes that the priests are Levites; and this secondary concern may also be detected in the textual uncertainty throughout Joshua 3–4 over how exactly to style the 'Levitical priests' responsible for carrying the ark over the Jordan.

The inherent importance of priests and Levites for the Chronicler, and a wish to underline the unique role of the Transjordanians: later editors of Joshua recognized the importance of both topics, but challenged significant details.

Then within both Joshua 13–22 and 1 Chronicles 2–7 we can detect traces of similar late adjustments. One good example relates to northern Transjordan, where half-Manasseh has clearly been added in vv. 18, 23–24 to the original Reuben and Gad of 1 Chronicles 5, as it has to the end of Joshua 13 (vv. 29–31) and throughout Joshua 22 (Auld 1980: 57–9) – cf. also Num 32:33, 39–42 and several other biblical passages. The Transjordan theme, which Chronicles and Joshua accentuated in their different ways and debated with each other, concerned originally only Reuben and Gad. In fact, it is the secondary addition of half-Manasseh in these various passages to an existing geographical concept which has complicated the geographers' discussion in our century of the extent of Gilead and Bashan.

A second instance is the introduction of Joseph to these tribal materials. In Chronicles, Manasseh and Ephraim are separately detailed among the northern tribes (7:14–19, 20–27) before we encounter a surprising summarizing mention of Joseph (whether all of 7:28–29, or only 7:29b, we shall discuss below). Similarly in Joshua, details about Ephraim (16:5–8, 10) and about Manasseh (17:1–7, 11–13) separately and information about their interrelationships (16:9; 17:8–10) appear to be the primary information, round which talk of Joseph (16:1–4 and 17:14–18) has thrown a secondary bracket.

Japhet (132–4) offers an interesting discussion of the midrash in 1 Chron 5:1–3, which explains deftly how the primogeniture of Joseph which replaced that forfeited by Reuben was legal, although it was Judah that 'surpassed all his brothers in strength and became the father of a great ruler'.

All the examples of Joshua as source listed in Japhet's summary (1993: 16) are drawn from the early chapters of 1 Chronicles. Yet, when she comes to discuss the Chronicler's special materials in 1 Chronicles 22–29 on the carefully planned transition from David to Solomon, she does acknowledge (1993: 400) the studies by Williamson and Braun, and does follow their account of how the picture in Deuteronomy 31 and Joshua 1 of the transfer of authority from Moses to Joshua had influenced the Chronicler. Neither David nor Moses lived to realize his mission, but both undertook many preparatory steps; both Joshua and Solomon were installed and instructed by the previous leader.

The links between Deuteronomy 31 and especially Joshua 1 and the lengthy and repetitive account in 1 Chron 22; 28–29 are undeniable. And it seems sensible to conclude that the Chronicler has drawn on the book of Joshua. Porter had drawn on arguments by Lohfink, and proposed earlier in the opposite direction – though in part from the same evidence – that 'The Succession of Joshua' was based on a royal pattern. There is in fact an interesting and complex tissue of links between three groups of passages: Deuteronomy–Joshua on the succession of Joshua, and Kings and Chronicles on that of Solomon. Each of the Joshua and Solomon texts has grown – and so it is clear that the tradition has identified important topics here. Williamson was readily able to dispose of some of Porter's arguments; but, I suspect, overstated his case when he claimed that the Chronicler based his version on Joshua, and 'did not even bother to include [1 Kgs 2:1–4] in his account' (1976: 354). Schäfer-Lichtenberger has annotated this discussion fully within her wider discussion of Joshua and Solomon (1995: 190–1).

I have more recently proposed (Auld 1994: 54) that the divergent accounts of the transition from David to Solomon, just as all of Samuel–Kings and Chronicles, are based on a shorter 'shared text':

When David was old and full of days,	23:1a // 1:1
he made Solomon his son king over Israel out of all his sons.	23:1b // 1:35
And he charged Solomon his son:	22:12 // 2:1b
Be strong and show yourself a man,	22:13 // 2:2b
and keep the statutes and ordinances of Yahweh,	22:13 // 2:3a
in order that you may succeed/prosper.	22:13 // 2:3b

The opening four verses of 1 Kings 2 as we know them may not have been familiar to the Chronicler – but their core was also his source. The pluses within 1 Kings 2:1–4 form two clusters. Some of them, typical of pluses throughout Kings and Chronicles, repeat elements from elsewhere in the Shared Text – in this case they anticipate language from Solomon's prayer, his second vision, and the Josiah story. The others use elements found also in Deuteronomy (31:14) and Joshua (1:6–9; but also 22:3; 23:14). Kings, differently from and more briefly than Chronicles, but no less significantly, emphasizes links between Moses/Joshua and David/Solomon. Yet were these emphases all the easier for the authors of Kings and Chronicles to develop because the installation of Joshua had been depicted in royal, or more precisely Solomonic, terms in the first place?

A complicating factor in this discussion is that Joshua 1 has also undergone revision by supplementation in several stages. The first part of this essay proposed the coexistence of different sorts of relationship between material in Joshua and 1 Chronicles, including influence from Chronicles to Joshua. Few would disagree that the defence of the Transjordanians in Joshua 22 from the charge of מעל is one of the latest portions of that book. But the same has often been argued of the *torah*-centred development in Josh 1:7–9 of the more military encouragement given the new leader in 1:6. Much of its language is distinctive and late: the key term הצליח, though found in Genesis 24 (×4); 39 (×3), Isa 48:15; 55:11 and Ps 37:7; 118:25, is most widely used in Chronicles (×13), Nehemiah (×2) and Daniel (×4) – and, significantly, is part of Psalm 1 (v. 3).

The picture of the Chronicler passing over the Deuteronomist's report of Solomon's installation in favour of his earlier chapter on the installation of Joshua is too simple. It was part of the critique of the kings by the Deuteronomist that he retrojected the significant beginnings of his people into an earlier age than that of David and Solomon. And the transition from David to Solomon, in a situation where there was not (yet) a dynastic expectation, provided him with a model for portraying a prepared transition from Moses to Joshua. The Chronicler in turn repainted his story of royal beginnings in colours learned from the very Joshua portrait that had used Solomon as model. And so the competition – or conversation – between 'Deuteronomist' and Chronicler continued.

12

WHAT MAKES JUDGES DEUTERONOMISTIC?*

Noth and the Deuteronomist

It just is: it is one of the books of the Former Prophets, and the Former Prophets of the Hebrew Bible are Deuteronomistic books – they constitute the larger part of the Deuteronomistic History which begins at the beginning of Deuteronomy and concludes at the end of Kings.

What was novel about Martin Noth's famous study in 1943 (1981) was not the perception that the books from Joshua to Kings were all influenced by the thought and language of Deuteronomy – that had been widely noted and long agreed. He contributed two further proposals. The one was negative: that the pre-Dtr source materials had few interconnections from book to book or even main section to main section. And the other was positive: that the Dtr connections made were the work of a single exilic historian. Arguing from his two observations, Noth concluded that the exilic Dtr created a connected history which had not existed before. Of course it was not the familiar books of Joshua, Judges, Samuel, and Kings which Dtr created – much more material was later added to the single framework he prepared; and this larger structure was only subsequently divided up. In the case of Judges, Dtr's contribution was something like chapters 2–12 only, little over half of the book we know: the fresh introduction in Judges 1 together with Samson (13–16) and the concluding chapters (17–21) – whatever the age and provenance of their materials – were all added later to what Dtr had made.

Many successors found Noth's proposals persuasive and unstable at the same time: most preferred to detect two or more Deuteronomists rather than Noth's one historian of the exilic period, and this tolerance of variety and even of dissent within Dtr ranks allowed more of the material within the Former Prophets to be assigned to Dtr hands than Noth had delimited. Both Veijola (1977), among the scholars indebted to Smend, and Boling (1975), among those indebted to Cross, ascribed the chapters at the end of the book to different Deuteronomistic hands. And this widening or loosening of the definition made it easier for Robert Polzin (1980) to retain Deuteronomist as the name for the author of the complex literary work he has explored in a rich quartet (I take the fourth volume in his set on trust) – and for SBL to welcome papers on

* Unpublished paper read at the SBL Annual Meeting in Philadelphia, November 1995.

Joshua to Kings in a section called 'Deuteronomistic History' rather than 'Former Prophets'.

There appear then to be three understandings available of Judges as Deuteronomistic:

(1) Noth was not concerned strictly with the book of Judges at all. His Deuteronomist reported a period of the Judges within the whole connected story from Horeb to Jerusalem's fall – and that episode is still to be found at the heart of the book of Judges.

(2) Several subsequent scholars who worked with methods he would have broadly recognized detected within the book of Judges a much larger authorial contribution than he had from Deuteronomists: not all of course from his first one, but also from successors who could be called his school.

(3) It has become conventional among most scholars of the Former Prophets to call the author or authors of these books the Deuteronomist(s).

Some of you will be – some of you are! – relieved that at least here within biblical studies there is a small area of agreement, or at least shared agenda. Ernst Würthwein's recent essay on the 'so-called Deuteronomistic History' (1994) still follows in essence Noth's account of the Dtr drafting of Judges 2–12, even although he now places this composition later than Samuel–Kings. But my own reaction is that Deuteronomistic has become too contested a term to be of much use in continuing discussion.

Judges without Deuteronomists

The most powerful reading of Judges in recent years of which I am aware – powerful though admittedly not comprehensive – is Mieke Bal's *Death and Dissymmetry*, exploring issues of coherence and counter-coherence, violence, parents and children, lethal power over women (1988). It may be only after we have extricated ourselves from the fascination of her argumentation that we realize that the terms Deuteronomic/istic have not been part of her discourse – and that we recognize the triumph of human interest over the national story-line not as lack but as liberation. I am not concerned here either to agree or disagree with Bal over many details of her reading of Judges – and larger issues too. But I do want to start by celebrating *Death and Dissymmetry* as a rich discussion of Judges: a discussion made all the richer by the absence from the table of any representative of the Deuteronomistic coalition. If Rabbi Akiva could endorse the Song of Songs as a sufficient ancient scripture on its own, without any of the

Torah, then let us promote Bal on Judges and be content without a word
said about Deuteronomists.

Though enthusiastically polemical on many matters, Bal herself does
not draw explicit attention to this loud silence. Indeed I wonder whether
one of her introductory remarks does not come short of the perceptive-
ness of what follows. Of course we can agree with her that 'it is not easy
to read the book without the burden of other readings obscuring it', and
look forward to her proposing 'a counter-reading, one that uses previous
readings polemically, analyzes their fallacies, and takes their insistent
falsifications and distortions of the text as a starting point.' Bal may be
right to suggest to us that the readings offered by the standard commentators have been skewed by their faithfulness to a tradition that goes
back at least as far as Ben Sirach. She notes how that ancient reader's
misreading of Judges in Ecclus 46:11–12 is actually the motto of
Boling's commentary. And she goes on to promise that in her study 'the
judges will not be celebrated, the ideology of the book will not be
repeated, and the faithfulness of the men toward their god will be
analyzed and related to their loyalty and disloyalty to their other
relatives rather than uncritically assumed'.

Good not to celebrate the judges – good to probe what is involved in
claims of men's faithfulness to their god – good to criticize thoroughly a
whole tradition of reading. But what is the ideology of the book of
Judges which she is concerned not to repeat? I wonder whether the clash
between Bal's own commitments and a reading tradition far from
conducive to them may have rendered her less than fair to a book whose
own commitments are much harder to track. And I wonder too whether
the familiar Dtr label, even although Bal is silent about it, has still
influenced her expectations of this text. After all, any strong sense of the
word Deuteronomistic implies a clear link with origins in the language
and thought of the book of Deuteronomy; and it is very hard to deny the
ideological commitment of the fifth book of Moses.

I recognize the danger – and probably even nonsense – of claiming
any text as an ideology-free zone. And yet – part of the fascination of
the book of Judges for me is that I cannot readily say what it is about as
a whole, or which causes it might be explicitly commending or even
implicitly sustaining. In fact I know much less now than when I wrote a
little commentary on Judges some ten years ago (Auld 1984). Many
readers have recognized that the outer chapters of the book, especially 1
and 17–21, are discontinuous with – or even subvert – the inner chapters
about the judges from Othniel and Ehud to Samson. But to say only that
is still to localize the phenomenon too severely. Questing subversive-
ness is in fact the character of the book through and through. The hero of
chapters 6–8, at the centre of the so-called inner core of the book, is a
Dr Jekyll and Mr Hyde. The Gideon, faithful to Deuteronomy 7, who
hacks down an Asherah; and the Jerubbaal, ominously resonant with

Jeroboam, are just the more obvious indicators. The much more important observation is that, whatever his name at any given point in the story, his words and actions are not easily judged.

Those who are made aware of the scandal at Gibeah and the chopping up of its victim's corpse observe in Judg 19:30 that nothing such had happened since Israel left Egypt; and they invite each other to 'consider it, take counsel, and speak'. That challenge reaches out of the pages of the story to grasp its readers too. They must also consider, take counsel – not just about this story in the book – and only then speak. I suspect, in fact, that to call the book Judges, as in manuscripts of both MT and LXX traditions, implies quite as much a misreading of the book as Ben Sirach's. It is the readers of this book who must judge throughout, from beginning to end, and not just in the middle where some few of the characters are said to 'judge Israel'. I prefer Philo's early – earlier? – description: 'the book of recorded judgements' (κρίματα – which almost always renders םיטפשמ). We readers are offered *in episode after episode* the opportunity to reconsider and further discuss our understanding of earlier issues – issues which require us to possess the discrimination of a Solomon. Jephthah, for example, sends us back to reread Gideon. The problems caused by Israel's vowed punishment of Benjamin send us back to re-evaluate Jephthah's fatal vow.

Qumran and LXX

I want to underscore that I am commending Bal's work for its own sake – though with the quibble that Judges' commitments are less obvious, or less *there-at-all* than most suppose. I am hoping, having reminded readers of how ably *she* can discuss Judges without ever using the D-word, that they may be the more open to the implications of the text-critical evidence. Before and after Noth, the most explicitly and uncontestably Dtr portions of the Judges text are Judg 2:6–3:6; 6:7–10; 10:6–16 (to which we should possibly add 3:7–11). Yet Judg 6:7–10 is absent from a relevant Qumran fragment. And LXX MSS of Joshua end with a two-verse plus over against MT which attaches the beginning of the Ehud story to the notices of the death and burial of Joshua and of Eleazar the priest. Just how integral are any of these Dtr passages to the book of Judges as a whole?

Wellhausen's surmise that Judg 6:7–10 was a late addition to the text appears confirmed by the absence of the passage from a fragment which links together what we know as vv. 3–6 and vv. 11–13. Noth and all who have followed him will have been wrong to attribute these verses to the Deuteronomist who shaped Judges 2–12 as the earliest draft of his story of the period of the Judges.

Judg 10:6–16 is a longer and more complex passage; and there is no textual testimony against its standing within earlier drafts of chapter 10. I just ask you to note four points in passing:

(1) Israel's dealings with Yahweh in response to the Ammonite crisis (10:9–16) are patterned exactly like Israel's dealings with Jephthah (11:4–11) in face of that same problem, and may well have been modelled on the latter.

(2) The Philistines are named, apparently retrospectively, among other neighbours in 10:6, 7, 11 whose gods Israel has served and from whom Israel has suffered. Yet this is a surprisingly anachronistic anticipation of their arrival in the main body of the biblical story, whether in the Samson chapters of Judges (13–16) or the accounts in Samuel of Saul's and David's struggles with them.

(3) The passages throughout the Former Prophets with which it shares significant elements are:

> Josh 24:15 (choosing gods 14), 23 (turning away foreign gods 16)
> 1 Sam (7–)12: 10a (we've sinned ... Baals 10b), 10b (save us 15b)
> 1 Kings 11:5 (Ashtoreth 6), 7 (gods of Moab 6)
> 2 Kings 23:13 (Ashtoreth 6)

Of these, only 1 Samuel 12 is listed among Noth's major Deuteronomistic creations. In Samuel's farewell, the Philistines do have an appropriate place; and we may suspect that Judg 10:6–16 is indebted to 1 Samuel 12 rather than part of the same composition.

(4) Mention together in 10:9 of Judah, Benjamin, and Ephraim is suspiciously reminiscent of 2 Chron 15:8; 25:5–7; 31:1.

However, the crucial passage is Judg 2:6–3:11. On the one side, and in terms of Dtr theory, 2:6–3:6 is the bridge passage crafted by Dtr himself and linking the period of Joshua to that of the Judges; and it is concluded, or immediately followed, by his own composition of a typical Judge episode: the Othniel story of 3:7–11. On the other side stands the aggravating piece of textual evidence, long known at the end of the LXX text of Joshua, drawn again to our attention by Rofé in 1982, and widely ignored since. To my surprise, I have to include here the recently published draft of Barnabas Lindars' work towards the International Critical Commentary on Judges (1994), which does pay close attention to the LXX. The one important exception of which I am aware is the adoption by Moenikes (1995) of much of Rofé's argumentation. The alternative final verse of Joshua reads:

> And the sons of Israel went each to their place and to their city. And the sons of Israel worshipped Astarte and Ashtaroth and the gods of the nations round about; and the Lord gave them over into the hands of Eglon the king of Moab, and he ruled over them for eighteen years.

Rofé demonstrated that this verse had a Hebrew *Vorlage*, and one that was known to the author of the Damascus Document; but he was, I think, less than successful in drawing literary-historical conclusions from his argument. And I fear that is also true of Moenikes' more recent work (1992; 1995).

If this plus is a condensed summary (the usual dismissive judgement), then it is interesting that the epitomizer has framed it by jumping right over Judg 1:1–2:5, and drawing 'the gods of the nations round about' from 2:12 (the Dtr prologue), Israel's service of Ashtoreth from 3:7 (the Othniel story) and the eighteen-year rule over Israel by Eglon of Moab from 3:14 (the Ehud story). However, if we reverse the argument and consider this to be an uncorrected fragment of an earlier version of the text, then it also preserves precious evidence of how the longer text was expanded from it.

One stage in the production of that familiar version was the crafting of a new first story about a typical judge (3:7–11): Othniel's name was taken from Joshua 15, 'Cushan the doubly bad' was invented as opponent, and almost everything said about him in 3:7–11 was drawn from subsequent heroes in Judges. Since Israel's service of Ashtoreth now led to oppression by Cushan rather than Eglon, the transition to Ehud and Eglon had to be reworked – and this was achieved in formulaic terms, and produced the new opening in 3:12–14.

It has long been argued that the virtual repetition of Josh 24:28–31 in Judg 2:6–9 testifies to Judg 1:1–2:5 also being a subsequent insert into this transitional text.

The intervening twenty verses, 2:10–3:6, preface the Othniel type-scene with a generalized meditation crafted from three main sources: 'the gods of the peoples round about them' (2:12) from our original transitional verse; most of its stock details from the Othniel story; and some significant wording from 2 Kings 17.

The Judges and their Book

With Noth and the Deuteronomistic reading of Judges, we have to conclude that portions like Judg 2:6–3:6; 6:7–10; and 10:6–16 were drafted both as commentary on the surrounding material and to draw the narratives of Judges closer together with the narratives of Joshua and of the monarchies. But Noth also held that these passages were penned by the same hand as linked the saviour heroes of Judges 3–12 together, and combined them with the list of minor judges. It is incumbent on us to re-evaluate the evidence, and ask again whether these were not late additions to an already complex book, rather than constitutive elements of its substratum – and we must go on to ask what this means for the label Deuteronomistic, or just how far Deuteronomistic is an appropriate description of such passages.

It is the promise of judges in the so-called Deuteronomistic prologue and the immediate appearance of Othniel as someone who 'judged Israel' that encourage us to receive the following heroes as judges. But of those that follow only Deborah, the five minor judges, and Samson (within the book of Judges), and Eli and Samuel (within the book of Samuel) are actually said to have 'judged Israel'! When the opening of Ruth or the comment in 2 Kings 23:22 on Josiah's passover talk about the period when the judges judged, who in history or in literature – and, since I do not know too much about the history, I would settle for the literature! – who did they have in mind? 2 Chron 35:18 tells us there had been no passover like Josiah's since the days of Samuel the prophet. And which of Kings or Chronicles altered that footnote? Ruth and Kings speak of a period of the Judges. But neither provides evidence that they were familiar with a book of Judges, even less of our (Deuteronomistic?) book of Judges.

INTERPRETATIONS

13

THE HISTORY OF INTERPRETATION OF THE BOOK OF JOSHUA*

Joshua the text raises acute questions of what context is appropriate for its interpretation. Is Joshua essentially a complete and integrated book which can properly stand on its own and be viewed in and for itself? Or is it only sensible to see its contents as part of something else: whether the Pentateuch, from which it may be a lost conclusion or a detached appendix; or the narratives of the Former Prophets, which may offer a single deliberately planned story? Of course the second alternative simply pushes back the equally vital question of how far the larger text of which Joshua might be a part might itself be an integrated work, rather than a haphazard deposit of tradition. How much or how little structure or planning can be detected in Joshua or its supposed wider context? Answers to questions like these determine whether we give priority to aesthetic or historical attempts to understand the book of Joshua. Is this text more like persons with whom we may readily deal and interact in the terms in which they present themselves? Or is it more like those people about whom we have to learn something of their family and their past before we can cope with the puzzle they represent? It may be impatience with such preliminaries that has led many readers to advocate simply taking the text 'as it is', as 'tradition' or 'the canon' has handed it down.

INTERPRETATION WITHIN THE TEXT, *OR* WHAT IS THE TEXT?

Such an apparently straightforward approach flounders on the facts as disclosed by text-critical studies in recent decades. The Hebrew (MT) and Greek (LXX) texts of Joshua, preserved separately by synagogue and church after their ancient division, exhibit significant differences; and only some of these are the result of random mistakes. The importance of the Septuagint (LXX) of Joshua as evidence for the history of the Hebrew text of Joshua before it was standardized in Masoretic tradition has long been appreciated, and at least since Hollenberg (1876). The important work of Holmes (1914), in part a defence of Hollenberg, broke ground in glimpsing the implications for the literary history of Joshua of some of the divergences between the ancient texts. Yet Margolis' magisterial treatment of the textual history

* From *Dictionary of Biblical Interpretation*, to be published by Abingdon Press. All rights reserved by Abingdon Press,

of the Greek Joshua (1931–8) and Noth's influential commentary on the Hebrew text (1938) combined to marginalize the significance of LXX for the understanding of Hebrew Joshua. A series of studies returning to and advancing Holmes's insights was inaugurated by Orlinsky (1989), and contributions have accelerated through the efforts of Auld, Rofé, Tov, Greenspoon, and Floss. (These have received thorough methodological grounding in the detailed and vital work by Trebolle-Barrera (1986) illustrating in portions of Judges, Samuel, and Kings the close relationship between textual criticism and literary history.) The implications of these studies have not yet reached a wide readership. Boling's textual notes (AB, 1975) do diligently note variation between Hebrew and Greek texts, and the divergent evidence of the available Qumran material. And several of the results of the above-mentioned scholars have been incorporated piecemeal into Butler's more important commentary (1983). However, a full-scale treatment of the whole book of Joshua from this perspective has still to be published; and Bieberstein (1995) and Den Hertog (1995) have urged caution.

EARLIER INTERPRETATION OF THE TEXT(S)

Ben Sirach epitomizes Joshua in a few verses (beginning of Sirach 46): successor to Moses, one who as a deliverer deserved his name, the one who brought Israel into her inheritance, splendid in fighting the Lord's battles. The passage from which most detail is drawn is Josh 10:10–15, with the sun held back, the hailstones, and all resistance destroyed at the descent.

The NT takes no explicit opportunity to exploit the fact that Joshua and Jesus share the same name – a feature prominent in patristic interpretation. The Letter to the Hebrews (4:8) contrasts the 'rest' offered by Jesus with what could not have been provided in full by Joshua, because Psalm 95 sees it as incomplete. The great review of examples of faith (Hebrews 11) passes over our book in two verses (30–31). James's letter (2:25) also mentions Rahab's 'justification by works'; while the Gospel of Matthew (1:5) counts her among the ancestors of the Messiah.

Josephus's account of Joshua in his *Antiquities* is mostly a rather wordy paraphrase of the whole text of the biblical book. Some of its additions, and even more its omissions, are interesting. The twelve stones at Gilgal form an altar; but there is absolute silence on the circumcision episode, and the passover is only mentioned. More understandably, the account of land division is both shorter and more orderly than Joshua 13–21, with the survey by geometricians (cf. 18:1–10) at its head. As if to compensate, the dispute over the eastern altar is even more leisurely than Joshua 22.

Origen's *Homilies on Joshua*, perhaps his latest work (around 250 CE), stress the first Joshua/Jesus as greater than the dead Moses of the law. The theme is already found in Justin Martyr and Irenaeus; but it appears to have been Origen's detailed exposition that had classical influence. The changing of the leader's name from Hoshea had been prophetic. The crossing of the Jordan was a procession with priestly ritual, not the undisciplined mob at the Red Sea. Moses settled only $2\frac{1}{2}$ tribes, and outside the land; Joshua the majority, and only he the Levites. Origen's other keynote has already been suggested: the spiritualizing of the land and the struggles within it. It is the soul that is the real area of conflict; heaven is symbolized by the promised land and its 'rest'. Such moves permitted Origen to oppose both the heretical disjunction between the cruel God of the OT and the loving one of the NT, and at the same time the fleshly literalism of the Jews. A fine example is the more 'dignified' interpretation he is able to give of the second circumcision of the people before the new passover in the promised land. In fact, his commentary on John had already mentioned the obvious literal sense of the passage. Here, however, Origen remarks that Jews must be asked how second circumcision is possible. For Christians, for whom the Law is spiritual, the difficulties of the passage are resolved in greater dignity: the first circumcision had marked the passage from idolatry to the Mosaic law; the second, accomplished by the stone that is Christ, marked the passage from the law and the prophets to the gospel faith. Theodore of Mopsuestia indulges in similar polemic when he suggest that Jews are regrettably unable to see that the circumcised perished and the uncircumcised were saved: the fathers died, and it was their sons who received the object of the promise.

Langlamet (1979) has provided a masterly survey of Rahab as she has been discussed in ancient and modern times – by the rabbis, among the fathers of the church, and in more recent scholarship (see also Baskin). Rabbis and early fathers almost outdid each other in the significance they found in this woman and her story. For some of the rabbis she was one of the four most beautiful women in the world (with Sarah, Abigail, and Esther); for others, one of the four most seductive (with Ruth, Jael, and Saul's daughter Michal). Her profession of faith was linked with those of Moses, Jethro, and Naaman; Joshua married her; and eight prophets were descended from her (including Jeremiah and Ezekiel in different lists). In short, as ideal proselyte, she was an example to all the nations of the world: any waverer could be challenged, 'Are you worse than Rahab?' Christian fathers made some similar points (already in Matt 1:5), and noted also: she was saved by her faith and her hospitality; the scarlet cord given her by the messengers of Joshua/Jesus was a sign of salvation by the Lord's blood; and her example is endorsed by Jesus' statement to religious leaders of his time that publicans and courtesans precede them into the kingdom.

The divinely instigated treatment of the Canaanites has long been a problem for commentators, whether as a straightforward moral issue, or as a precedent from within their own scriptures felt by politically vulnerable Jews to be all too dangerous in Christian hands. Medieval rabbis suggested that Joshua, before his invasion, had offered the inhabitants of Canaan by letter a three-fold invitation to submit.

Calvin's commentary on the book happens to be his last literary work too, from the closing months of his life in 1563/4. His long experience as a leader and his failing health both illumine his exposition. The removal of Moses, 'as if God, after cooping up his people in a corner, had left his work in a shapeless and mutilated form', and his replacement by Joshua 'suggests the very useful reflection, that while men are cut off by death, and fail in the middle of their career, the faithfulness of God never fails'. Again, on the dispute in chapter 22 over the altar of the Transjordanian tribes, he comments irenically but firmly:

> Nothing was farther from their intention than to innovate in any respect in the worship of God. But they sinned not lightly in attempting a novelty, without paying any regard to the high priest, or consulting their brethren, and in a form which was very liable to be misconstrued.

Leadership and literary sensitivity combine to influence his discussion of how the two closing speeches by Joshua himself are related: in chapter 24 Joshua 'explains more fully what he before related more briefly. For it would not have been suitable to bring out the people twice to a strange place for the same cause.'

EARLIER MODERN DISCUSSION: JOSHUA AND PENTATEUCH

The synthesis of Wellhausen on the composition of the Hexateuch (1889^2), which was to remain authoritative for 60 years, was heavily indebted to two immediate predecessors. Hollenberg (1874) had declared that Pentateuchal criticism gave new life to the study of Joshua. In a detailed article he argued first that Josh 1; 8:30–35; 23; and parts of 24 had been composed by the Deuteronomist who had added Deuteronomy 1–4 and portions of the final chapters to the basic speech of Moses in Deuteronomy 5–28; and then that this major author had also made numerous smaller contributions to the 'Jehovistic' Joshua traditions. Kuenen (1886) was to concur in almost all details, though he argued against ascribing this Deuteronomic recension to a single author. Wellhausen's move (towards the end of his influential study) from Pentateuch to Joshua was introduced in carefully chosen words: unlike Judges–Kings, Joshua was an appendix to the Pentateuch which assumed it at all points – without the same material being edited in it in the same way. In fact, he was to argue that the sources had been more substantially altered in the editing of Joshua than in the Pentateuch. In his discussion of the Deuteronomist's role, Wellhausen made only minor alterations to the proposals of Hollenberg and Kuenen, agreeing with Hollenberg that Deuteronomic style could be found even in late additions unrepresented in LXX (e.g. 20:4–6).

The commentary of Keil and Delitzsch (1869), while admitting that Joshua is more closely connected to the Pentateuch in form and content than any other book, insists that it is not a literary appendix: their relationship is like that of Joshua to Moses himself. Even if it was not composed till some time after Joshua's death, this does not affect its historico-prophetic character; for both the content and form of the book show it to be an independent and simple work composed with historical fidelity, and a work which is as thoroughly pervaded with the spirit of the OT revelation as the Pentateuch itself. The third volume of Dillman's Hexateuch commentary (1886), on Numbers–Joshua, is more sympathetic to Wellhausen and Kuenen. Once separated from the more authoritative Pentateuch, Joshua had not been so carefully corrected – hence its many preferable LXX readings. However, historically it cannot be separated from the Pentateuch. He offers some arguments against preferring LXX just because it is shorter. Steuernagel's third volume on the historical books (1900) covers Deuteronomy–Joshua and offers a concluding introduction to the Hexateuch. Five sections of the latter concern composition, and only one treats the book of Joshua as historical source: the miraculous and popular form in which religious conviction clothes itself in the book is worthless for the political history of Israel; it has meaning for the history of religion only as a sign that Israel was a people with lively religious thought.

The earlier Cambridge Bible volume, by Maclear on the AV (1880), stands very much in the Greek patristic tradition, with Joshua presented as a 'type' prefiguring Jesus the Christ. He notes that the undoubtedly terrible severity of the work of Joshua was often used as an objection against OT morality, but quotes Ewald:

> It is an eternal necessity that a nation such as the majority of the Canaanites then were, sinking deeper and deeper into a slough of discord and moral perversity, must fall before a people roused to a higher life by the newly awakened energy of unanimous trust in Divine Power.

Maclear continues: 'When ... God entrusted the sword of vengeance to Joshua, was ever campaign waged in such an unearthly manner as that now inaugurated by the leader of the armies of Israel?' And he ends by quoting a sermon of Thomas Arnold: 'The Israelites' sword in its bloodiest executions, wrought a work of mercy for all the countries of the earth ... they preserved unhurt the seed of eternal life.'

Cooke's later volume (1878, 1917[2]) based on the RV, is a whole
thought-world away. After an account of the book's literary origins very
like that of Wellhausen, Cooke explains that the Deuteronomic
redactor

> tells about Joshua, not as he really was, but as the writers of the 7th cent.
> pictured him; the portrait, if it can be called one, is not a study from the life,
> but the creation of a fervid believer and patriot. We may be sure that nothing
> like the wholesale slaughter of the natives and irresistible victories of the
> Israelites ever took place. ... Far more ancient and vivid than anything we
> find in the OT is the picture of early Canaan given by the Amarna tablets.

Like Hollenberg, Kuenen and Wellhausen, he is good in his treatment of
LXX.

The divorce between the message of Joshua and the facts of history
was already clear in Steuernagel and Cooke. It was not successfully
overcome by Garstang, despite that archaeologist's attempt to define the
'Foundations of Biblical History' (1931). However, a more enduring
historical response was to come from German colleagues.

THE LEGACY OF ALT AND NOTH

Alt's three volumes of *Kleine Schriften* (1953) contain a dozen major
papers relevant to the historical evaluation of Israel's settlement, the
role of Joshua and, most distinctively, the topographical information in
our book; behind this he detected archival administrative source
material (from the end of the Judaean monarchy in the case of the
town lists in 15:21–62). Noth adopted Alt's methods and argued (1935)
that a list of Judaean localities in twelve districts had been combined
with a system of tribal boundaries to produce most of the material in
Joshua 13–19. It is their studies that provided the methods and set the
standards for the major works that followed by Aharoni, Kallai, and
Simons.

In his commentary on Joshua (1938), Noth reaffirmed that the
topographical material had had its own prehistory, and argued that even
the narratives had a literary background distinct from Genesis in which
Deuteronomistic affiliations were most easily detectable. Noth
(1943/81) then addressed all the biblical narratives where consensus
recognized Dtr edition, arguing first that Joshua–Kings represented a
self-contained whole: the retrospective and anticipatory passages
(Joshua 1; 23; Judges 2; 1 Samuel 12; 2 Kings 17) had no exact parallels
in OT, and had much in common with each other in subject.

> If we take the perfectly sound approach of interpreting the relatively simple
> and clear conditions in Joshua–Kings, without regard to the findings of

literary criticism elsewhere, and postpone discussing the very controversial 'Hexateuch' questions in their application to Joshua, we can reach only one conclusion.

However, Joshua 1 is certainly not the beginning: the links of this chapter with the Moses story and, in particular, the account of the settlement of some tribes in Transjordan, show that these matters have already been treated in Dtr's work. Noth finds that with little difficulty the chronological details in the other books can be seen to square with the information in 1 Kings 8:1 that the temple was dedicated 480 years after the exodus. (In the case of Joshua this depends on his claim that Josh 14:10 is part of a passage once linked to Dtr's 11:23!) His review of Dtr's contribution to the account of the occupation of Cisjordan differs little in essence from Hollenberg's (1874). A series of separate etiological stories relevant to the Israelites' successful incursion had been combined into a well-rounded whole with a few heroic legends. Dtr obviously took the whole of this over and altered it only by adding an introduction and epilogue and some supplementary material. In a significant comment on the nature of the composition, he writes that these Deuteronomistic passages,

> brought in at every suitable opportunity ... come to make good literary sense if they are not just the monotonously repeated statement of the pet idea of an 'editor,' intended to accompany and interpret a piece of tradition already existing in finished form, but rather meant to play a part in transforming elements totally diverse in form, scope and content, into a single literary unit.

The fact that despite these elements the separate parts of the work seem disunited and heterogeneous is explained because Dtr consciously committed himself to using the material available to him. Novelty and faithfulness hand in hand! In 1953 Noth published a fresh edition of his commentary on Joshua, stating more decisively what he had anticipated in 1938: that the book should be read independently of the Pentateuch (i.e. Genesis–Numbers). Von Rad, Mowinckel, and Fohrer continued to assert close links between Joshua and the Pentateuch. Auld (1980) and Rose (1981) responded suggesting that even more of the Pentateuch depended on material in Joshua than Noth had claimed.

Noth's thesis of a Deuteronomistic History was to capture the imagination of almost all non-conservative scholars, although important details of his argument were challenged by many followers. Commentaries on Joshua for over 30 years (e.g. by Hertzberg, Gray, Miller and Tucker, and Soggin) were to operate within his structure. Smend (1971) challenged Noth's view that the addition of the topographical traditions was achieved editorially by anticipating in Josh 13:1 Dtr's words in 23:1 about Joshua's age. His reversal of the relationship of these two verses allowed him to propose (a) that DtrH did contain a report of land-division; and (b) that Joshua 23 was simply the most detailed of several additions to the original history by a second Deuteronomistic author (DtrN). Dietrich was to follow with a study on Kings (1972), inter-posing a third redaction (DtrP). Their lead was followed by Veijola, and summarized by Smend himself (1978). Cross's discussion (1973) focused on the later chapters of Kings and led him to propose that the original Dtr History was composed before the fall of Judah and in honour of Josiah. This history was brought up to date in exile, and supplemented with elements more critical of kingship. Cross's more summary views have been adjusted and advanced by Nelson (1981a). Hoffmann, in a study of the religious reforms related by Dtr (1980), argued against both these trends: (a) that Dtr was a unity (apart from quite insignificant exceptions), and (b) that very much more of Joshua–Kings had been drafted by Dtr than Noth had allowed. Mayes proposed (1983) that with a little adjustment on each side the similarities between the Smend and Cross 'schools' would be clear.

Unhappily for our purposes, with the exception of Smend's article (1971) – and of course Noth's original epoch-making commentary – very little of the above discussion has actually been based on close study of Joshua. There is a real danger that study of our book is now quite as much at the mercy of broader theories about a Deuteronomistic History as it was once misread as the conclusion of a Hexateuch.

Soggin's introduction and his commentary on Judges have endorsed the modifications argued by Smend and his followers. The volume by Boling and Wright (AB), by contrast, stands more in the American tradition of Cross and Nelson. Unhappily, it is also a very uneven volume: the introduction had been prepared by G. Ernest Wright before his death in 1974, and so was out of date on its publication in 1982; then, since Boling did not write the introduction, the methods under-lying his puzzling approach to matters of textual and literary history remain rather obscure despite further exposition in articles (1983, 1985).

Different stages of the discussion were well reviewed by individual scholars: Jenni, Radjawane, Smend (1978), Auld (1980), Butler, Mayes, and Weippert (her survey of what she in nice understatement calls a polyphonic situation, published in 1985, includes studies up to 1981). When the studies mentioning the Deuteronomist in Joshua since those reviewed by Weippert are considered, 'chaotic' might be a more adequate term than 'polyphonic'. Van Seters (1983) attributed most of Joshua–Kings to a first Dtr, lightly touched up by a second; Peckham (1984) most of Joshua–Samuel to the second Dtr, seeing his work as a monumental commentary built into and on to a once-brief narrative of Dtr 1. And Begg confidently talked (1986) of the 'Deuteronomisticity' of Joshua 7–8 on the basis of its structural contribution to the whole, whether words and ideas from Deuteronomy are found in it or not. All believed in a Deuteronomistic History – but not in Noth's, and each in a different one. Was it time to revalue this currency – or to move on to a different standard? Two collaborative projects, one on the legacy of Noth and the other on Israel constructing her history, led to valuable publications edited by McKenzie and Graham (1994) and De Pury, Römer, and Macchi (1996). Schäfer-Lichtenberger provided a wealth of documentation in her careful comparison of Joshua and Solomon (1995); and Auld also reviewed (1995) some Joshua issues in the light of his work on Kings.

A LITERARY READING?

Polzin's attempt (1980) to read the first half of the Deuteronomistic History (Deuteronomy–Judges) after the example of the Russian 'formalist' literary critics may have been underrated. He offers sensitive and attractive readings of many parts of Joshua. The text is studied 'as it is', unreconstructed, mostly by attention to the shifting perspectives or points of view in different 'planes' of the text: phraseological, temporal, spatial, psychological and ideological. The reader is invited into ever-richer readings of the text; and the deepest, the ideological level, is reached through the more superficial. Polzin makes particular use of the interplay between the narrator, God, and Moses or Joshua, especially when one is quoting, and sometimes slightly misquoting, another.

The detail of the Rahab story (chapter 2) is allowed to interrupt the action of conquest so long because, once it is seen that the story of Rahab is really the story of Israel told from the point of view of a non-Israelite, the larger themes of the justice à and mercy of God *vis-à-vis* Israel can then be recognized as central to the very story itself and its position as the initial episode in Dtr's account of the occupation of the land. The valuable distortions brought about by constant shifts in perspective offer the reader a much more adequate image of the occupation of the land as the fulfilment of God's word than the flat, universalized, and pat evaluations of the voice of authoritarian dogmatism, the reflexes of whose simplistic ideology can be still heard in the categorical assertions of, say, 4:10b. Chapter 22 helps us see why the $2\frac{1}{2}$ tribes are so prominent in the book: they are like the other 'aliens' – Rahab, the Gibeonites, Caleb, the Levites, and dependants in the book of Joshua. All of them are representative versions of the same typology – the Transjordanian tribes are a permanent representation of the obedience to God's law that never quite makes it. As Phinehas testifies to these 'outcasts': 'We know this day … that you have saved the people of Israel from the hand of the Lord' (Josh 22:31).

Greenberg has noted how Kaufmann's reading of Joshua (1985), while less critical historically, was holistic before that became fashionable. There is sensitive but less co-ordinated literary comment in Boling, Butler, and Auld (1984), who do draw attention to humour and irony, and warn against too straight a reading of the text. Butler, a master of fair-minded review, encourages the search for historical development in the interpretation of the Joshua traditions; and claims that their 'final, canonical message ... is made clear by the Deuteronomistic structural markers'. It is vital that the import of the book of Joshua be sought in its text, and not in a reconstruction of whatever history may underly it: the commentaries of Boling and Hamlin commend a liberationist Joshua who owes more to the historical endeavours of Mendenhall and Gottwald than to close reading of the biblical book.

Polzin's reading of Deuteronomy–Judges (complemented by subsequent volumes on the books of Samuel) has received valuable support from the articles by Gunn and Rowlett and the volumes by Eslinger, Hawk, Mitchell, and Mullen. Rowlett (1992) particularly neatly sketches contrasts such as the fate of outsider Rahab and insider Achan with respect to the Jericho 'ban', or of insider Transjordanians on the wrong side of the Jordan and outsider Gibeonites on the right side; and Carroll explores the myth of the empty land. Winther-Nielsen (1995) has made a thorough appeal to discourse analysis as a more objective umpire among the competing witnesses cited by synchronic and diachronic readers alike.

None of the commentaries of the 1990s has embraced these newer literary approaches, though each is novel in its own way. Ottosson reads Joshua as a plea for a new David in the period of Josiah. His interest in the topographical chapters is reflected also in Svensson's dissertation. Fritz, whose work replaces that of Noth in the HAT series, remains remarkably faithful to the broad lines of his predecessor's approach, although the Deuteronomist, whether Josianic or exilic, now displaces Noth's early monarchic *Sammler* as the first collector of the materials. He too offers a fresh account of the topographical materials. Ahituv's modern Hebrew volume (1995) is intended as a 'scientific' commentary, but also for a wide readership in Israel. It unpacks idioms from the older tongue, offers a transcription of all the Joshua Qumran fragments, and explores several issues with contemporary resonance: the conquest and the question of the land left over; the Canaanite 'ban': *halakha* and fact; the righteous generation of the conquerors; the dating of the geographical lists. The bibliography is quite detailed on such points of interest, but makes little concession to more literary approaches. The most recent commentary available, by Hess (1996), emphasizes evidence for early dating, but is well informed and judicious throughout. These commentaries make little use of the more radical historical assessments by Ahlström, Coote, Davies, Lemche, Thompson, and Whitelam; and Ahituv in particular is more at home with compatriot historians such as Weinfeld and Na'aman.

Tov (1981 and repeatedly) has drawn attention to the relevance of the LXX for the literary history of the Bible. His discussion (1986) of the strange story of the altar on Ebal, which appears in a different position in the Hebrew and Greek Bibles, suggests this is a late addition to the narrative, filed differently by different editors. The apparent link in 4QJosh[a] of the end of this story with the beginning of Josh 5:2–3 has allowed Kempinski, Rofé (1994), and Auld (1995) to give this discussion a new twist. Tov developed a series of arguments (1987) to support the claim that the shorter LXX *Vorlage* has (by and large) been expanded into the longer familiar Hebrew rather than shortened from it. He assumes, apparently without argument, that the short Hebrew text translated into Greek around 200 BCE had existed for centuries. However, might the familiar expanded Hebrew instead be much more recent than often thought?

Auld's studies on the tribal lists (1980, 1987) and those of Wüst (1975), whose major project remains only half-published, have suggested that much of the historico-geographical information in Joshua 13–21 on the division of the land between the various tribes of Israel is more heavily re-edited and harmonized than Alt and Noth allowed – or Aharoni and Kallai, who have largely followed their methods. Kallai did not take the opportunity of the translation of his major study (Hebrew 1967) to answer some of these criticisms. However, Cortese has been very critical of Auld's work. Garbini has argued that details suggesting the Persian period are not so much supplements to an older tradition as indicators of the age of much of the biblical narrative tradition.

The discussion between Rofé and Rösel over the traditions that interlock at the end of Joshua and the beginning of Judges, but rather differently in MT and LXX, is quite vital for answering the first question posed in this article: in what context should we view the book of Joshua – in and for itself, or as part of a longer story, whether we call that a Deuteronomistic History or not? Tov has been soberly providing the text-critical tools. Others must try to stand on his shoulders and attempt a riskier view. Two samples are the detailed study of Joshua 2 by Floss (1982–6) and Trebolle-Barrera's correlation of textual and literary work at the beginning of Judges (1986). That is where the most exciting action may be in Joshua studies in the next years.

RE-ORIENTATION

Joshua, Moses and the Land

As was already observed in the Orientation to this volume, the first four essays and the ninth provided much of the foundation for the novel argument in the two central chapters (IV and V) of *Joshua, Moses and the Land* (1980). The three opening chapters of that book review scholarship on Joshua and its links with the Pentateuch in the generation following the first edition of Martin Noth's commentary on Joshua (1938).

Chapter IV is concerned with 'The Distribution of the Land in Joshua', related in Joshua 13–22. First it restates and develops the conclusions of essay 2 in this volume on the first introduction to the land-division (Josh 13:1–7); the second introduction, drafted in three stages (14:1–5); and the principle of lot imported late into Joshua 13–17. It then argues that half-Manasseh has been added to the materials on Reuben and Gad east of the Jordan, and that the passages on Joseph in Josh 16:1–4 and 17:14–18 represent a secondary bracket round Ephraim and Manasseh. It next explores the work of the land commission in 18:1–10b – the story about the survey by the official representatives introduces the report of the allotment to the final seven tribes in Joshua 18–19. It was from its first mention in that story that the principle of lot was generalized forwards into Joshua 13–17. Then the corrective notes scattered through Joshua 13–19, many of them adapted in Judges 1 and so studied in essay 9 above, are reviewed for evidence of the earlier text to which they were added as supplements. Then, finally, there is discussion of the concluding formulae in 19:49–51 and the appendices in Joshua 20–21 (treated much more fully in essays 3–5 in this volume).

The results of this fourth chapter are offered under five main heads (1980: 66–7):

1. The main narrative stratum of Joshua did offer an account of the distribution of the land, including brief mention of Moses' grant east of the Jordan to Reuben and Gad, and description of the ten territories west of the Jordan. This was concluded by the original wording of 19:49a (now found only in the Greek version following 21:42), followed naturally by 21:43–45.

2. There were several minor but cautious corrections of this first draft. Though these were broadly homogeneous, they need not have been added at one time.

3. The major reorganization which gave that earlier draft its present shape had two aspects. The simple pattern of ten western territories all described in similar terms was broken when Ephraim and Manasseh were bracketed together and became sections of Joseph. This was part of a re-edition to achieve a two-stage process of distribution. Priority was now given to two groupings: Judah and this new Joseph. The seven remaining descriptions were furnished with a new narrative introduction (18:1–10) plus the explicit statement repeated at the beginning of them all, that it was by lot that each territory had been assigned to the tribe in question.

4. The added hypothesis of a half-Manasseh in northern Transjordan led to new territorial description in 13:29–31 and compensatory adjustments in 17:1–6.

5. The major appendices on cities for the Levites (21) and cities of refuge (20) were presented in language similar to secondary framing materials such as 14:1b–5 and 19:51.

Chapter V, on 'The Distribution of the Land in Numbers', has surprising and exciting results. It explores connections in the Moses traditions with the materials just reviewed from Joshua. The earliest mention of land division in Numbers (26:52–54), uses the same term (חלק – 'divide') as the primary introduction to the theme in Joshua (13:1, 7). The principle of division by lot was introduced at the end of this passage by the secondary addition of 26:55–56, and was repeated where appropriate within Numbers 32–36 by the secondary insertion of 33:54 into 33:50–56 and 35:7 into 35:1–8. Half-Manasseh is even more obviously a late arrival to the story of the Transjordanian tribes in Numbers 32 than to Joshua 13–22; and the consequent tally of only $9\frac{1}{2}$ tribes west of the Jordan (when there appear to be 10) has been inserted after the description of the land in Num 34:1–12. The listing of tribal leaders in Num 34:16–29 (where Manasseh has reverted to being a complete unit!) shares with Joshua 15–19 and Judges 1 several features which are unusual within the Bible as a whole. In fact this Numbers order (Judah, Simeon, Benjamin, Dan, Manasseh, Ephraim, Zebulun, Issachar, Asher, Naphtali) may have been drawn without change from an earlier draft of Joshua 15–19. Just one change has been made in Judges 1 (itself based on Joshua – see essay 9): Dan has been moved to the end by virtue of its northerly migration. Joshua has subsequently made this change too, and also two more: the 'demotion' of Simeon to the final seven and the transposition of Ephraim before Manasseh – possibly in deference to the story in Genesis 48 of Jacob/Israel's blessing of Joseph's sons. In Numbers, as in Joshua, it seems that the material on the Levitical cities was drafted without knowledge of the material on the cities of refuge.

The first part of *Joshua, Moses and the Land* documented an impasse in literary study of the book of Joshua. It was text-critical work on Joshua, based on essays 1–4 and 9 in this volume, which led to novel proposals to circumvent that literary impasse. The most exciting aspect of *Joshua, Moses and the Land* was the close convergence between these proposals on Joshua and the results of a fresh scrutiny of what the book of Numbers had to say on the distribution of Israel's new land. This stage by stage convergence I naturally took as confirmation of both analyses. Martin Noth had been right to propose that the lines and direction of influence stretched from Joshua to the end of Numbers, rather than from the Pentateuch to Joshua.

The only attempt I know of at a rebuttal of the whole range of the earlier studies is found in rather intemperate responses by Cortese: an article followed by a monograph. However, these hardly represent detailed critique. The former (1985) includes on its first page the complaint that *Joshua, Moses and the Land* had been over-enthusiastically reviewed in another Italian journal (in *Henoch* (1982) by Garbini). My response to the detail of his first critique can be found in essay 5 above, published in 1990. Cortese's monograph on *Josua 13–21* from the same year disputes my claim that Noth had described Joshua 13–21 as Deuteronomistic; and dismisses as absurd any attempt to locate the beginning of the development of Joshua 13–21 in a period as late as the Exile. The first point is simply answered by reference to the middle of Noth's discussion of 'Das deuteronomistische Josuabuch' (1953: 9–10). The second I have simply never stated. What I have argued could in fact be given a conservative rather than a radical gloss: I followed Smend against Noth in ascribing to the primary Deuteronomistic historian, rather than a secondary hand, the earliest detectable introduction to the narrative in the second part of Joshua (13:1, 7); and I offered criteria for detecting behind that primary historian's description of ten territories a still earlier listing of six central and northern holdings (1980: 84, 106). Cortese had noticed this suggestion (1990: 69), but not appreciated how it undercut his accusation that I placed the beginnings of the material in the exilic period.

Critique of the textual and literary observations in these essays has hitherto been offered only piecemeal. A prime reason for issuing together all these studies of Joshua and of its relationships with other biblical books is that, as I begin to prepare a large commentary on Joshua (ICC), I am hoping for more thorough critique from colleagues who have often addressed some of these interconnected arguments, but not a wide enough range of them. It is not sufficient to evaluate the discussion of the cities of the Levites or the refuge cities on its own, without probing at the same time the distinctive testimony of the Septuagint in Joshua 5 or 8 or the complexities of how tribes are differently listed in the Hebrew or Greek texts. The evidence for the

integrity and distinctiveness of the Greek witness to the text of Joshua
has been a cumulative one. It will only ultimately be found to lack
cogency after a demonstration step by step that much of the path taken
has been wrongly directed.

Prospects

The history of interpretation (essay 13) has underscored just how open
the discussion still is of many of the questions explored in the earlier
dozen essays. It may be useful in closing to spell out, in a little greater
detail than was possible there, some contemporary trends.

TEXTUAL ISSUES

The preceding essay ended with mention of the discussion between
Rofé and Rösel on the transition from Joshua to Judges, and on the
correlation of textual and literary work. Noth recognized in his pioneer-
ing study that questions of Deuteronomistic relationships were more
controverted in Joshua 23–24 and Judges 1–2 than elsewhere in his
History; and he had to pause (1943/81: 6–9) in an otherwise rapid
sketch to criticize Rudolph's arguments (1938) for a twin-stratum
approach. Blum has returned to the attempt to untie these compositional
knots in a substantial contribution to the Brekelmans Festschrift (1997).
For Judges 1 he depends heavily, though not uncritically, on the
monograph by Becker on the period of the Judges and monarchy.
Becker attempts a substantial critique of my study on Judges 1 (essay 9).
He states (1990: 31), but does not appear to argue, that the Greek text of
Joshua has been adjusted towards Judges 1; and deduces that I was
wrong to claim that the LXX of Joshua gives us privileged access to the
source of both Joshua (MT) and of Judges 1. It should be noted that
Lindars, in the published draft of the opening chapters of what should
have been his ICC commentary on Judges (1995), does not commit
himself on my main case on Joshua, but does cite Auld (1975)
frequently and mostly with approval.

The work of Floss has been thoroughly reviewed in Bieberstein's
comprehensive study of Joshua 1–6 (1995). This is very well-informed
and carried forward over a broad front. He has not just briefed himself
thoroughly about archaeology at *tell es-sultan*. He also offers a very
detailed stratigraphical sketch of the development of Joshua 1–6, with
Josh 3:1, 5, 13b–14a, 16 and 6:1–3, 4b, 5, 11, 14–15, 20c–21 presented
as the first small structure on bedrock. The introduction to his treatment
of Joshua 6 is typical, and may be translated as follows:

To be sure, above all Steuernagel (1900) and Holzinger (1901) and also
Holmes (1914) and Benjamin (1921) gave preference to the smoother version
preserved in G, yet this was little noted by later authors who were concerned
with a literary-critical analysis. And those more recent authors like Chesman
(1967), Orlinsky (1969), Auld (1976), Greenspoon (1982) and Tov (1986),
who in principled opinions vehemently advocated G as the earlier version,
have not let any corresponding consistent text-critical analysis of the unit
under consideration accompany their determined attitudes. (1995: 230)

Yet, as a comment on Joshua 6 this hardly seems fair. The very few
remarks on Joshua 6 in Auld (1976; 1979) clearly pretended to no close
study of that chapter, and simply noted that some features of MT and
LXX noted in Joshua 6 resembled elements of other chapters which had
been discussed much more fully.

The most striking difference between MT and LXX within Joshua
1–6 is over circumcision and passover in chapter 5. Here Bieberstein
agrees that the shorter and ambiguous ושב, without שנית, was the original
reading in 5:2 and that LXX should also be followed in reading vv.11,12
without 'on the morrow [after the passover]'. However, he mounts a
detailed defence of MT over LXX in the central section where the
differences are greater (198–206).

Den Hertog's Giessen doctoral thesis (1996) offers an even more
fundamental contribution to the study of Greek Joshua. He starts with a
review of the pertinent literature on the Manuscript groups, in which
Margolis' division is shown to be basically solid (3–21). Here Den
Hertog has the great benefit of close familiarity with the Septuaginta-
Unternehmen in Göttingen, where he has helped collect materials for the
new Göttingen edition of Joshua being prepared by Udo Quast. A
review of Brooke–McLean, Rahlfs, and Margolis follows (22–8); and
then a discussion of each of the (not very many) differences between the
texts reconstructed by Rahlfs and Margolis (29–114). Den Hertog's
discussion of the date and place of the translation follows; and involves
a review of the relationship between Greek Joshua and the LXX
versions of Genesis, Exodus, Numbers, Deuteronomy, Judges, and
Psalms. He deduces that the translation was not later than the first half of
the second century BCE, and was made outside Palestine – probably in
Egypt (115–50).

A careful excursus (151–6) treats Josh 5:4–6. Auld is warned against
concentrating on quantitative rather than qualitative discrepancies
between MT and LXX; and it is noted that the Latin Vulgate is less
dependent on LXX than often claimed. Den Hertog notes that MT in
Josh 5:4–6, with its three clauses opening with כל העם ('all the nation')
was an ideal candidate for corruption by homoeoarcton; and proposes
that LXX represents a bettering of a mistakenly shortened *Vorlage*.

Discussion of the canonicity of the Hebrew and then the Greek text
follows (157–66). And the final chapter (167–85) – the most important

in Den Hertog's view – studies the translation technique of the Greek under four main headings: the use of the article with proper names; the rendering of construct state linkages; participial constructions and the forming of principal and subordinate clauses; and, finally, aspects determined by content. An assessment of Den Hertog's work in the volume on Jesus/Joshua in the Bible d'Alexandrie is eagerly awaited.

Fritz's commentary (1994: 1–2) replaces Noth's in the Handbuch zum Alten Testament series, yet follows its predecessor with its rather disappointing lack of interest in the LXX. Fritz cites the first essay in this volume, but not the second – exactly like Ahituv (1995: 64). He also sets his readers on the wrong track by describing the LXX-*Vorlage* as proto-masoretic instead of pre-masoretic, and by suggesting that additions in LXX are likely to go back (only) to the translator rather than to this Hebrew *Vorlage*. Bieberstein has contributed a review of Fritz's commentary, particularly detailed in text-critical matters (1996).

Schäfer-Lichtenberger (1995: 192) adds to the German voices cautioning against citing LXX as crown witness for an originally shorter Hebrew text. Hess shows himself very thoroughly informed, text-critically as otherwise, yet highlights in his Introduction (1996: 18–20) examples which tend to diminish the significance of potential rivals to the Masoretic text.

Svensson's work on the towns and toponyms of Joshua 14–21 (1994) pays close attention to LXX and other ancient versions, yet in an idiosyncratic though highly interesting way. As his title suggests, he is less interested in the whole text than in the places mentioned within the text and their names. Yet, on the other hand, he also probes the implications of five substantial pluses (or minuses) when MT and LXX are compared. The town list including Bethlehem (15:59a), Gezer as dowry of Pharaoh's daughter (16:10a), Dan's northern migration (19:47a, 48a), and the doublet of Josh 19:49–50 at the end of the list of Levitic cities (21:42a–d) are all part of LXX but not MT (a possible problem is that he does not include as a fifth example the Levitic cities from Reuben, though he admits these 'are lacking in the best manuscripts'). Then Josh 20:4–6, the casuistic element in that short chapter on refuge cities, is absent from LXX but part of MT. It is with reference to these variations that Svensson makes the observation that LXX is actually longer than MT – something which is not true of Joshua as a whole (Tov has reckoned Joshua LXX some 4–5 per cent shorter than MT) or even of Joshua 14–21 in particular.

Another recent Swedish publication concentrates on earlier chapters in Joshua (2–8) in an equally fresh way. Winther-Nielsen's *Functional Discourse Grammar of Joshua* seeks to answer among other questions 'How close is the match between syntactic and pragmatic relations in Joshua 2?'; 'Can episode demarcation and drama explain unusual features in the grammar of the stories on Jordan, Jericho and Ai in Joshua 3–8?'; and 'Is the Book of Joshua coherent in structure and theme?' The author warns against 'fus[ing] the MT with variant readings prior to textual analysis' (22), and is critical of Floss (1982; 1986) for establishing an eclectic text of Joshua 2 rather than making the extant MT the basis for his meticulous linguistic description of the text.

Not least because the manuscript fragments from the Dead Sea coast relating to Joshua are so few, discussion of them is hard to control. The fact that they share more readings with MT than with LXX where these diverge has reinforced some apologists for the traditional Hebrew text. The fact that (perhaps) the most interesting of the fragments attaches the beginning of the story of the circumcision to the end of the story of the stone altar (see essay 10 above) has led some to propose that it was part, not of a variant biblical text, but of a parabiblical recombination of biblical texts (e.g. Hess 1996: 20). Bieberstein notes (1995: 76) that Josephus also reports the building of an altar just after the crossing of the Jordan.

TERRITORIAL TEXTS

Ottosson, Fritz, Aḥituv, and Hess have all offered fresh perspectives on the geographical materials in Joshua in their recent commentaries. Rich seams of relevant information (literary, text-critical, geographical, historical) have been mined by Svensson and compactly, even tersely, presented in his doctoral study with a wealth of tables and charts. This work recognizes a large debt to Ottosson.

The topics which may have seen the most lively discussion in recent years have been the refuge and Levitical cities. Rofé uses the MT plus in Josh 20: 4–6 and its 'Deuteronomistic' language to argue for a Kaufman-like source hypothesis, with D-elements added to an existing P-text represented by the shorter LXX. Fritz mentions Auld and Rofé in his discussion of refuge (1994: 202–6). However, he does not engage with them, nor with Cortese who discusses Joshua 20–21 in some detail (1990: 77–85).

It has already been noted (p. 51 above) that my historical conclusion that the irregular number of cities ascribed to Judah (and Simeon) – nine, not a multiple of four – must derive from a source, not a theory, has been adopted by Na'aman. And so it is interesting now to find Ofer agreeing with Na'aman (his editor!) on the realistic background of the non-schematic part of the list relating to Judah (Ofer 1994: 116).

Kartveit offered a carefully critical review (1989: 70–7), to which Auld made brief response (1990). Kartveit provides a useful bibliography in his brief return to the topic of these cities (1989: 159–63), in which he develops the view that these cities are a late supplement to 1 Chronicles 1–9.

Many issues discussed by Ben Zvi (1992) are apparently responding to Auld (1978; 1979), though this is not acknowledged point by point. He argues fully and compellingly that the authors of Joshua 21 have drawn on several different biblical texts; and that the chapter cannot have been drafted before the post-monarchical period.

Commentators on Chronicles have also joined the discussion. Williamson (1982: 68) writes of a forceful challenge, but does not take sides: 'whatever be the truth of the matter . . .'. He does, however, note how the order of Levitical clans in the list of cities in vv. 39ff. (Kohath–Gershom–Merari) agrees with the immediately preceding part of the chapter (6:16–32). There is also some discussion of Auld (1979) in Japhet (1993: 147ff.), where Kartveit (1989) and Na'aman (1986) are also both cited – but not Auld (1990). There are preliminary responses in essay 11 (especially on p. 114 above).

The clarity of Richard Hess's recent review of Joshua's 'composition' (1996: 31–42) renders unnecessary a further attempt at comprehensiveness in similarly short compass. However, Hess is less interested and I rather more interested in questions relating to the separateness or connectedness of the 'book' of Joshua – in questions, that is, often discussed in connection with the so-called 'Deuteronomists'. What is or should be the fundamental unit of reading or of meaning? Is Joshua a book quite complete on its own? Or, alternatively, is Joshua simply a component part of the Former Prophets, or of the Deuteronomistic History? Or, in middle position, is Joshua at least a sequel to Deuteronomy and closely linked to it? I raised somewhat similar questions in connection with the book of Judges towards the end of essay 12 above; and discuss them more fully in a contribution on the Former Prophets to McKenzie and Graham (eds), *The Hebrew Bible Today*.

The section on 'Literary approaches' in the essay above on the history of interpretation mentioned a series of recent 'final form' readings of Joshua, and suggested that these gave some support to Polzin's reading of the whole text as the work of the Deuteronomist. This is, however, true only up to a point. Unlike studies devoted to Joshua alone and making little or no mention of 'Deuteronomistic' matters, Polzin has presented his reading of Joshua within a volume devoted to Deuteronomy–Judges as a connected text, and within a series in which he has already analysed 1 and 2 Samuel and in which he will treat Kings. Until his Kings volume completes his project, critique must remain preliminary. However, issues from Deuteronomy do bulk much larger in his reading of Joshua than in his reading of the books of Samuel.

Rowlett's (1992) article was also mentioned in the history of interpretation. That has been followed by her 'new historicist' approach to *Joshua and the Rhetoric of Violence* (1996). This fuller analysis begins with an account of methods, and ends (156–80) with a reading of Joshua 'focused on the processes of marginalization within the text and how the rhetoric of violence expressed in military language is used to set and negotiate boundaries of inclusion, exclusion and marginality' (29). Yet the central discussions are more conventional. A sketch of the historical context of Joshua, indebted to Cross, Nelson, and Robert and Mary Coote, suggests the relevance of Joshua to Josiah's concerns. A good review of scholarship on divine warfare gives qualified endorsement to the monograph of Sa-Moon Kang (1989). Then the long discussion of the conventional language of war in the ancient near east agrees with Van Seters that Assyrian parallels are the most relevant for biblical material. The following detailed study of the rhetoric of violence in the opening chapter of Joshua includes a careful critique of Lohfink's much-cited proposal that there was an actual genre of installation.

Fritz sees no literary way behind the Deuteronomistic *Grundschicht* (1994–6) that dates from the very end of monarchy or beginning of the exilic period (9). That is an identifiable unit, but only part of a larger composition. It has no connections with Pentateuchal J (as conventionally understood); and the base-narrative of Joshua 6–9 reads like the realization of the commands in Deut 7:1ff. and 20:16ff. The view he advocates on Joshua 13–24, that the core of these chapters was also part of this *Grundschicht*, he attributes to Auld (1980: 52–71).

1 Chronicles 6 is secondary to Joshua 21 – against Auld (Fritz 1994: 210)—but it is useful for the reconstruction of some place-names in the source chapter. Numbers 35 assumes that Joshua 20 and 21 are linked. Na'aman is supported in deriving many of the names in Joshua 21 from Joshua 13–20: it is not a 'strange text', as Schmitt had suggested, but a piece of Midrash literature, as proposed by Holzinger (Fritz 213). The more recent discussion in Auld (1990) is not cited by Fritz—or in fact by Aḥituv.

There is a very thorough discussion of Joshua 1 in Schäfer-Lichtenberger's detailed study of the authority and legitimacy of the successor in the Old Testament, with particular reference to the cases of Joshua and Solomon (1995: 190–209). Her discussion of the laws on king and prophet in Deuteronomy should be compared with that of Dietrich in de Pury *et al.* (1996).

My work on Samuel and Kings (Auld 1994), followed by essays 10 and 12 above, has led me to share aspects of the increasing scepticism about the existence of a connected Deuteronomistic History, voiced also in different ways by Westermann and Würthwein. I am inclined to read only Joshua and Judges as individual works, but Samuel–Kings as a single account of the monarchic period. Joshua has a particularly close connection with Deuteronomy. Its opening chapter starts—and without any resumptive repetition—just where the narrative in Deuteronomy 31 and 34 has left off. It finishes unproblematically, noting how the death of its hero was also the end of an era. Then the opening of 1 Samuel offers a good introduction, in promise and in threat, to everything that follows. Judges may be read as a secondary link between Joshua and what the Greek Bible describes as the four books of Reigns or Kingdoms—what the Hebrew Bible (followed by most modern English translations) calls two books each of Samuel and Kings.

The royal story underlying Samuel–Kings should perhaps be thought of as the root-work that supports the whole growth of Deuteronomy–Kings, and even of Genesis–Kings. The royal Davidic story was first anticipated in the stories from Moses to the Judges, and then a fresh and still 'earlier' preface supplied in the groundwork of Genesis–Numbers. We should also pay attention to larger panels or recurring patterns in Deuteronomy–Kings. The first royal figures, David and Solomon, are handled at greater length than any that follow—as were Moses and Joshua at the very beginnings. The succession of Solomon to David and that of Joshua to Moses are very similarly portrayed. The deaths of Solomon and Joshua are each followed by a breakdown in central authority. Both Kings and Judges concentrate on the increasing disorder that ensues in northern Israel; and both contrast the north with Judah.

These repeated similarities may reinforce our impression that a deliberate pattern is being created. The new extended preface in Deuteronomy, Joshua, and Judges permits a fresh reading of the older story of David's line. We readily recall that we have encountered analogous situations before; and we are prepared for the importation here and there in the royal story of values and language from the newer Mosaic narratives. The new primary stress on Torah, and no longer on King and Temple, are indicative of the interests of the exilic or post-exilic situation.

BIBLIOGRAPHY

Aharoni, Y. (1967), *The Land of the Bible* (2nd edn, 1979; London: Burns & Oates).

Ahituv, Sh. (1995), *Joshua: Introduction and Commentary* (Mikra LeYisra'el; Jerusalem: Magnes).

Ahlström, G. W. (1982), *Royal Administration and National Religion in Ancient Palestine* (Leiden: Brill).

— (1993) *The History of Ancient Palestine* (Sheffield: Sheffield Academic Press).

Albrektson, B. (1993), 'Grundtext och urtext: om underlaget för svenska översättningar av Gamla testamentet', in A. G. Auld (ed.), *Understanding Poets and Prophets: Essays in Honour of George Wishart Anderson* (JSOTSup 152; Sheffield: JSOT Press), 23–37.

Albright, W. F. (1945), 'The List of Levitic Cities', in *Louis Ginzberg Jubilee Volume* (New York), 49–73.

Alt, A. (1953), *Kleine Schriften*, vols I–III (München: C. H. Beck).

Auld, A. G. (1976), 'Studies in Joshua: Texts and Literary Relations' (unpublished Ph.D. thesis, Edinburgh).

— (1979a), 'Joshua: the Hebrew and Greek Texts', *SVT* **30**, 1–14.

— (1979b), 'The "Levitical Cities": Texts and History', *ZAW* **91**, 194–206.

— (1980), *Joshua, Moses and the Land* (Edinburgh: T. & T. Clark).

— (1983), 'Prophets through the Looking Glass: between Writings and Moses', *JSOT* **27**, 3–23.

— (1984), *Joshua, Judges and Ruth* (Daily Study Bible; Edinburgh: St Andrew Press).

— (1986), *Kings* (Daily Study Bible; Edinburgh: St Andrew Press).

— (1987), 'Tribal Terminology in Joshua and Judges', *Le Origini di Israele*, 87–98.

— (1989), 'Gideon: Hacking at the heart of the Old Testament', *VT* **39**, 257–67.

— (1990), 'The Cities in Joshua 21: the contribution of textual criticism', *Textus* XV, 141–52.

— (1992), 'Salomo und die Deuteronomisten: eine Zukunftsvision?', *ThZ* **48**, 343–55.

— (1993), 'Solomon at Gibeon: History Glimpsed', *Avraham Malamat Volume* (Eretz Israel 24; Jerusalem: Israel Exploration Society), 1–7.

— (1994), *Kings Without Privilege* (Edinburgh: T. & T. Clark).

— (1995), 'Reading Joshua after Kings', in J. Davies (ed.), *Words Remembered: Texts Renewed. Essays in Honour of John F. A. Sawyer* (JSOTS 195; Sheffield: Sheffield Academic Press).

— (1998), 'Former Prophets', in S. L. McKenzie and W. P. Graham (eds), *The Hebrew Bible* (Louisville, KY: Westminster/John Knox).

— (*in press*), 'The Deuteronomists and the Former Prophets', in S. L. McKenzie and L. Schearing (eds), *Those Elusive Deuteronomists* (Sheffield: Sheffield Academic Press).

Avi-Yonah, M. (1951), *Historical Geography* (2nd edn; Jerusalem).

Bal, M. (1988), *Death and Dissymmetry: The Politics of Coherence in the Book of Judges* (Chicago Studies in the History of Judaism; Chicago and London: University of Chicago Press).

Barr, J. (1989), *The Variable Spellings of the Hebrew Bible* (The Schweich Lectures 1986; Oxford: Oxford University Press for the British Academy).

Becker, U. (1990), *Richterzeit und Königtum. Redaktionsgeschichtliche Studien zum Richterbuch* (BZAW 192; Berlin: de Gruyter).

Begg, C. T. (1986), 'The Function of Josh 7,1–8, 29 in the Deuteronomistic History', *Bib* **67**, 320–34.

Benjamin, C. D. (1921), *The Variations between the Hebrew and Greek Texts of Joshua: Chapters 1–12* (Leipzig: W. Drugulin).

Ben Zvi, E. (1992), 'The List of the Levitical Cities', *JSOT* **54**, 77–106 (especially 86ff.).

Bertheau, E. (1845), *Das Buch der Richter und Rut* (Exegetisches Handbuch zum AT 6; Leipzig: Weidmann'sche Buchhandlung).

Bieberstein, K. (1994) *Lukian und Theodotion im Josuabuch, mit einem Beitrag zu den Josuarollen von Hirbet Qumran* (BNB 7; München: Inst. Bibl. Exegese).

— (1995), *Josua – Jordan – Jericho. Archeologie, Geschichte und Theologie der Landnahme-erzählungen Josua 1–6* (OBO 143; Freiburg (CH): Universitätsverlag).

— (1996), Review of V. Fritz, *Josua* in *ThLZ*.

Blenkinsopp, J. (1976), 'The Structure of P', *CBQ* **38**, 275–92.

Blum, E. (1990), *Studien zur Komposition des Pentateuch* (BZAW 189; Berlin: de Gruyter).

— (1997), 'Der kompositionelle Knoten am Übergang von Josua zu Richter: ein Entflechtungsvorschlag', in M. Vervenne and J. Lust (eds), *Deuteronomy and Deuteronomic Literature: Festschrift C. H. W. Brekelmans* (BETL 133; Leuven: Peeters).

Boling, R. G. (1975), *Judges* (Anchor Bible; New York: Doubleday).

— (1983) 'Levitical History and the Role of Joshua', in C. L. Meyers and M. O'Connor (eds), *The Word of the Lord Shall Go Forth* (Winona Lake, IN: Eisenbrauns), 241–61.

— (1985), 'Levitical Cities: Archaeology and Texts', in A. Kort and S

Merschauser (eds), *Biblical and Related Studies Presented to Samuel Iwry* (Winona Lake, IN: Eisenbrauns), 23–32.

Boling, R. G. and G. E. Wright (1982), *Joshua* (Anchor Bible; New York: Doubleday).

Braun, R. L. (1973), 'Solomonic Apologetic in Chronicles', *JBL* **92**, 503–16.

— (1976), 'Solomon, the Chosen Temple Builder: The Significance of 1 Chronicles 22, 28, 29 for the Theology of Chronicles', *JBL* **95**, 581–90.

Brooke, A. E. and N. McLean (1940), *The Old Testament in Greek* III, Part I (Cambridge University Press).

Brueggemann, W. (1972), 'The Kerygma of the Priestly Writers', *ZAW* **84**, 397–413.

Budde, K. (1887), 'Richter und Josua', *ZAW* **7**, 93–166.

— (1897), *Das Buch der Richter* (KHAT; Freiburg: Mohr).

Butler, T. C. (1983), *Joshua* (WBC; Waco, TX: Word).

Callaway, J. A. (1968), 'New Evidence on the Conquest of Ai', *JBL* **87**, 312–20.

Calvin, J. (1984), *Commentaries on the Book of Joshua* (Edinburgh: Calvin Translation Society).

Carroll, R. P. (1992), 'The Myth of the Empty Land', in D. Jobling and T. Pippin (eds), *Ideological Criticism of Biblical Texts* (Semeia 59), 79–93.

Cooke, G. A. (1917), *The Book of Joshua in the Revised Version* (CBC, 1878; 1917²; Cambridge University Press).

Coote, R. P. (1990), *Early Israel: a new horizon* (Minneapolis: Fortress).

Coote, R. P. and K. W. Whitelam (1987), *The Emergence of Early Israel in Historical Perspective* (Sheffield: Almond).

Cortese, E. (1985), 'Gios 21 e Giud 1 (TM o LXX?) e l'''abbottonaura'' del Tetrateuco con l'Opera deuteronomistica', *RiB* **33**, 375–94.

— (1990), *Josua 13–21: Ein priesterschriftlicher Abschnitt im deuteronomistichen Geschichtswerk* (OBO 94; Freiburg (CH): Universitätsverlag).

Cross, F. M. (1958), *The Ancient Library of Qumran and Modern Biblical Studies* (New York).

— (1973), *Canaanite Myth and Hebrew Epic* (Cambridge, MA: Harvard University Press).

Dahood, M. (1968), *Psalms II* (Anchor Bible; New York: Double-day).

Davies, P. R. (1992), *In Search of 'Ancient Israel'* (JSOTS 148; Sheffield: JSOT Press).

Delekat, L. (1964), 'Zum hebräischen Wörterbuch', *VT* **14**, 7–66 (especially 13–23).

Dietrich, W. (1972), *Prophetie und Geschichte* (FRLANT 108; Göttingen: Vandenhoeck & Ruprecht).

—(1996), 'Histoire et Loi: Historiographie deutéronomiste et Loi deutéronomique à l'example du passage de l'époque des Juges à l'époque royale', in de Pury *et al.*, 297–323.

Dillmann, A. (1886), *Die Bücher Numeri, Deuteronomium und Josua* (KHC; Leipzig: S. Hirzel).

Douglas, M. (1993), *In the Wilderness: The doctrine of defilement in the Book of Numbers* (JSOTS 158; Sheffield: JSOT Press).

Dupont-Sommer, A. (1956), 'Une stèle araméenne d'un prêtre de Ba'al trouvée en Égypte', *Syria* **33**, 79–87.

Durrell, L. (1958), *Balthazar* (London: Faber & Faber).

Eslinger, L. (1989), *Into the Hands of the Living God* (JSOTS 84, Bible and Literature Series 24; Sheffield: Almond).

Finkelstein, I. (1988), *The Archaeology of the Israelite Settlement* (Jerusalem: Israel Exploration Society).

Floss, J. P. (1982–6), *Kunden oder Kundschafter: Literaturwissenschaftliche Untersuchung zu Jos 2* I: *Text, Schichtung, Überlieferung* (ATSAT 16); II: *Komposition, Redaktion, Intention* (ATSAT 26; St Ottilien: Eos).

Fohrer, G. (1968), *Introduction to the Old Testament* (London: SPCK).

Frick, F. S. (1985), *The Formation of the State in Ancient Israel: a survey of models and theories* (Sheffield: Almond).

Friedman, R. E. (1981), *The Exile and Biblical Narrative: The Formation of the Deuteronomistic and Priestly Works* (HSM 22; Chico, CA: Scholars Press).

Fritz, V. (1994), *Das Buch Josua* (HAT I/7; Tübingen: J. C. B. Mohr).

Garbini, G. (1988), *History and Ideology in Ancient Israel* (London: SCM).

Garstang, J. (1931), *Joshua, Judges (The Foundations of Bible History)* (London: Constable & Co.).

Geus, C. H. J. de (1976), *The Tribes of Israel* (Assen: Van Gorcum).

Gottwald, N. K. (1980), *The Tribes of Yahweh: A Sociology of the Religion of Liberated Israel, 1250–1050 B.C.E.* (London: SCM).

Gray, J. (1986), *Joshua, Judges and Ruth* (NCBC, 1967; 1986[2]; London: Marshall, Morgan and Scott).

Greenspoon, L. J. (1983), *Textual Studies in the Book of Joshua* (HSM 28; Chico, CA: Scholars Press).

—(1992), 'The Qumran Fragments of Joshua: Which puzzle are they part of and where do they fit?', in G. J. Brooke and B. Lindars (eds), *Septuagint, Scrolls and Cognate Writings* (SCS 33; Atlanta, GA: Scholars Press), 159–94.

Gressmann, H. (1922), *Die Anfänge Israels (von 2.Mose bis Richter und Ruth)* (Göttingen: Vandenhoeck & Ruprecht).

Gunn, D. M. (1987), 'Joshua and Judges', in R. Alter and F. Kermode (eds), *The Literary Guide to the Bible* (London: Collins), 102–21.

Hamlin, E. J. (1983), *Inheriting the Land: A Commentary on the Book of Joshua* (ITC; Edinburgh: Handsel).

Haran, M. (1961), 'Studies in the account of the Levitical cities', *JBL* **80**, 45–54, 156–65.

Hawk, L. D. (1991), *Every Promise Fulfilled: Contesting Plots in Joshua* (Literary Currents in Biblical Interpretation; Louisville, KY: Westminster/John Knox Press).

Hayman, A. P. (1993), 'Qohelet, the Rabbis and the Wisdom Text from the Cairo Geniza', in A. G. Auld (ed.), *Understanding Poets and Prophets. Essays in Honour of George Wishart Anderson* (JSOTS 152; Sheffield: Sheffield Academic Press), 149–65.

Den Hertog, C. G. (1996), 'Studien zur griechischen Übersetzung des Buches Josua' (unpublished Giessen dissertation).

Hertzberg, H. W. (1953), *Die Bücher Josua, Richter, Ruth* (ATD 9; Göttingen: Vandenhoeck & Ruprecht).

Hess, R. (1996), *Joshua* (TOTC; Leicester: Inter-Varsity Press).

Ho, Craig Y. S. (1995), 'Conjectures and refutations: is 1 Samuel xxxi 1–13 really the source of 1 Chronicles x 1–12?', *VT* **45**, 82–106.

Hoffmann, H.-D. (1980), *Reform und Reformen* (ATANT 66; Zürich: Theologischer Verlag).

Hollenberg, J. (1874), 'Die deuteronomischen Bestandtheile des Buches Josua', *TSK* **47**, 462–506.

—(1876), *Der Charakter der alexandrinischen Übersetzung des Buches Josua und ihr text-kritischer Werth* (Moers: J. G. Eckner).

Holmes, S. (1914), *Joshua, the Hebrew and Greek Texts* (Cambridge University Press).

Jacob, B. (1974), *Genesis* (New York: Ktav).

Japhet, S. (1993), *I & II Chronicles* (OTL; London: SCM).

Jenni, E. (1961), 'Zwei Jahrzehnte Forschung an den Büchern Josua bis Könige', *TRu* **27**, 1–32, 87–146.

Johnstone, W. (1990), *Exodus* (Old Testament Guides; Sheffield: JSOT Press).

—(1993), 'The Deuteronomistic Cycles of "Signs" and "Wonders" in Exodus 1–13', in A. G. Auld (ed.), *Understanding Poets and Prophets: Essays in Honour of George Wishart Anderson* (JSOT Sup 152; Sheffield: JSOT Press), 166–85.

Kallai, Z. (1967), *Historical Geography of the Bible; The Tribal Territories of Israel* (ET 1986; Jerusalem: Magnes).

Kang, Sa-Moon (1989), *Divine War in the Old Testament and in the Ancient Near East* (BZAW 177; Berlin: de Gruyter).

Kartveit, M. (1989), *Motive und Schichten der Landtheologie in I Chronik 1–9* (Coniectanea Biblica, OT Series 28; Stockholm: Almqvist & Wiksell).

Kaufmann, Y. (1985), *The Biblical Account of the Conquest of Canaan* (with a preface by M. Greenberg; Jerusalem: Magnes Press).

Keil, C. F. and F. Delitzsch (1869), *Joshua, Judges and Ruth* (Edinburgh: T. & T. Clark).

Kempinski, A. (1993), '"When History Sleeps, Theology Arises": A Note on Joshua 8:30–35 and the Archaeology of the "Settlement Period"' (*Malamat Volume* EI 24; Jerusalem: Israel Exploration Society), 175–83.

Kittel, R. (1895), *History of the Hebrews* (Theol. Transl. Library, 3; London).

Kochavi, M. (1972), 'The Survey in the Land of Judah', in *Judea, Samaria and the Golan, Archaeological Survey in 1968* (Jerusalem), 17–91 (Hebrew).

Kuenen, A. (1886), *An Historico-Critical Enquiry into The Origin and Composition of the Hexateuch* (London: Macmillan).

Langlamet, F. (1969), *Gilgal et les récits de la traversée du Jourdain* (Cahiers de la Revue Biblique; Paris: J. Gabalda).

— (1979), 'Rahab', *SDB* **6**, 1065–92.

Leibowitz, N. (1976), *Studies in Bereshit (Genesis)* (3rd edn; Jerusalem: World Zionist Organization).

Lemche, N.-P. (1988), *Ancient Israel: A New History of Israelite Society* (The Biblical Seminar; Sheffield: JSOT Press).

— (1993a), Review of M. Ottosson, *Josuaboken*, in *JBL* **112**, 512–13.

— (1993b), 'The Old Testament – A Hellenistic Book?', *SJOT* **7**, 163–93.

Lindars, B. (1994), *Judges 1–5* (Edinburgh: T. & T. Clark).

Liver, J. (1950–), '*mšpḥḥ*', in *Enzyklopedia Miqra'it* (Jerusalem), 582–8.

Lohfink, N. (1977), 'Wachstum', in *Unsere grossen Wörter. Das Alte Testament zu Themen dieser Jahre* (Freiburg: Herder), 156–71.

— (1978), 'Die Priesterschrift und die Geschichte', *Congress Volume. Göttingen 1977*, VT Suppl. 29, 189–225.

MacLear, G. F. (1880), *The Book of Joshua* (CBC; Cambridge University Press).

Margolis, M. A. (1931–8), *The Book of Joshua in Greek* (Paris: Geuthner).

Mayes, A. D. H. (1983), *The Story of Israel between Settlement and Exile: A Redactional Study of the Deuteronomistic History* (London: SCM).

— (1985), *Judges* (Old Testament Guides; Sheffield: JSOT Press).

Mazar, B. (1960), 'The Cities of the Priests and the Levites', *VTS* **7**, 193–205.

Miller, J. M. and G. M. Tucker (1974), *The Book of Joshua* (CBC; Cambridge University Press).

Miller, P. D. (1973), *The Divine Warrior in Early Israel* (HSM 5; Cambridge, MA: Harvard University Press).

Mitchell, G. (1993), *Together in the Land. A Reading of the Book of Joshua* (JSOTS 134; Sheffield: JSOT Press).

Mittmann, S. (1975), *Deuteronomium 1:1–6:3 literarkritisch und traditionsgeschichtlich untersucht* (BZAW 139; Berlin: de Gruyter).

Moenikes, A. (1992), 'Zur Redaktionsgeschichte des sogenannten Deuteronomistischen Geschichtswerkes', *ZAW* **104**, 333–48.

—(1995), *Die grundsätzliche Ablehnung des Königtums in der Hebräischen Bibel* (BBB 99; Weinheim: Beltz Athenäum).

Moore, G. F. (1895), *Judges* (ICC; Edinburgh: T. & T. Clark).

Mowinckel, S. (1964a), *Erwägungen zur Pentateuch Quellenfrage* (Oslo: Universitetsforlaget).

—(1964b), *Tetrateuch-Pentateuch-Hexateuch. Die Berichte uber die Landnahme in den drei altisraelitischen Geschichtswerken* (BZAW 90; Berlin: de Gruyter).

Mullen, E. T. Jr (1993), *Narrative History and Ethnic Boundaries: The Deuteronomistic Historian and the Creation of Israelite National Identity* (SBL Semeia Studies; Atlanta, GA: Scholars Press).

Na'aman, N. (1986), *Borders and Districts in Biblical Historiography* (JerBS 4; Jerusalem: Simor).

—(1994), 'The Conquest of Canaan in the Book of Joshua and in History', in I. Finkelstein and N. Na'aman (eds), *From Nomadism to Monarchy: Archaeological and Historical Aspects of Early Israel* (Jerusalem: Israel Exploration Society), 218–81.

Nelson, R. D. (1981a), *The Double Redaction of the Deuteronomistic History* (JSOTS 18; Sheffield: JSOT Press).

—(1981b), 'Josiah in the Book of Joshua', *JBL* **100**, 531–40.

Noth, M. (1935), 'Studien zu den historisch-geographischen Dokumenten des Josuabuches', *ZDPV* **58**, 185–255.

—(1938), *Das Buch Josua* (HAT 1.7, 1953²; Tübingen: J. C. B. Mohr).

—(1943), *Überlieferungsgeschichtliche Studien* I (ET of Part I (1981), *The Deuteronomistic History*, JSOTS 15; Sheffield: Sheffield Academic Press).

(1950), 'Überlieferungsgeschichtliches zur zweiten Hälfte des Josuabuches', *Bonner Biblische Beiträge* I, 152 67.

Ofer, A. (1994), ' ''All the Hill Country of Judah'': From a Settlement Fringe to a Prosperous Monarchy', in I. Finkelstein and N. Na'aman (eds), *From Nomadism to Monarchy. Archaeological and Historical Aspects of Early Israel* (Jerusalem: Israel Exploration Society), 92–121.

Origen (1960), *Homélies sur Josué* (SC 71, ed. A. Jaubert; Paris: Editions du Cerf).

Orlinsky, H. M. (1969), 'The Hebrew *Vorlage* of the Septuagint of the Book of Joshua', *SVT* **17**, 187–95.

Otto, E. (1975), *Das Mazzotfest in Gilgal* (BWANT 107; Stuttgart: Kohlhammer).

Ottosson, M. (1991), *Josuaboken. En programskrift for davidisk restauration* (Studia Biblica Upsaliensia I; Stockholm: Almqvist & Wiksell).

Peckham, B. (1984), 'The Composition of Joshua 3–4', *CBQ* **46**, 413–31.

Polzin, R. (1980), *Moses and the Deuteronomist: A Literary Study of the Deuteronomic History*, I: *Deuteronomy, Joshua, Judges* (Bloomington: Indiana University Press).

Porter, J. R. (1970), 'The Succession of Joshua', in J. I. Durham and J. R. Porter (eds), *Proclamation and Presence: Old Testament Essays in Honour of Gwynne Henton Davies* (London: SCM Press), 102–32.

—(1992), Review of M. Ottosson, *Josuaboken*, in *SOTS Book List 1992*, 83–4.

Pritchard, J. B. (1954), *The Ancient Near East in Pictures Relating to the Old Testament* (Princeton: Princeton University Press).

Pury, A. de, T. Römer and J.-D. Macchi (1996), *Israël construit son histoire: L'historiographie deutéronomiste á la lumière des recherches récentes* (Le Monde de la Bible 34; Génève: Labor et Fides).

von Rad, G. (1938), *Das formkritische Problem des Hexateuchs* (BWANT 26; Stuttgart).

—(1943), 'The Promised Land and Yahweh's Land in the Hexateuch', in *The Problem of the Hexateuch and Other Essays* (1966; Edinburgh: Oliver & Boyd), 79–93.

—(1950), 'Hexateuch oder Pentateuch', *VF* 1947/50, 52–6.

Radjawane, A. N. (1974), 'Das deuteronomistische Geschichtswerk. Ein Forschungsbericht', *TRu* **38**, 177–216.

Rofé, A. (1982), 'The End of the Book of Joshua according to the Septuagint', *Henoch* **4**, 17–36.

—(1985), 'Joshua 20: Historico-Literary Criticism Illustrated', in J. H. Tigay (ed.), *Empirical Models for Biblical Criticism* (Philadelphia: University of Pennsylvania Press).

—(1994), 'The Editing of the Book of Joshua in the Light of 4QJosh[a]', in J. G. Brooke (ed.), *New Qumran Texts and Studies Relating to the Bible*.

Rogerson, J. W. (1978), *Anthropology and the Old Testament* (Oxford: Blackwell).

Rose, M. (1981), *Deuteronomist und Jahwist: Untersuchungen zu den Berührungspunkten beider Literaturwerken* (ATANT 67; Zürich: Theologischer Verlag).

Rösel, H. (1980), 'Die Überleitungen vom Josua– ins Richterbuch', *VT* 30, 342–50.

Rosenbaum, M. and A. M. Silbermann (1929), *Pentateuch with Targum Onkelos, Haphtaroth and Rashi's Commentary* (London: Shapiro, Valentine and Co.).

Ross, J. P. (1973), 'The "cities of the Levites" in Joshua XXI and I Chronicles VI' (unpublished Ph.D. thesis, Edinburgh University).

Rothstein, J. W. and Hänel, J. (1927), *Das erste Buch der Chronik* (Kommentar zum Alten Testament XVIII/2; Leipzig: Deichert).

Rowlett, L. L. (1992), 'Inclusion, Exclusion and Marginality in the Book of Joshua', *JSOT* **55**, 15–23.

—(1996), *Joshua and the Rhetoric of Violence. A New Historicist Analysis* (JSOTS 226; Sheffield: Sheffield Academic Press).

Rudolph, W. (1938), *Der 'Elohist' von Exodus bis Josua* (BZAW 68; Berlin: de Gruyter).

Schäfer-Lichtenberger, C. (1995), *Josua und Salomo. Eine Studie zu Autorität & Legitimität des Nachfolgers im Alten Testament* (SVT 58; Leiden: Brill).

Seebass, H. (1984), 'Zur Exegese der Grenzbeschreibungen von Jos. 16,1–17,13', *ZDPV* **100**, 70–83.

—(1985), 'Josua', *BN* **28**, 53–65.

Simian-Yofre, H. (1984), '*mth*', in *Theologisches Wörterbuch zum Alten Testament* IV, 818–26.

Simons, J. (1959), *The Geographical and Topographical Texts of the OT* (Leiden: Brill).

Smend, R. (1971), 'Das Gesetz und die Völker', in H. W. Wolff (ed.), *Probleme Biblischer Theologie* (München: Kaiser), 494–509.

— (1978), *Die Entstehung des Alten Testaments* (Stuttgart: Kohlhammer).

Soggin, J. A. (1972), *Joshua* (2nd edn 1988, Old Testament Library; London: SCM).

—(1976), *Introduction to the Old Testament* (London: SCM).

—(1984), *A History of Israel: from the Beginnings to the Bar Kochba Revolt, AD 135* (London: SCM).

Steck, O. H. (1978), *World and Environment* (Biblical Encounters Series; Nashville: Abingdon).

Steuernagel, C. (1899), *Das Buch Josua* (HAT; Göttingen: Vandenhoeck & Ruprecht).

—(1900), *Deuteronomium und Josua* (HAT; Göttingen: Vandenhoeck & Ruprecht).

Strange, J. (1993), 'The Book of Joshua: A Hasmonean Manifesto', in A. Lemaire and B. Otzen (eds), *History and Tradition of Early Israel: Studies presented to Eduard Nielsen* (SVT 50; Leiden: Brill), 136–41.

Svensson, J. (1994), *Towns and Toponyms in the Old Testament, with Special Emphasis on Joshua 14–21* (CB [OT] 38; Stockholm: Almqvist & Wiksell).

Talstra, E. (1993), *Solomon's Prayer. Synchrony and Diachrony in the Composition of 1 Kings 8, 14–61* (Contributions to Biblical Exegesis and Theology 3; Kampen: Kok Pharos).

Thompson, T. L. (1992), *The Early History of the Israelite People* (Leiden: Brill).

Tov, E. (1981), *The Text-Critical Use of the Septuagint in Biblical Research* (Jer BS 3; Jerusalem: Simor).

—(1986), 'The Growth of the Book of Joshua in the Light of the Evidence of the LXX Translation', in S. Japhet (ed.), *Studies in Bible* (SH31; Jerusalem: Magnes), 321–39.

—(1987), 'Some Sequence Differences between the MT and LXX and their Ramification for the Literary Criticism of the Bible', *JNWSL* **13**, 151–60.

—(1992a), *Textual Criticism of the Hebrew Bible* (Minneapolis: Fortress).

—(1992b), '4QJosh[b]', in Z. J. Kapera (ed.), *Intertestamental Essays in Honour of Jozef Tadeusz Milik* (Krakow: The Enigma Press).

Trebolle-Barrera, J. (1986), 'Historia del Texto de los Libros Historicos e Historia de la Redaccion Deuteronomistica (Jueces 2, 10–3, 6)', in D. Muñoz Leon (ed.), *Salvacion en la Palabra: Targum – Derash – Berith* (Madrid: Ediciones Cristiandad), 245–55.

Tsafrir, Y. (1975), 'The Levitic city of Beth-shemesh in Judah or in Naphtali?', in *Nelson Glueck Memorial Volume* (EI 12; Jerusalem: Israel Exploration Society), 44–5 (Hebrew: Eng. Sum. 119).

Ulrich, E. (1994), '4QJosh[a] and Joshua's First Altar in the Promised Land', in J. G. Brooke, (ed.), *New Qumran Texts and Studies Relating to the Bible*.

Umhau Wolf, C. (1946), 'Terminology of Israel's Tribal Organization', *JBL* **65**, 45–9.

Van Seters, J. (1983), *In Search of History* (New Haven: Yale University Press).

Vawter, B. (1977), *On Genesis: a new reading* (New York: Doubleday).

Veijola, T. (1975), *Die ewige Dynastie* (AASF B/193; Helsinki: Academia Scientiarum Fennica).

—(1977), *Das Königtum in der Beurteilung der deuteronomistischen Historiographie: eine redaktionsgeschichtliche Untersuchung* (AASF B/198; Helsinki: Academia Scientiarum Fennica).

Webb, B. G. (1987), *The Book of Judges: An Integrated Reading* (JSOTS 46; Sheffield: JSOT Press).

Weinfeld, M. (1972), *Deuteronomy and the Deuteronomic School* (Oxford: Clarendon Press).

—(1993), *The Promise of the Land: The inheritance of the land of Canaan by the Israelites* (Berkeley: University of California Press).

Weippert, H. (1985), 'Das deuteronomistiche Geschichtswerk: Sein Ziel und Ende in der neueren Forschung', *TRu* **50**, 213–49.

Wellhausen, J. (1885), 'Pentateuch and Joshua', *EncBrit* 9 18, 505–14.

—(1889), *Die Composition des Hexateuchs* (2nd edn; 1899[3]; Berlin: G. Reimer).

Westermann, C. (1974), *Genesis 1–11* (BK AT I/1; Neukirchen-Vluyn: Neukirchener Verlag).

Whitelam, K. W. (1996), *The Invention of Ancient Israel: the silencing of Palestinian history* (London: Routledge).

Whybray, R. N. (1967), 'ענות in Exodus xxxii 18', *VT* **17**, 122.

Wildberger, H. (1965), 'Das Abbild Gottes', *ThZ* **21**, 245–59, 481–501.

Williamson, H. G. M. (1976), 'The Accession of Solomon in the Books of Chronicles', *VT* **26**, 351–61.

—(1982), *1 & 2 Chronicles* (New Century Bible; London: Marshall, Morgan & Scott).

Winther-Nielsen, N. (1995), *A Functional Discourse Grammar of Joshua* (CB (OT) 40; Stockholm: Almqvist & Wiksell).

Woudstra, M. H. (1981), *The Book of Joshua* (NICOT; Grand Rapids, MI: Eerdmans).

Würthwein, E. (1994), 'Erwägungen zum sog. deuteronomistischen Geschichtswerk: Eine Skizze', in *Studien zum deuteronomistischen Geschichtswerk* (BZAW 227; Berlin: de Gruyter), 1–11.

Wüst, M. (1975), *Untersuchungen zu den siedlungsgeographischen Texten des Alten Testaments*, 1: *Ostjordanland* (Wiesbaden).

Younger, K. L. Jr (1990), *Ancient Conquest Accounts. A Study in Ancient Near Eastern and Biblical History Writing* (JSOTS 98; Sheffield: JSOT Press).

Zobel, H.-J. (1986), '*mšphh*' in *TWAT* **V**, 86–93.

INDEX OF AUTHORS CITED

INDEX OF HEBREW WORDS

INDEX OF NAMES

INDEX OF BIBLICAL REFERENCES

173

13–17	19, 24, 140	15	20, 24, 125
13–16	9	15. 1	15, 24, 31, 39, 42, 69
13	19, 20, 24, 53, 115	15. 13–19	44
13. 1–7	140	15. 13	30, 32, 44
13. 1	20, 21, 135, 141–2	15. 21–62	134
13. 2–5	113	15. 26–32	114
13. 7–12	21	15. 50	62
13. 7–8	1, 116	15. 51	62
13. 7	20, 74, 141–2	15. 59	11, 61, 62, 145
13. 7b-13	54	15. 63	21
13. 8ff	20, 22	16	24
13. 13	21, 115	16. 1–4	118, 140
13. 14	1, 21, 22, 54, 116	16. 1	24, 31, 42
13. 15–32	21, 22, 54	16. 4	116
13. 15–31	23	16. 5–8	118
13. 15	15, 23, 24, 39, 69	16. 8	15, 39, 69
13. 16	20, 24	16. 9	118
13. 18	32	16. 10	21, 108, 111, 118, 145
13. 24	15, 39, 69	17	9, 24
13. 29–31	74, 117, 141	17. 1–7	74, 118
13. 30	24	17. 1–6	24, 141
13. 32	23, 39	17. 1	15, 24, 31, 39, 40, 42, 69
13. 33	1, 21, 22, 23, 24, 54	17. 4	51
14–21	74, 145	17. 5	39
14–19	69	17. 7	15, 24, 69
14	19, 23, 24	17. 8–10	118
14. 1–5	23, 24, 57, 69, 140	17. 11–13	21, 118
14. 1b–5	141	17. 11–12	113
14. 1–4	15	17. 14–18	116, 140
14. 1–3	23	18–19	24, 64, 140
14. 1	24	18	2, 9, 19, 21, 64, 66
14. 2b–4	116	18. 1–10	24, 130, 140–1
14. 3	39	18. 1	65, 66
14. 4	22, 23	18. 2–10	66, 116
14. 5	23	18. 7	21, 22, 39, 74
14. 6–15	44	18. 11	15, 45, 69
14. 10	135	18. 21	15, 69
15–19	141	19	9, 15, 53
15–17	20	19. 1–9	114